D1617383

Employment and Human Rights

University of Pennsylvania Press
Pennsylvania Studies in Human Rights
Edited by Bert B. Lockwood, Jr.

A complete listing of the books in this series
appears at the back of this volume.

Employment and Human Rights

The International Dimension

Richard Lewis Siegel

HD
4903
.S47
1994
West

University of Pennsylvania Press

Philadelphia

Copyright © 1994 by the University of Pennsylvania Press
All rights reserved,
Printed in the United States of America

Library of Congress Cataloging-in-Publication Data
Siegel, Richard Lewis
    Employment and human rights: The International Dimension / Richard L. Siegel.
        p.   cm. — (Pennsylvania studies in human rights)
    Includes bibliographical references and index.
    ISBN 0–8122–3211–9
    1. Right to labor.   2. Human rights.   3. Unemployment.   4. Full employment
policies.   I. Title.   II. Series
HD4903.S47   1994
331.01′1—dc20   93–32175
                                                                    CIP

To the memory of my father

Contents

Acknowledgments

Many individuals and organizations provided vital assistance to this project. For library research, I am particularly indebted to Steven Zink, Duncan Aldrich, and the entire staffs of the Government Publications and Reference departments of the Getchell Library of the University of Nevada, Reno, for their resourceful help. Other assistance was provided by the libraries of the Columbia University Law School, the New York University School of Law, and the University of London.

Initial work on this book was accomplished as a result of the invitations by Paul Martin, Louis Henkin, and others to attend symposia and serve as a Human Rights Fellow at Columbia University's Center for the Study of Human Rights. Interviews for the project were conducted at the International Labor Organization, Organization for Economic Cooperation and Development, United Nations, and European Community. Other interviews were conducted with experts and officials in leading national and international trade unions, women's rights organizations, and employer organizations, as well as national ministries of social affairs, foreign affairs, and employment. The University of Nevada, Reno, contributed funds for the necessary travel and provided sabbatical leave time. Those interviewed were promised anonymity, and their comments are identified in this book only with their organizational affiliation.

The manuscript benefited greatly from critiques of particular chapters or of the entire manuscript by Jack Donnelly, Gösta Rehn, Alex Groth, Sumner Rosen, Bert Lockwood, Jr., David Reichardt, Stuart Nagel, Larry Wade, and Marvin Soroos. Research assistance was ably provided by Winfield Scull, David Reichardt, and Robin Pulliam. Indispensable word processing support that often improved the language of the manuscript was provided by Kenna Boyer, Marilyn Woosley, Daniel Siegel, Larissa Faulkner, and Waiman Kwok. Special gratitude is expressed to Bert Lockwood, Jr., the series editor, and to the editors of the University of Pennsylvania Press, especially Timothy Clancy and Alison Anderson.

Finally, thank you to my children, my parents, my brother and sister, and to Marsha for their contributions to my well being during the course of this project.

Chapter 1
Unemployment: The Case for an International Response

This is a study of national and international responses to unemployment and the evolution of thought about this problem on the part of scholars and policy-makers. Emphasis is put on the international aspects of the responses as well as on the effort of writers, political leaders and organizations to place the goal of full employment and the issue of employment opportunity squarely within the rubric of internationally recognized human rights.

Employment and unemployment are related in this work to various theories of political economy, to a variety of historical and contemporary political movements, and to the construction and transformation of contemporary international regimes and global policies. The place of employment in the evolving post-1945 "International Bill of Rights" is also reviewed. Yet the employment issue involves more than economic policy, political movements, and human rights. It also relates closely to poverty, and basic human needs, human nature, jurisdictional issues among branches and levels of government, social insurance, and governmental stability and turnover.

More than many other spheres of public policy, employment and unemployment involve trade-offs that challenge our ordering of values. For many experts there are almost always trade-offs between levels of employment and inflation. Some also perceive trade-offs between the relatively activist national government and intergovernmental efforts that may ameliorate or reduce unemployment and the perceived threats to individual liberty inherent in such activism.[1]

1. See Friedrich A. Hayek, *The Road to Serfdom* (Chicago: University of Chicago Press, 1944) and *The Constitution of Liberty* (Chicago: University of Chicago Press, 1960).

While unemployment is a subject that lends itself to seemingly objective quantitative analysis, it is an area of study and policy laden with ideological and partisan conflicts. The reasons for this are readily clear: employment lies at the nexus of such issues as the scope of government responsibility and private power; of equity and inequity based on gender, class, and race; and of societal determination of whether the interests of an unemployed minority should be sacrificed for a greater good. Issues involving employment are at the crossroads of many ideologies. Not only socialism and Marxism-Leninism but also creeds ranging from Roman Catholicism to versions of conservatism and liberalism have stressed employment opportunity and pondered its denial. Reasons for this include the crucial role played by employment in economic and social policy and the strong tendency of various strands of European social thought in particular to stress the situation of the worker.

The subject of employment is an exceptionally confusing one due to conflicting ideas about the roles of work and workers in contemporary societies. Ralf Dahrendorf has noted that in modern societies full-time employment is increasingly a "privilege" available to a declining proportion of the adult population.[2] He is not the first or latest theorist of work to contemplate life without employment for a large proportion of those seeking and needing employment.

Many observers accept the idea that social insurance, public assistance, family provision, and other societal mechanisms can substitute for employment. Others stress that our concern with employment should lie principally with the coercion, exploitation and excess that have historically been associated with it. Yet both of these perspectives functionally deflect efforts to concentrate on human fulfillment and opportunity associated with employment.

In order to develop a thorough analysis of responses to unemployment it is necessary to explore a variety of intellectual pathways. The subject of employment has remained a relatively esoteric one, but the issues that underlie national and international efforts to deal with that problem are diverse and intriguing. In the following sections the subject of unemployment is introduced together with its connection to the principal analytical approaches explored in this book.

I have written this book out of a recognition that employment is a neglected subject, especially for political scientists, and from a sense that only through international processes will current trends of neglect of massive unemployment be challenged. My route to this book has

2. Ralf Dahrendorf, *The Modern Social Conflict: An Essay on the Politics of Liberty* (New York: Weidenfeld and Nicolson, 1988), p. 144.

been a varied one, having come to the subject of employment after explorations of such subjects as the welfare state, civil liberties, and international human rights.

When writing and debating about social insurance and public assistance I regularly contemplated the relationship of these welfare policies to the world of work. I did not do this as an ideologue or partisan of any school or movement. Neither arguments for imposed work or for welfare rights seemed altogether convincing. However, such various thinkers as Frances Fox Piven and Friedrich Hayek provoked me to think harder and deeper about the relationship between work and social welfare.

Other thoughts and connections arose from involvement with civil liberties and human rights throughout my adult life. The American tradition of civil liberties is not a consistent friend of employment rights. It is true that the American Civil Liberties Union (ACLU) emphasized in its formative years the rights of union members and leaders to associate and to express dissenting views. Yet the core tradition of the ACLU and its closest allies is rooted in an eighteenth-century philosophy of rights, one that defines rights as civil and political, rarely as social or economic.[3] During thirteen years of service on the National Board of Directors of that organization I was often asked to help restructure that philosophy of rights in the direction of socioeconomic goals. I often heard arguments that connected the rights to subsistence and work to the core values of civil liberties. These arguments were not always convincing, given the constraints on the ACLU imposed by the Bill of Rights, its own history and principles, and American jurisprudence. Yet I did not dismiss the idea that the American concept of civil liberties, like that of American civil rights, required the incorporation of elements of social and economic rights as substantive rights and not merely through the guarantees of equal protection and due process of law associated with such rights.

The views that led to the writing of this book were also shaped by my reading and participation in the world of international human rights. In that sphere the issue of unemployment is usually ignored. It is not difficult to understand this given such concerns of international human rights activists as genocide, political prisoners, disappearances, and torture. These conjure up perceptions of wholesale murder and the depths of inhumanity to man, woman and child. I would not dream of denigrating the centrality of such "gross violations" of fundamental human rights, some of which led directly to significant advances in the

---

3. See Samuel Walker, *In Defense of American Liberties: A History of the ACLU* (New York: Oxford University Press, 1990).

international machinery designed to forestall their repetition and perpetuation. Yet the study of international human rights broadens one's thinking and raises consciousness about less obvious issues even as it deepens knowledge and commitment about known outrages. For me this involved the discovery of "socioeconomic human rights," including rights to subsistence and employment.

Motivations for exploring issues of subsistence and employment in this book also emerged in part from a sense of neglect of such issues by too many scholars, national governments, and international human rights organizations. The dominant, though certainly not the exclusive, emphasis of those who have devoted considerable attention to socioeconomic rights has been on such subjects as starving and disease-ridden children.[4] Arguably, famine and worldwide neglect of our capabilities to lessen the trauma of disease are the essence of contemporary Holocaust. Images of mass unemployment cannot match the intensity of television pictures of starving and diseased babies or of homeless adults in India or America. Yet the raw numbers of the unemployed and underemployed also reach into the hundreds of millions. These numbers also represent misery and hopelessness, and often trigger crises of sickness, homelessness, hunger, violence, and early death. The situation of these hundreds of millions are neglected because they are often invisible, because many believe that society is taking care of the unemployed through the welfare state, and because unemployment is one social problem that is periodically planned for by national macroeconomic policy-makers. Indeed unemployment is viewed as contributing to the solution of such problems as the control of price and wage inflation. Interestingly, unemployment is like many gross violations of human rights violations in being a price that a ruling elite or even a majority of the population is willing to pay periodically to achieve other ends.

As such, employment seems worth studying as an underappreciated public policy issue and as a matter deserving consideration as an aspect of human rights. As a political scientist I note the rarity of this issue as a concern of my discipline. Yet unemployment is far too important to be left to economists alone. Indeed, employment and unemployment have played significantly different roles in politics and political philosophy than in economics.

4. See Henry Shue, *Basic Rights: Subsistence, Affluence, and U.S. Foreign Policy* (Princeton, NJ: Princeton University Press, 1980); "Symposium, UN Convention on Children's Rights," *Human Rights Quarterly* 2, 1 (February 1990): 94–178; Philip Alston and Katarina Tomaševski, eds., *The Right to Food* (Boston: M. Nijhoff, 1984).

The Extent of Unemployment

If global policy is driven by the worsening of problems, a stronger international response to the unemployment problem might have been expected in such periods as the Great Depression, the aftermath of the 1973–74 oil shock, and the recession of 1981–1983. The Organization for Economic Cooperation and Development (OECD) reported that the unemployment rate for its twenty-four mostly developed member countries rose from 3.0 percent in 1970 to 8.7 percent in 1983; the latter figure translates to 33 million people needing jobs.[5] The International Labor Office noted in 1982 that the problem was then much worse in Africa, Asia, and Latin America, where "no less than 40 to 45 percent of the total labor force, almost 330 million adult men and women, are either out of work or underemployed."[6]

The economic recovery that benefited many fortunate countries between 1983 and 1989 failed to change the basic situation. At the close of that period the United States stood out for its job-producing capacity, managing to temporarily reduce its reported unemployment rate to 5.1 percent. Yet experts continued to express concerns about the low wages in that country for many new service jobs and the likely future negative effects on employment from stubborn budgetary and trade deficits as well as private and governmental debt. Few other developed countries matched the overtly favorable U.S. employment trends in the 1980s. In Western Europe, the overall unemployment rate peaked at 11 percent in 1985 before beginning a gradual improvement until 1990. Yet the average unemployment rate for West Germany, France, and Britain was virtually unchanged from 1982 to 1988.[7]

The OECD reported in 1990 that "unemployment rates in most OECD countries are above those recorded at the peak of the last recovery in 1978–79."[8] The stubbornness of the problem in Western Europe is illustrated by the experience of Spain, where the unemployment rate rose above 20 percent in 1986 despite a stunning rise of 12.8 percent in annual industrial production.[9] Levels for the OECD countries stalled and then worsened in the wake of the new recession of 1990–1993. Although overall OECD unemployment stabilized at 6.4

5. OECD, *Employment Outlook, September 1984* (Paris: OECD, 1984), pp. 21–23.

6. International Labor Conference, 69th Sess., 1983, *Employment Policy*, Report VI (1) (Geneva: ILO, 1982), p. 3.

7. *The Economist*, May 13, 1989, p. 111.

8. OECD, *Employment Outlook, July 1990* (Paris: OECD, 1990), p. vii.

9. *The Economist*, September 20, 1986, p. 115.

percent in 1989, that in various Southern European member states remained above 10 percent and worsened as the 1990s began.[10]

By 1988 unemployment was clearly a growing and very serious problem in the Soviet Union and in some now formerly Communist nations of East-Central Europe, worsened by Soviet *perestroika* and by Eastern Europe's foreign debt repayment problems.[11] It was revealed in 1988 that as many as 16 million Soviet administrators and workers faced layoffs by the year 2000, and that at least one million people were already jobless in Uzbekistan alone.[12] Overall Soviet unemployment was authoritatively estimated at 8.4 million, or 6.2 percent, in a 1989 publication.[13] By 1990 leading intergovernmental organizations suggested the possibility of a Soviet unemployment rate of 9–12 percent in the first year of full transition to a market economy.[14] Ruinous subsidies and monetary policies have slowed the advent of mass unemployment in Russia and various other post-Soviet republics, but the specter of disastrous unemployment remains in the near-term picture. Recent trends have also been very negative for much of the developing world. Various economic plagues hit many regions simultaneously during the 1980s, including softness in commodity prices and widespread debt crisis. With evidence of major employment problems mounting, much of this rooted in rapid population growth as well as rapid urbanization, International Labor Organization (ILO) Director-General Francis Blanchard ascribed Third World employment problems as being "still more dramatic" in 1985, noting that the attainment of ILO employment goals was "more remote than ever."[15] A subsequent ILO report indicated that, in the Latin American and Caribbean region as a whole during 1980–85, "Salaried jobs have shrunk in absolute terms while the population has grown. There are 3 million more unemployed than in 1980. Some 8 million more people have been forced into precarious, low-productivity jobs or self-employment."[16]

In 1988 the ILO estimated Third World unemployment at 70 mil-

10. OECD, *Employment Outlook, July 1990*, p. 35.

11. *The Economist*, December 26, 1987, pp. 15–18; "*Pravda* Puts Layoffs in Perspective," *Current Digest of the Soviet Press* XL, 10 (1988): 7–8. "Glasnost and Unemployment," *The Economist*, December 26, 1987, pp. 15–18; "Tackling the Challenge of Unemployment," *Current Digest of the Soviet Press* XL, 4 (February 24, 1988): 1–7.

12. *New York Times*, January 22, 1988, p. A5.

13. I. F. Adirim, "A Note on the Current Level, Pattern and Trends of Unemployment in the USSR," *Soviet Studies* LXI (July 1989): 460.

14. International Monetary Fund et al., *A Study of the Soviet Economy* (Paris: IMF, World Bank, OECD, and European Bank for Reconstruction and Development, 1991), 2: 149.

15. *Employment and Poverty in a Troubled World: Report of a Meeting of High Level Experts on Employment* (Geneva: ILO, 1985), pp. 1–2.

16. *ILO Information* 16, 1 (February 1988): 4.

lion, with "close to 500 million underemployed and some 900 million living in extreme poverty.[17] Trends toward higher unemployment in various parts of the Third World continue in the wake of increasing foreign debt pressures, unstable commodity prices, imposed austerity, and rapidly increasing labor forces entering the employment market. This contrasts with recent or projected declines in domestic labor forces in various industrialized countries.

Overall levels of unemployment represent only one perspective on the problem. Higher overall unemployment generally understates truly horrendous situations for such groups as school dropouts, new secondary school graduates, the long-term unemployed, older "redundant" workers, the illiterate and physically/mentally handicapped, and certain racial and religious minorities. It is also important to note declines in the percentage of jobs providing middle-class incomes, fringe benefits, and employment security, especially in the United States.[18]

Qualitative aspects of employment remind us that employment, like such other basic needs as shelter and nutrition, may be provided only in part. Those underemployed or employed only part-time or seasonally may be subsumed under official counts of the employed, together with "discouraged" workers, thereby skewing the totals.

There is also the need to consider "what price employment?" The total number of jobs can be increased, at least in the short term, by such means as substandard wages, the lack of employment security, the absence of fringe benefits, neglect of safety, and featherbedding. As has been widely discussed in recent years in the U.S. context, good jobs can be replaced by bad ones. Employment can not be disconnected from these issues, which speak to the quality of employment and the standard of living that is made possible.

Impacts of Unemployment

It can be argued that various other socioeconomic concerns affect individuals and families more directly than employment and qualify more easily as basic needs or rights. Employment is often treated as a means to other ends, as either an unwelcome and unavoidable obligation of mankind or as a source of income that often can be replaced by charity, help from kinfolk, inheritance, social security, or public assistance benefits.

17. International Labour Conference, 75th Sess., 1988, *Human Rights: A Common Responsibility*, Report of the Director-General, Part I (Geneva: ILO, 1988), p. 10.

18. "America's Shrinking Middle," *The Economist*, November 12, 1988, pp. 84–85.

Indeed, it is argued in various scriptural passages as well as by some secular writers that employment is a dread visitation on humankind. In the Genesis version work is imposed as a punishment for moral failure. In some contemporary secular versions of the descent of the human race, industrialization meant that most people were excluded from self-reliant subsistence, and reduced to dependence on paid labor. Marxists were not alone in finding irredeemable horror in labor relations, characterized by such terms as exploitation and alienation. Many recent critiques of employment focus on environmental and safety hazards as well as on refined techniques for domination of men and women by managers and technology.

Nevertheless, hundreds of millions of people struggling without the safety nets of meaningful social insurance, ownership of fertile agricultural land, or adequate communal assistance face starvation and death as a result of long-term unemployment and acute underemployment. Even in highly developed welfare states the consequences of unemployment are often dire. Bertram Gross and Shirley Williams reflect a substantial literature on the social impacts of unemployment when they link it to consequences ranging from loss of self-respect and the onset or exacerbation of physical or mental illness to increased drug abuse, family breakdown, violence, street crime, and suicide.[19] Noel Whiteside's interesting study suggests that unemployment does not so much create poor health as reveal and exacerbate preexisting physical and psychological impairment.[20] Yet Johns Hopkins University researchers suggest that every percent of the American unemployment rate is associated with more than 20,000 deaths annually from heart disease alone.[21]

Literature on the psychological aspects of unemployment has been abundant, with a rather recent synthesis by Peter Kelvin and Joanna Jarrett updating earlier work by Marie Jahoda, Paul Lazarsfeld, Hans Zeisel, and E. Wight Bakke.[22] Kelvin and Jarrett stress the blurring of

19. Bertram Gross, "Toward Global Action," in Gross and Alfred Pfaller, eds., *Unemployment: A Global Challenge*, Vol. 492 of the Annals of the American Academy of Political and Social Science (Newbury Park, CA: Sage Publications, 1987), pp. 182–194; Shirley Williams, *A Job to Live: The Impact of Tomorrow's Technology on Work and Society* (New York: Viking Penguin, 1985), pp. 21–24.

20. Noel Whiteside, "Unemployment and Health: An Historical Perspective," *Journal of Social Policy* 17, 2 (April 1988): 191.

21. Kenneth Pelletier, "The Hidden Hazards of the Modern Office," *New York Times*, September 8, 1985, p. F3.

22. Marie Jahoda, Paul Lazarsfeld, and Hans Zeisel, *Marienthal: The Sociography of an Unemployed Community* (Chicago: Aldine Atherton, 1971); E. Wight Bakke, *The Unemployed Man: A Social Study* (New York: E. P. Dutton, 1934); Peter Kelvin and Joanna

the impacts of poverty and unemployment on those who share both conditions, the displacement of unemployed people from various settings, and their need to fill time and reorient themselves. They also emphasize that Western attitudes concerning unemployment are unpredictable and ambivalent, perhaps because of their finding that "moral significance does not attach to work as such, but to 'not living off others.'"[23]

Other effects on individuals have been identified. An Italian Labor Minister pointed out: "Having a job means having certain rights which are connected with participation in a modern democratic society."[24] Dahrendorf adds that, for individuals, paid employment "has been the key both to the entitlement structures of modern societies and to their growth potential."[25]

The impacts of unemployment on the broader society are also substantial. In recent years various governments have behaved as though high levels of unemployment pose little threat to national social or political stability and do not even threaten the reelection of incumbent governments. Manfred G. Schmidt, Jeremy Richardson, and Roger Henning perceived few signs of system-threatening stress in Western democracies in the face of high unemployment.[26] Yet such signs exist in various forms. One is the strain placed on national budgets and social insurance systems when high unemployment levels lower levels of contributions and add to outlays.[27] Another is the cumulative debilitating effects of long-term employment on particular groups. Distinct concerns confront political leaders in the face of unemployment bulges in the inner cities, older industrial regions, youth reaching their mid-twenties without experiencing regular employment, older adults losing industrial jobs without evident prospects for reemployment, and women unable to satisfy the needs of their one- or two-parent families for their paychecks.

Jarrett, *Unemployment, Its Social Psychological Effects: A Commentary on the Literature* (Cambridge: Cambridge University Press, 1985).

23. Kelvin and Jarrett, *Unemployment*, p. 109.

24. Gianni de Michelis, "Technology and Unemployment: A Role for Government," in *Interdependence and Co-operation in Tomorrow's World* (Paris: OECD, 1987), p. 171.

25. Ralf Dahrendorf, "Changing Perceptions of the Role of Government," in Dahrendorf, ed., *Europe's Economy in Crisis* (New York: Holmes and Meier, 1982), pp. 118–119.

26. Jeremy Richardson and Roger Henning, "Public Responses to Unemployment: Symbolic or Placebo Policies," in Richardson and Henning, eds., *Unemployment: Policy Responses of Western Democracies* (Beverly Hills, CA: Sage Publications, 1984), p. 316; Manfred G. Schmidt, "The Politics of Unemployment: Rates of Unemployment and Labor Market Policy," *West European Politics* 7 (July 1984): 18–21.

27. Oliver J. Blanchard and Lawrence H. Summers, "An Austerity That Wrecked Europe," *New York Times*, February 8, 1987, p. F3.

Dahrendorf stresses the power of large-scale unemployment to further divide societies by intensifying the effects of divisions based on race, nationality, and class. He sees societies split into majorities with and minorities without employment, the latter including subgroups of virtually unemployable people.[28] One of the remarkable phenomenon of the 1980s was the tolerance by many national governments of such growing divisions in their societies, apparently counting on the willingness of millions of the unemployed to be bought off by welfare benefits and to be restrained from protest by the de-energizing impacts of despair.[29] Yet such assumptions have been increasingly challenged in the 1990s. Unemployment has contributed to deep crises of national division and intolerance.

International Dimensions

Certain aspects of the unemployment issue are already the subjects of major studies, these including numerous analyses of national employment policies in leading industrial countries.[30] Works offering theories of the economic roots of unemployment and advocating particular public policies designed to ameliorate large-scale unemployment have also been numerous.[31]

For several reasons this work focuses on the international dimensions of employment policy. One is a perceived growing belief among scholars as well as leaders of national and intergovernmental agencies that effective employment policy must transcend national boundaries and incorporate intergovernmental coordination if not international authority. Pressures for such coordination are rooted in elite awareness that such critical economic factors as movement of investment funds and currencies, setting of interest rates, currency valuation, and maintenance of currency reserves are increasingly beyond the power of national governments alone. Such international coordination or regulation is also prompted by the presence in many countries of large numbers of foreign workers, leading to the violation of the interna-

28. Dahrendorf, "Changing Perceptions," p. 118.

29. Richardson and Henning, "Public Responses to Unemployment," p. 315.

30. See Gregg M. Olsen, ed., *Industrial Change and Labor Adjustment in Sweden and Canada* (Toronto: Garamond, 1988); and Richardson and Henning, "Public Responses to Unemployment."

31. See Andrew J. Pierre, ed., *Unemployment and Growth in the Western Economies* (New York: Council on Foreign Relations, 1984); Lyn Squire, *Employment Policy in Developing Countries: A Survey of Issues and Evidence* (New York: Oxford University Press, 1981); Morley Gunderson, Noah M. Meltz, and Sylvia Ostry, eds., *Unemployment: International Perspectives* (Toronto: University of Toronto Press, 1987).

tional human rights standards of equal treatment in employment and social benefits. Further, it is indisputable that the need to facilitate social learning from other nations' experience has increased enormously and thus the international community has developed structures and processes to facilitate exchanges of information about policies and their implementation.

The decision to focus on the international dimension also facilitates reconsideration of critical theoretical issues concerning the boundaries and relationships between foreign and domestic policy as well as the requisite conditions for developing viable international cooperation in many issue-areas. Despite the high priority placed on the problem of unemployment by the International Labor Organization as early as 1919, the employment policy area has remained centered in national and local government domains. There are numerous reasons why policy responsibility may continue to be centered at a particular level of government even when rational or objective arguments can be marshaled for a strong international role. The norms and processes of incremental policy change alone tend to delay significant reallocations of functions. This was evident when Ronald Reagan, at the peak of his presidential power in the early 1980s, failed to promote a major reallocation of federal and state functions. Such fundamental reallocations have been rare at the national or international levels. Although the European Community (EC) has achieved centralization of power in Brussels in such policy areas as agricultural subsidies and competition policy, it has not yet reversed national predominance in certain other policy areas for which confederal or federal divisions of labor have been planned.[32]

What conditions are necessary or sufficient to allow a policy area to pass a threshold of strong international involvement? The inherent seriousness of the subject matter is not decisive taken alone. Though such issues as genocide and mass starvation have eventually been addressed internationally, many would stress the extraordinary hesitancy to allow this level of involvement. There is frequent conflict between national governments' senses of relative powerlessness in many policy areas and their perceived need to preserve national sovereignty and autonomy. In almost all cases the national government, at least the leading ones in the particular issue area, must decide whether a particular form of international cooperation or authority is justified, needed, or unavoidable. This study begins with the hypothesis that such developments are most often incremental byproducts of other

32. Paul G. Taylor, *The Limits of European Integration* (New York: Columbia University Press, 1983).

decisions. My perception is that new areas of international involvement result most often from the expansion of international jurisdiction through bureaucratic politics and reactions of major national and international actors to existing or impending crises.

It is common for international regimes, the means through which international influence is brought to bear in a particular issue area, to assume jurisdiction or influence in only certain aspects of policy in a given area. In social policy, for example, the principle of non-discrimination has often opened up international involvement, while the sufficiency of national provision of most social benefits has rarely received consistent or intensive international attention. Issues of discrimination and individual liberty have helped drive international interest in such problems as apartheid and forced labor. Yet the essence of employment policy is aggregate opportunity to work as well as the degree of acceptance of public responsibility for unemployment and underemployment, and these issues have yet to be fully addressed by any international regime.

Regimes and Global Policy

The nature of international involvement in social and economic policy is central to this study. Social scientists have devoted considerable attention to international policy regimes and have begun to address global policy studies. Both approaches are aimed at the analysis of policies in issue areas with strong international components, and regime analysts are also very interested in the structures, processes, and norms of the national and international organizations that make and implement policy.

It is possible to argue that an "international employment regime" has begun to emerge, with responsibilities for fostering principles, enforcing rules, and promoting supportive policies at the national and international levels. The concept and approach of international regime, as developed by political and other social scientists during the past two decades, provides criteria for evaluating the progress of globalization or regionalization of particular policy issues. It has grown out of the literature of international law but today incorporates elements of the political, economic, and legal context in which a particular policy issue is managed. Such a regime has begun to be established to a significant degree at the levels of the global community (United Nations, World Bank, International Labor Organization), Western industrial states (Organization for Economic Cooperation and Development), and Western European states (European Community, Council of Europe). Such international agencies provide forums utilized by their own staffs as well as by participating national governments, firms, trade unions, and other interested parties to advance full employment, this as part of broader efforts on behalf of social and economic stability and development. This book addresses the degree to which the right to work and full employment principles are served by a regime in which many of the primary players are less than fully devoted to these principles and in which major structural weaknesses and resource limitations are evident.

Most national governments exhibit a limited willingness to accept regional and global or regional direction regarding employment, even as they acknowledge that real benefits can derive from international coordination and exchange of knowledge. International regimes that have major impacts typically facilitate the exchange of ideas and information, coordinate and enhance investment of capital, and prescribe and enforce rules that limit the discretionary powers of national governments. Despite widespread national governmental reluctance to accept international involvements other than the facilitation of communication and financial assistance regarding employment, political pressures from inside and outside national boundaries have forced some governments—most notably those in Western Europe—to accommodate significant other international influences on their employment policies. These have included internationally endorsed policies ranging from the protection of the rights of foreign workers and women to the facilitation of expanded job training. A system has also begun to be developed for calling nation states from various continents to account when they patently ignore the principle of full employment, this centered in the International Labor Organization. Yet such legitimate processes have had to function in a global political environment in which many national governments seem to be far more interested in making symbolic gestures on behalf of employment than in making tangible and lasting progress in this field.

Given the seriousness of unemployment and underemployment throughout much of the world, and the severe social costs inflicted by these phenomena, effective international responses might well have been expected decades ago. Thus employment would seem a likely addition to such "global policy" problems identified by Marvin Soroos as being addressed by international institutions as nuclear proliferation, economic development, human rights, ocean resources, pollution, and telecommunications.[33] The problem of widespread unemployment meets virtually all the criteria that Soroos suggests may

33. Marvin S. Soroos, *Beyond Sovereignty: The Challenge of Global Policy* (Columbia: University of South Carolina Press, 1986).

trigger international treatment of a major problem and at least some of his criteria for considerations of a problem as "global."[34]

Soroos argues that global policy issues are regarded as of special interest to the international community. However, global concern with unemployment and underemployment in various countries has not been nearly as "special" an interest of the international community as, for example, apartheid or nuclear proliferation. Such forthright addressing of employment by international authorities was most evident from about 1944 to 1948 and in the second half of the 1970s. The "Declaration of Philadelphia" adopted by the 1944 International Labor Conference was a strong call for "effective international and national action" on behalf of full employment in the context of the memory of the Great Depression and the strong sense of international solidarity resulting from military victory.[35] This era culminated in the inclusion of the right to work (employment) in the 1948 Universal Declaration of Human Rights and the subsequent U.N. covenants. The nature of the reference to the right to work in the United Nations International Covenant on Economic, Social, and Cultural Rights (adopted 1966, ratified 1976) was resolved in debates in the Commission on Human Rights in 1951–52 and in the Third Committee (Social, Humanitarian and Cultural) of the General Assembly in 1956 and 1957.[36]

Although international interest in levels of unemployment and underemployment never disappeared in subsequent decades, nothing approaching special interest occurred again until the second half of the 1970s. During that period, concern for unemployment was stimulated by the economic and social impacts of oil price increases and the rapid growth in the labor force in many countries. The pattern of the 1940s was repeated: an intense, but short-lived, interest arose in important sectors of various national governments as well as in such intergovernmental organizations as the International Labor Organization (ILO), the Organization for Economic Cooperation and Development (OECD), and the European Community (EC). Even in the context of crisis, however, many national governments refused to allow unemployment to be placed near the top of the international agenda. By the second half of the 1980s, lower unemployment rates muffled national

34. Ibid., pp. 70–72.

35. International Labour Conference, 26th Sess., 1944, *Record of Proceedings* (Montreal: ILO, 1944), p. 623.

36. See A. Glen Mower, Jr., *International Cooperation for Social Justice: Global and Regional Protection of Economic/Social Rights* (Westport, CT: Greenwood Press, 1985), esp. pp. 7–46.

and international responses, paralleling the ebbing of interest in the 1950s.

How does a global policy approach to an international issue such as employment relate to regime theory? Soroos suggests:

The regime and policy approaches have much in common, but whereas regimes are oriented toward a more encompassing problem area, policies are responses to a more narrowly defined problem. . . . Furthermore, whereas the regime approach focuses on the international arrangements that have evolved for devising a cooperative response to matters pertaining to a certain problem area, policies are the actual course of actions adopted to deal with a specific problem. Thus, the two approaches have a complementary relationship in the sense that regimes are the institutional environment within which international policies are made.[37]

This distinction is consistent with Friedrich Kratochwil and John Gerard Ruggie's view of regimes as "governing arrangements" and with Robert Keohane's conception of them as enabling mechanisms that aid attempts to design cooperative arrangements by easing information transfer, decreasing transaction costs, and facilitating enforcement of agreements.[38] However, other conceptions of international regimes argue that institutional arrangements are as much the result and expression of policies as the mechanism for their selection.[39]

Regime development choices are especially important for employment policy because major policy-makers have not agreed on comprehensive policy approaches set out in treaties or conventions. Important structural decisions have included the development of mechanisms for limited macroeconomic policy coordination by the leading Western industrialized states in the 1980s,[40] the substantial supplements to members' regional development and vocational training programs provided through the European Community, and the shift from imple-

37. Soroos, *Beyond Sovereignty*, p. 21.

38. Friedrich Kratochwil and John Gerard Ruggie, "International Organization: A State of the Art or an Art of the State," *International Organization* 40 (Autumn 1986): 759; see also Robert Keohane, *After Hegemony* (Princeton, NJ: Princeton University Press, 1984), pp. 244–245.

39. Joseph S. Nye, Jr., "Nuclear Learning and U.S.-Soviet Security Regimes," *International Organization* 41 (Summer 1987): 375; Nicholas G. Onuf and V. Spike Peterson, "Human Rights from an International Regime Perspective," *Journal of International Affairs* 37 (Winter 1984): 329–333.

40. Robert D. Putnam and Nicholas Bayne, *Hanging Together: Cooperation and Conflict in the Seven-Power Summits*, rev. ed. (Cambridge, MA: Harvard University Press, 1987), pp. 237–238.

mentation of standards to technical assistance and other guidance by the ILO.

Regime and policy approaches also overlap in the emphasis placed on various goals, principles and values.[41] Global and international policy responses regarding employment are characterized by the striking inconsistency between their lofty principles and goals and the overall weakness of most actual policy responses. Principles and goals appear in international policy statements relating to employment that are framed in economic and human rights terms. For example, they assert the existence of "the right to work," prohibit slavery and forced labor, value freedom of transnational movement of labor and services, emphasize non-discrimination and equal opportunity, and affirm national government responsibility for the creation and maintenance of full employment.

A policy approach is most distinct from the focus of regime analysis when it stresses specific choices about how to apply the regime's approaches and powers. This includes choices about the intensity and scope of international regulation as well as levels of spending.

Full Employment and the Right to Employment

The goal of full employment and the principle of a right to employment are central to at least the declared policies of the international employment regime. This results from certain peculiarities of the historical and philosophical evolution of this policy area as well as the efforts of certain political leaders and experts to increase the importance of the issue area and strengthen its norms by linking it to fundamental human rights.

Even as genocide and "disappearances" continue to be reported in various countries, indicating the need for increased vigilance against gross violations of civil and political rights, interest in various social and economic rights has also grown. Lists of social and economic rights usually start with such basic needs as food, income, shelter, and medical care. Some interpreters, including major international organizations, count as socioeconomic rights such controversial concepts as paid vacations and parental leaves. From my perspective, the socioeconomic rights that have gained the most attention in the past several decades include food and employment.

Food—the right to eat—is at the core of our perception of subsis-

---

41. Stephen D. Krasner, "Structural Causes and Regime Consequences: Regimes as Intervening Variables," *International Organization* 36 (Spring 1982): 186; Soroos, *Beyond Sovereignty*, pp. 129–136.

tence requirements and is effectively if only periodically dramatized by televised images of famine and starvation. Although controversy continues regarding the priority to be given to developmental agricultural investment, erosion control, and food relief, the centrality of food to subsistence is beyond debate.[42]

Employment shares a direct relationship with food and water as a requisite for subsistence in many societies. For millions of people unemployment or underemployment, together with a lack of access to fertile agricultural land, means inadequate income, misery, and early death. Such gloomy realities underline the tremendous present need to place full employment at the center of public policy and human rights, this requiring enlightened global perspectives as well as effective national policies.

At both the national and international levels, one conceptual approach to the unemployment problem has been the recognition and promotion of a right to employment. At various historical junctures dating back at least to seventeenth-century Europe, the right to employment has risen from obscurity or apathy to become a focal point of the writings of influential advocates. Less frequently it has emerged as a central theme of prominent political movements.

It seems fitting at the advent of the 1990s, in the wake of virtually unprecedented political and socioeconomic changes in many parts of the world, to reexamine the case for including employment as an internationally recognized human right and full employment as a public policy goal. This is an appropriate time to look back at the fruits of years of effort to prescribe and implement this nationally and internationally declared right, and to analyze why there has been such limited progress toward full employment and the effective right to work. To do this it is necessary to evaluate current demands for a more effective right to employment in the context of historical experience as well as current social, economic, and political realities.

This study explores the antecedents of the international recognition of the right to work in diverse European and American writings of the past four hundred years, in writings and statements that have been labeled utopian, revolutionary, socialist, Christian and conservative. The concept of a right to work fascinated scholars, devotees of socioeconomic experiments, and would-be leaders of political movements long before many now widely recognized human rights were asserted. As scholarship became increasingly specialized, authorities in such varied disciplines as philosophy, economics, law, sociology, history,

42. Shue, *Basic Rights*.

and political science contributed to the prescription and implementation of the concept, and also challenged its appropriateness, legitimacy and feasibility. In subsequent phases of discussion and prescription, the right to work has been a focal point of debate by advocates of competing ideologies and of interests promoted and opposed by national governments and international agencies, as well as the national and transnational spokespersons for trade unions, business enterprises, social groups, and other actors affected by the assurance or non-assurance of work.

The roots of Western concern for social and economic protection in general, of which the advancement of a right to employment is a part, is reviewed first. Some readers will be surprised to learn of the vital role of traditional conservative paternalism in this regard. Concern for full employment is inextricably linked to traditional efforts by charitable institutions as well as local government bodies to assure subsistence in the face of life's major risks. The forms of such efforts have not changed to the degree that many analysts of the contemporary welfare state would have us believe. Although social insurance is little more than one hundred years old, regularized provision of income and in-kind benefits was already widespread in much of Europe from the sixteenth century, and even government-ensured employment can be traced back for centuries.

Marxist and other versions of nineteenth-century socialism certainly played a major role in highlighting the gaps in the traditional safety nets, and also contributed much to the documentation of human rights abuses attributed to European and North American early industrialization and imperialism. The specter of socialism encouraged conservative and liberal political leaders to further advance social protection in the nineteenth and twentieth centuries. Yet Marxism long retained major doctrinal barriers to the advancement of social protection, these including reluctance to promote social reform in capitalist states. Further, the continuing influence of strong attachment to the work ethic by various disciples of Marx and Lenin, including Josef Stalin and Nikita Khrushchev, limited the commitment to social protection of many contemporary devotees of Marxism-Leninism. Indeed the right to employment has been combined most effectively with the expansion of social security not in Marxist-Leninist Eastern Europe but rather in certain mixed ideological and institutional political and economic systems of contemporary Western Europe.

The subject of socioeconomic rights generally, and employment rights in particular, provided numerous opportunities for thinkers and officials identified with widely varying ideological orientations to learn from each other and to adopt major themes from their adversaries. The right to employment evolved from conceptions of national solidarity and welfare state obligations in the century before World War II. It first received broad international recognition in the post-1945 era, with its inclusion in the United Nations Universal Declaration of Human Rights and International Covenant on Economic, Social, and Cultural Rights as well as in the Council of Europe's European Social Charter.[43] Additional support can be found in various conventions and recommendations concerning full employment ratified through the Organization for Economic Cooperation and Development and the International Labor Organization (most notably those adopted in 1964 and 1984) and the myriad relevant legal steps taken by the organs of the European Community.

Although the idea of a human right to employment has been repeated often in international legal instruments, its prescription by international agencies has been characterized by compromise and dilution, and its implementation and promotion has virtually always disappointed its advocates. The diverse sources of such disappointment include the gamesmanship of national and international organizations, the lack of consensus among experts and political representatives concerning the most effective ways to deal with unemployment, and honest disagreements about social and economic priorities.

Difficulty of implementation does not, however, set the right to employment apart from many well-established "fundamental human rights." The sad truth is that most core human rights (e.g., the rights not to be tortured or not to be detained without charges) are violated by governments all too frequently, and individual victims rarely secure effective redress of grievances.

Yet the right to employment involves some unique problems of legitimacy. Some observers view employment as merely a means to obtain basic needs, something that can be replaced by income maintenance. Others view it as hopelessly bogged down by such problems as individual qualifications, association with "forced labor," the inability of the state to provide jobs directly in largely private enterprise economies, and the perceived costs of guaranteed employment in terms of

43. For the debate within the United Nations over the right to work article in the International Covenant on Economic, Social and Cultural Rights, see U.N. Commission on Human Rights, *Official Records*, April 21, 26, 27 and May 5, 1952. The disputed issues changed little when this right was debated by the ILO Committee on Employment in 1983–84.

less competitive firms, industries, and national economies. As a result, the right to work has all too often been relegated by scholars and governments to the level of a platitude rather than a human right that rallies commitment.

Few advocates have been able to state confidently the basis or specific nature of such a right. It has usually been left unclear whether implementation of a right to employment would be limited to promoting action by governments on behalf of full employment or would also involve enforcing legal claims by individuals to guaranteed jobs. There has also been too little clarification regarding the relationship of the right to employment to such issues as job security, equal opportunity for various groups, income maintenance, education, training, forced labor, and the duty of work.

Efforts to provide a right to employment have inevitably been affected by the lack of clarity and precision about what is being prescribed. Rights and law are widely misunderstood terms. Ronald Dworkin and others have helped us to understand that the process of prescribing rights at both the national and international levels may emphasize principles, rules, norms, and policies.[44] Principles declare certain goals to be worthy ones. They reinforce the case for a particular decision without requiring that decision. In contrast, legal rules are specific prescriptions or proscriptions that presumably must be obeyed in each instance. Those responsible for setting out the right to work struggled with the question of whether rules could be established that would be enforceable in courts or other forums. Some contended that efforts should be limited to enhancing recognition of a principle that would be furthered by various policies. These did not turn out to be entirely either/or choices. Opportunities existed for promoting rules in such spheres as non-discrimination, job security, forced labor and free movement of labor while leaving the broader aspects of the right to work and full employment largely in the sphere of policy. Such issues have long been highly charged, largely because the right to be employed involves basic value judgments, the allocation of scarce resources, and the regulation of profit-oriented behavior.

The central questions about international efforts to promote the right to work and full employment lead to ever deeper exploration of the contemporary international political economy and the role of human rights in the international system. Paradoxes lie at every juncture. The right to work has been proclaimed without reconciling its various

44. Ronald W. Dworkin, "The Model of Rules," *University of Chicago Law Review* 35 (1967): 14–26.

ideological roots. Additionally, full employment is asserted frequently in legal and policy documents that do not come to grips with the varying perspectives of economists and other experts regarding the relationship of full employment to economic growth and stability.

One paradox is that such concepts as the right to work and full employment have always carried a mystique that make their proclamation politically useful but their implementation politically inconvenient. One must be for full employment as one is for motherhood. Yet international organizations and national governments often place employment (as motherhood) quite low on their list of priorities.

A related paradox is the use by various agencies and authorities of the term "right" in relation to employment even though no consensus exists as to its appropriateness. Has this term essentially been appropriated from the language of political and civil rights even though most advocates viewed full employment in the context of the duties of states or employers rather than the rights of individuals?

The purpose of this study is to explore the roots of such paradoxes. Such fields as intellectual history, law, organizational behavior, economics, and political science inform such a search while challenging scholars to integrate and reconcile their often sharply different assumptions and findings about the evolving role of the international system in the promotion of the right to employment and full employment.

Conclusion

The case for a global response to the problem of unemployment is shaped by each of the perspectives introduced in this chapter. First, there is the scope and severity of the problem. Although unemployment and underemployment often lack the starkness of starvation and torture, they share the ability to engender severe physical and psychological effects. They are also inextricably tied to our increasingly interdependent global and regional economies, and normally cannot be expected to be brought into an acceptable range without cooperation from leading economic powers, major multinational corporate and financial institutions, and the major intergovernmental organizations operating in the social and economic fields.

This global response must be built on a common conception of an unacceptable threshold of unemployment and underemployment that should and will trigger an effective international response that augments and intensifies national efforts. This is what "full employment" must mean in a practical sense. It is necessary to affirm the duty of each nation-state to protect and advance the cause of full employment as defined in this paragraph. Employment and human rights regimes can also do much to affirm state duties and to limit the inclinations of various actors in economic regimes to neglect employment in favor of other social and economic values and goals.

Chapter 2
The Right to Employment and the Evolving Welfare State: 1600–1900

Employment has been integrally connected with the evolution of the Western welfare state for more than a millennium. In the past five hundred years many thinkers have struggled to develop solutions to poverty or means to ameliorate its effects. From time to time some writers and statesmen have addressed the possibility of government promotion of employment as the key to the problem of poverty or as a major part of the solution.[1] We focus here on the ideological origins of thought about poverty and employment, particularly ideas about the right of individuals to be employed and the duties of the state to assure work and subsistence. Are such ideas narrowly based on socialist ideology, or do they have broader ideological and pragmatic roots? Do contemporary conceptions of social and economic rights have broad enough support to overcome renewed classical liberal assertion of a more limited role of the state in the struggle against unemployment and poverty?

One of the propositions to be examined in this chapter is that something termed "social rights" evolved from the late nineteenth century as part of an expanding conception of national citizenry. The late British social historian T. H. Marshall has had enormous influence on the human rights literature with his thesis of a three-stage development of the rights of citizens ending with the emergence of social

1. See Gertrude Himmelfarb, *The Idea of Poverty: England in the Early Industrial Age* (New York: Alfred Knopf, 1984); John A. Garraty, *Unemployment in History: Economic Thought and Public Policy* (New York: Harper and Row, 1978); Merritt Ierley, *With Charity for All* (New York: Praeger, 1984); Samuel Mencher, *Poor Law to Poverty Program* (Pittsburgh: University of Pittsburgh Press, 1974).

rights.[2] Marshall's work draws a rather sharp line between such rights, identified with the availability of social protection programs to every citizen as a matter of legal right, and earlier approaches to social protection that were based on means tests—programs that "had little direct effect on social inequality" and that were "not woven into the fabric of citizenship."[3]

A second issue to be addressed is the relationship between centuries of paternalistic ideas about the socioeconomic welfare of the poor, which led to programs designed to promote social protection at the local and national levels, and current interpretations of internationally prescribed social and economic rights. Did the organized international human rights community, during the quarter century following World War II, seek to go beyond paternalistic conceptions that focus on the duties of states rather than the rights of individuals? Or, alternatively, did that community merely prescribe a lowest common denominator of state duties in the name of human rights?

Another proposition to be reviewed here is that the recognition of socioeconomic rights at the international level owes a special debt to socialist doctrine.[4] Various scholars have built theses to this effect on the fact that certain social and economic rights were first expressed in constitutional documents of regimes that openly identified themselves with socialist principles and programs.[5] Can such a viewpoint be squared with the abundant evidence of non-socialist origins of various conceptions of social protection and the social duties of the state? Is the concept of social rights dependent on an approach to social justice that emphasizes equality rather than liberty or national solidarity?[6]

Contemporary Recognition of Social Rights and International Human Rights

At the root of any analysis of the evolution of socioeconomic rights is the question of the definition of rights, particularly human rights. The

2. T. H. Marshall, *Class, Citizenship, and Social Development* (Garden City, NY: Double-day, 1964), 105.

3. Ibid.

4. Burns Weston, "Human Rights," *Human Rights Quarterly* 6, 3 (August 1984): 265.

5. See Imre Szabo, "Historical Foundations of Human Rights and Subsequent Development," in Karel Vasak, ed., *The International Dimensions of Human Rights* (Westport, CT: Greenwood Press, 1982), 1: 19.

6. See Douglas M. Johnston, "The Foundations of Justice in International Law," in Ronald St. John Macdonald, Johnston, and Gerald L. Morris, eds., *The International Law and Policy of Human Welfare* (Alphen aan den Rijn, Netherlands: Sijthoff and Noordhoff, 1978), pp. 118–119.

Marshallian conception of a social right assumes the development of a legal claim that can be asserted by individuals as citizens. Such legally enforceable rights undoubtedly exist in most nation-states today, and certainly have existed in various countries for well over a century.

Yet these same nation-states have been rather reluctant to mandate such individual rights for citizens (much less for all residents or nationals) through intergovernmental organizations. Some of this reluctance stems in part from the continuing variations in welfare state programs even among proximate industrial states, with some rooting various social rights in constitutional law and others depending on statute alone.[7] This hesitancy also reflects major differences among governments regarding willingness to accept supranational policing of the provision of socioeconomic rights and, in some cases, claims that their federal systems pose special problems. Nonetheless, contemporary socioeconomic needs and demands are frequently expressed in post-1945 international human rights instruments as rights. This reflects the broad (yet far from unchallenged) support during the third quarter of this century for a sweeping conception of human rights designed in part to redeem wartime and postwar promises of social justice. Yet when socioeconomic rights were drafted as part of international human rights instruments there was a dominant tendency, at the global and regional levels, to sharply limit the legal obligations and entitlements associated with social and economic "rights" ranging from social insurance to employment. The outcomes were usually conceptually closer to what Joel Feinberg has termed "manifesto rights" than to the much more substantial sense in which Henry Shue, among others, advocates "subsistence rights."[8]

Rights do not appear to be the key operative concept in leading contemporary international documents purporting to prescribe social and economic rights. Statements of welfare rights in such instruments as the United Nations International Covenant on Economic, Social and Cultural Rights and the Council of Europe's European Social Charter are designed primarily to highlight the broad context of state responsibilities regarding health, welfare, education, and employment, while only minimally advancing meaningful individual entitlements.[9]

7. Louis Henkin, "Rights: Here and There," *Columbia Law Review* 81 (1981): 1582–1610.

8. Joel Feinberg, *Rights, Justice, and the Bounds of Liberty: Essays in Social Policy* (Princeton, NJ: Princeton University Press, 1980), p. 153; Henry Shue, *Basic Rights: Subsistence, Affluence, and U.S. Foreign Policy* (Princeton, NJ: Princeton University Press, 1980), pp. 22–29.

9. International Covenant on Economic, Social and Cultural Rights, opened for signature December 16, 1966, entered into force January 3, 1976 (Appendix IV, this

The limits of such documents are widely known. While some strengthen legal claims on grounds of equal protection and non-discrimination, they have rarely been meaningfully invoked in relation to inadequate social and economic provision for the minimal needs of any nation's residents or citizens, individually or in the aggregate. The U.N. Covenant on Economic, Social and Cultural Rights allows for rights to be established "progressively," "to the maximum of [each state's] available resources," subject to the promotion of the general welfare, and not necessarily in relation to non-nationals.[10] Even the Council of Europe, whose member states had little need to equivocate about their implementation of most areas of social rights, found it necessary in 1961 to incongruously employ the comprehensive language of rights while allowing ratifying states to initially remain unbound regarding any two of seven articles in the "compulsory nucleus" of the European Social Charter.[11]

We can apply a variety of authoritative tests of "welfare rights" in the instruments noted above. For Carl Wellman, a right is "a system of normative elements that, if respected, confers autonomy concerning the exercise or enjoyment of some specified core upon its possessor in face of one or more second parties."[12] Dworkin speaks of individual rights as "political trumps" that should overcome challenges based on assertions of collective goals.[13]

I have no difficulty conceiving of welfare rights in such terms as Wellman's and Dworkin's, and I accept in principle conceptualizing various of them as legal rights. Such tests are approached in various leading international human rights instruments regarding equal protection claims as well as claims to rights based on a traditional political-civil conception of liberty (e.g., freedom of trade union association).[14] Yet the international prescription and implementation of most social and economic rights are rooted in the view that primary welfare rights, entitlements to particular benefits or social protections, are inherently subject to the limits of states' financial, physical, and administrative resources.[15]

There are, of course, variations in the degree to which primary social

---

volume); European Social Charter, signed October 18, 1961, entered into force February 26, 1965 (Appendix III, this volume).

10. International Covenant on Economic, Social and Cultural Rights, Articles 2 and 4.

11. European Social Charter, Article 20.

12. Carl Wellman, *Welfare Rights* (Totowa, NJ: Rowan and Littlefield, 1982), p. 31.

13. Ronald Dworkin, *Taking Rights Seriously* (Cambridge, MA: Harvard University Press, 1977), p. xi.

14. International Covenant on Economic, Social, and Cultural Rights, Article 8.

15. Ibid., Article 2.

rights are qualified in major international instruments. For example, social security is prescribed more forthrightly than the right to work, reflecting its broader institutionalization and acceptance. Although social security standards of European and global intergovernmental organizations have clearly focused on equality and national reciprocity in treatment, such agencies have also fostered the "right to protection" in relation to inclusion of additional categories of persons, a broader range of covered risks, and more generous minimum benefits.[16] Yet since the late 1970s there has been a major effort to constrain and sometimes roll back various aspects of social insurance in many Western industrialized states, with emboldened opponents arguing that high costs and certain other aspects of its provision reduce the economic competitiveness of various countries.[17] It is not clear that international labor standards have contributed significantly to the counter-effort to maintain and advance social benefits in those states.

Demands concerning the right to employment have provided major challenges to intergovernmental organizations. Although such a right is asserted in numerous instruments promoted by global and regional intergovernmental organizations, including the United Nations and Council of Europe, the global community has been quite restrained regarding its advocacy. Indeed, a major effort to strengthen the concept of a right to work in the Employment Policy (Supplementary Provisions) Recommendation adopted by the International Labor Organization (ILO) in 1984 was largely rebuffed by a broad coalition of member states.[18]

The avoidance of the term "right to work" in most ILO instruments has helped the ILO committee concerned with the application of labor standards to be free to ignore such a right in its regular reviews of compliance with that organization's conventions and recommendations. Yet that committee has agreed to help the United Nations to review national reports and other information relating to the right to work and related articles in the Economic and Social Covenant. For this purpose the committee has interpreted Article 6, dealing with the right

16. Richard L. Siegel, "The Transnationalization of Domestic Policy: Social Security in Western Europe and the United States," in Forest L. Grieves, ed., *Transnationalism in World Politics and Business* (New York: Pergamon Press, 1979), p. 73.

17. See Hugh Heclo, "Toward a New Welfare State?" in Peter Flora and Arnold J. Heidenheimer, eds., *The Development of Welfare States in Europe and America: Conference on Social Policies in the 1980s* (New Brunswick, NJ: Transaction Press, 1981, pp. 398–406; *The Welfare State in Crisis: An Account of the Conference on Social Policies in the 1980s* (Paris: OECD, 1981).

18. International Labour Conference, 70th Sess., 1984, *Record of Proceedings* (Geneva: ILO, 1984), pp. XVII–XXXV, 32/1–28, 39/1–14.

to work, to involve "general measures to promote equality of opportunity and treatment in employment," "policies and measurements
pursued with a view to achieving full employment," and issues of
forced labor that relate to "free choice of employment."[19]

This committee's approach, fully consistent with the language of the
Economic and Social Rights Covenant, supports the contention that
most contemporary intergovernmental organizations prefer to deal
with social and economic rights in terms of equal protection and government interference with individual liberty. They rarely utilize a regulatory approach that reaches beyond such parameters, and in particular tend to avoid passing judgment on alleged denials of the rights of
individuals to subsistence, work or other basic needs.

Drawn from the international implementation of rights to social
security and work, such lessons cast doubt on the significance of the
line separating historic social protection and contemporary social or
welfare rights. If national governments feel free to reduce as well as
augment most areas of social protection without great concern for
international reactions, then the conceptual gap between sixteenth- or
eighteenth-century European social protection and contemporary international assertions of social rights may well be less significant than
many are prepared to concede. Although nation-states generally appear to accept social and economic rights as legal rights, the rights are
still implemented in a manner that reflects older conceptions of social
protection. We seek in the following pages to review early perspectives
and experience concerning socioeconomic rights generally and the
right to employment in particular.

Early Roots of Socioeconomic Rights

T. H. Marshall emphasized that, although social rights were linked to
the earlier developed political and civil rights, they were essentially
products of the late nineteenth and the twentieth centuries. This perspective is part of a broader tendency to emphasize differences between earlier and contemporary paternalistic and conservative traditions and the brave new offerings of this century's welfare states. In
order to review such historical relationships it is necessary to reconsider various countries' social legislation, as prescribed and implemented, and to reexamine the social policy implications of schools of

19. U.N. Economic and Social Council, *Implementation of the International Covenant on
Economic, Social and Cultural Rights* (New York: United Nations) E/1983/40, April 15,
1983, pp. 8–9; see also "Human Rights—U.N. Monitors Progress," *Free Labour World* 5
(Nov.–Dec. 1984): 24–26.

social and political thought not generally identified with a socially active state. Several prominent authorities have recently encouraged such reconsiderations.

Gertrude Himmelfarb, in one of most intensive reviews of British intellectual thought concerning poverty and welfare, notes that "an Old Corruption Radical . . . would have located social as well as civil rights in the eighteenth century, with its 'moral economy' and paternalistic 'old society.'"[20] Though various European nation states were far more repressive than benevolent toward the poor from about 1550 to 1850, numerous more or less "paternalistic old societies" evolved during that long period.

Socioeconomic rights have rather deep roots that are, in addition to socialist ones, also feudal, mercantilist, Methodist, utilitarian, radical conservative, Roman Catholic—and even classical liberal. Such diverse perceptions and forces as aristocratic paternalism, fear of social disintegration, utopian musings, belief in "the idea of progress," and political leaders' awareness of the need to integrate additional elements of the population into a solidary citizenry cumulatively contributed far more than the various socialist schools to the recent emergence of an international consensus concerning the social duties of government.[21]

The modern state's legal responsibilities to the poor are linked to obligations accepted by European feudal towns, principalities, and other local jurisdictions above and beyond those long implemented by the Church.[22] From the sixteenth century the rising nation-states moved erratically from what Hugh Heclo has termed "exhortations for local parish support" of the poor to legislation that mandated local tax collecting and direct provision for certain categories of the poor. They also developed various administrative mechanisms to ensure such assistance.[23] Maurice Bruce traces the English Poor Law in terms of "the slow widening of the area of responsibility, from the parish, through the Union (1834) to the Local Authority (1930), and eventually . . . to the nation as a whole."[24] At each of these levels of responsibility a sense of state obligations was evolving, driven forward by various strands of social thought termed radical and conservative, as well as utopian and practical.

The relating of employment to poor relief was advanced by the

20. Himmelfarb, *Idea of Poverty*, p. 268.
21. See Robert Nisbet, *History of the Idea of Progress* (New York: Basic Books, 1980).
22. Marc Bloch, *Feudal Society*, trans. L. A. Manyon, 2nd ed. (London: Routledge and Kegan Paul, 1962), 2: 408.
23. Hugh Heclo, *Modern Social Politics in Britain and Sweden: From Relief to Income Maintenance* (New Haven, CT: Yale University Press, 1974), p. 50.
24. Maurice Bruce, *The Coming of the Welfare State* (London: B. T. Batsford, 1968), p. 7.

dramatic proliferation of writings on this subject in seventeenth-century England. Although some English radicals of that era were long surprisingly reluctant to advocate direct state underwriting of programs for the relief of destitution and the provision of work, often preferring private support, others joined conservatives in offering what they viewed as practical proposals for state-sponsored relief. Various more or less radical seventeenth-century English writers viewed as inadequate the authorities' emphasis on systems of work-houses to assure subsistence. The motivations of various pamphleteers included concerns for increasing national production, reducing crime, and elevating the morals of the poor. The idea of a right to food or subsistence gained advocates among these publicists.[25] Although work had not yet gained wide recognition as an object of right, even among the leading radical schools, the provision of employment was a principal focus of such radical and not so radical authors as Samuel Hartlib, Peter Chamberlen, William Goffe, Gabriel Plattes, Caspar Stiblinus, Gerard Winstanley, Peter Cornelious Plockhoy, Robert Burton, Sir Mathew Hale, Richard Haines, John Bellers, and Sir Ambrose Crowley.[26]

Ideas developed in England during the tumultuous seventeenth century centered on a catalytic role for the state in originating new productive enterprises, often focusing on the task of raising and investing capital. The idea of public works was certainly not new to the seventeenth century. What was striking was the variety of proposals for public and private investment in employment-generating projects that were stimulated by an era of new industries and changing patterns of international trade. Some have identified the origins of modern state social and economic planning in the ideas of various English writers in the 1630s and 1640s.[27]

Various strains of seventeenth-century English radicalism developed a vision of an uncomplicated and permanent full employment society, whether stimulated by state creation of additional factories (Chamberlen) shipbuilding and fisheries (Goffe), supply of hemp and flax directly to the poor (Hartlib), or redistribution of the common land and promotion of collective or state farms (Winstanley). The needs to markedly increase overall demand for domestic production and to

25. Joyce Oldham Appleby, *Economic Thought and Ideology in Seventeenth-Century England* (Princeton, NJ: Princeton University Press, 1978), pp. 53–54.

26. J. B. Davis, *Utopia and the Ideal Society: A Study of English Utopian Writing, 1516–1700* (Cambridge: Cambridge University Press, 1981), pp. 300–367.

27. Charles Webster, ed., *The Intellectual Revolution of the Seventeenth Century* (London: Routledge and Kegan Paul, 1974), p. 378.

increase the value of labor on a national basis were already widely understood by the writers noted here.

Most seventeenth-century (and subsequent) utopian approaches to problem-solving were to have limited immediate impact, partly due to their emphasis on implementation in withdrawn communities. Nonetheless, as expressed by J. C. Davis, "the fact that we expect institutions, new or reformed, legislation or educational programs, to solve, or at least cope with, most of our social problems owes much to that utopian tradition of thought."[28]

If the largely unconsummated radicalism of seventeenth-century England produced little lasting progress toward the modern welfare state, other forces shaped a truly extraordinary social experiment in that country at the end of the eighteenth century. Under the English Speenhamland system, which functioned at the local level from 1785 to 1834, the authorities subsidized the wages of a large proportion of laborers in relation to established formulas. Karl Polanyi, though critical of some of Speenhamland's ultimate effects on agricultural laborers, viewed it as establishing in practice a "right to live."[29] This right was proclaimed in 1793 by the authors of the French Declaration of the Rights of Man.[30] Contemporaneously, the Prussian Civil Code that came into force in 1794 asserted that "it is the duty of the State to provide the sustenance and support of those of its citizens who cannot . . . provide subsistence themselves."[31] This Code also included a state commitment to provide work to the dependent. More than two hundred and fifty years of European national paternalism were culminating in such policies even as counter-attacks from liberals were being mobilized with varying strength in much of Europe.

The seventeenth- and eighteenth-century social and economic

28. Davis, *Utopia and the Ideal Society*, p. 9.

29. Karl Polanyi, *The Great Transformation* (Boston: Beacon Press, 1957), p. 78. Polanyi also emphasizes the national administration of the English Poor Law through the Crown's Justices of the Peace between 1590 and 1640. For a discussion of the paternalism of the English magistrates see Peter Dunkley, "Paternalism, the Magistracy and Poor Relief in England, 1795–1834," *International Review of Social History* XXIV (1979), Part 3: 371–397.

30. Richard B. DuBoff, "Economic Thought in Revolutionary France, 1789–1792," in *French Historical Studies* 4 (1966): 434–451. The preamble of the Declaration proclaimed, "Society is obliged to provide for the subsistence of all its members, either by giving them work or by supporting those who are unable to work."

31. Gaston V. Rimlinger, *Welfare Policy and Industrialization in Europe, America and Russia* (New York: John Wiley, 1971), p. 94. This code preceded by only two years William Pitt's aborted proposal to Parliament concerning such social programs as pension funds, family allowances and state-provided education. Also see Himmelfarb, *Idea of Poverty*, pp. 74–75.

thought and policies discussed above were bridges to the utopian socialist and pre-socialist proposals for relief, training and employment offered by Robert Owen and Louis Blanc, among others, in the first half of the nineteenth century.[32] The ideas of rights to subsistence and employment were implemented briefly and experimentally in revolutionary France in 1848 in the form of large-scale state provision of employment. With the early collapse of such programs, leadership in the development of state obligations again shifted to such conservatives as Napoleon III and Bismarck.

Positions concerning the state's duties to the poor were often not polarized on ideological lines. As noted by Polanyi, "Syndicalism, capitalism, socialism, and anarchism were indeed almost indistinguishable in their plans for the poor" as late as the first half of the nineteenth century.[33] These eclectic origins are indicated in Bruce's portrayal of nineteenth century British social legislation as inspired by "in part Christian concern for fellow men, in part the humanism of the late eighteenth century and the social legacy of the French Revolution, and in part—for long, the least part—the socialism which . . . endeavored to find scientific remedies for the injustices of industrial society."[34] In the century following the French revolution, the advocates of progressive development of social legislation designed to protect the poor against unemployment and hunger represented virtually the entire political spectrum. Prominent advocates included William Pitt, Thomas Paine, Louis Blanc, Benjamin Disraeli, Otto von Bismarck, Johann Fichte, Pope Leo XIII, Napoleon III, and John Stuart Mill.[35] Some of these figures carried forward elements of conservative traditions of feudal and mercantilist religious and secular ideas. Others echoed earlier radical themes nurtured by such developments as the Reformation and England's Glorious Revolution. The evident ideological diversity represented by the proponents of greater social protection, including the right to employment, is illustrated in the following pages via brief summaries of the contributions of radicals Paine and

32. Plans for national systems for training and employment were advanced early in the nineteenth century by Robert Owen and, in the context of the 1840s, by Louis Blanc. Both of these writers are closely linked to the origins of nineteenth century socialism.

33. Polanyi, *Great Transformation*, p. 108.

34. Bruce, *Coming of the Welfare State*, p. 13.

35. See, for example, Nisbet, *History of the Idea of Progress*, pp. 227–279, 272–273; Joseph N. Moody, "Leo XIII and the Social Crisis," in Edward T. Gargan, ed., *Leo XIII and the Modern World* (New York: Sheed and Ward, 1961), pp. 65–88; Leo Loubère, *Louis Blanc* (Evanston, IL: Northwestern University Press, 1961); George Lichtheim, *The Origins of Socialism* (New York: Praeger, 1969), pp. 80–82, 104–107.

Blanc and the distinctly non-radical Emperor Napoleon III, Chancellor Otto von Bismarck, and Pope Leo XIII.

The individuals and groups discussed below advanced employment-related ideas and programs that anticipated aspects of the twentieth century welfare state and, in some instances, the prescription by governments and international organizations of the right to work. For some of them support of such rights and benefits was an endorsement of a belief rooted in natural law and concepts of distributive justice. For others it was a vote for the possible and necessary, support for the capability of the emerging discipline of economics and of public administration to assure that all citizens seeking employment could be assured of a job, a decent wage, reasonable working conditions, and insurance against the loss of the ability to work.

Revolutionary Traditions: The Comité de Mendicité, Thomas Paine, and Louis Blanc

Although Thomas Paine and Louis Blanc are separated by half a century, they are connected by their association with the heritage of the French Revolution. Paine helped the revolutionary Assembly to draft the Declaration of the Rights of Man. Blanc was a prolific historian of those revolutionary events as well as a major actor in the revolutionary months of 1848.

Provision of work by the state was at the heart of the approach to public relief legislated during the first five years of the revolution. Ground for such an approach had been prepared during the several decades before 1789 by both authors and administrators, including Jacques Necker and Jacques Turgot. Although many proposed ideas were not implemented before the revolution, interest in public workshops and public works was then already high in various parts of France. Turgot put such a policy into practice during his term as Intendant at Limoges, which included efforts to complete particular projects as well as to create jobs.[36] Broad support for such efforts was also evident in the writings of such Enlightenment figures as Jean Jacques Rousseau and the Marquis de Condorcet, each providing justifications in the spirit of egalitarianism and progress.[37]

---

36. Rimlinger, *Welfare Policy and Industrialization*, p. 28; Alan Forrest, *The French Revolution and the Poor* (New York: St. Martin's Press, 1981), p. 101.

37. Garraty, *Unemployment in History*, p. 61; Stuart Hampshire, "Introduction," in Marquis de Condorcet, *Sketch for a Historical Picture of the Progress of the Human Mind*, trans. June Barraclough (London: Weidenfeld and Nicolson, n.d.).

The revolutionary Assembly's Comité pour l'Extinction de la Mendicité expressed a strong governmental commitment to job creation together with a program for centralizing critical aspects of social service and direct poor relief.[38] Although reflecting homage to free enterprise and the need for efficiency and economy in public programs, from 1790 to 1794 the Comité was instrumental in securing central government support for public workshops, public works, new central government allocations to various institutions and poor funds, and experiments in social insurance. These revolutionary programs were short-lived for reasons that included financial constraints on the central government, evident waste and fraud in programs, and perceived negative impacts on private employers in regard to wages and work discipline.[39] By 1792 the emphasis on public workshops and works began to recede, and soon there were also sharp reductions in other central government welfare programs.

The political environment of the first several years of the revolutionary era provided the backdrop for Thomas Paine to extend his radicalism beyond narrowly defined political issues. Paine undoubtedly embodied contradictions concerning the roles of the state regarding poverty and unemployment that paralleled those of the Comité. The radical publicist's credentials as a progenitor of the welfare state have been sharply disparaged by Himmelfarb and others. She contends that Paine offered merely "another version of the poor law," a legal and moral commitment to the poor in times of need.[40]

Much could be added to Himmelfarb's deprecation of Paine's contribution to the welfare state and the right to work. His proposed state-sponsored workplace was a variation of the traditional asylum, and he thought in terms of assisting only several tens of thousands of the unemployed.[41] Yet Himmelfarb seems to underestimate the significance of millions of copies of Paine's pamphlets, which repeatedly emphasized the concept of rights in relation to a wide range of social and political demands. Paine is credited with collaborating with Condorcet in preparing a draft Declaration of the Rights of Man in January 1783 that developed several aspects of the concept of the right to

38. Du Boff, *Economic Thought in Revolutionary France*, pp. 443–444; Forrest, *French Revolution and the Poor*, p. 99. According to Forrest, emphasis was placed on outdoor projects demanding hard physical labor and tens of thousands of workers were employed at least seasonally.

39. Forrest, *French Revolution and the Poor*, pp. 109–112.

40. Himmelfarb, *Idea of Poverty*, p. 88.

41. Thomas Paine, "The Rights of Man, Part II," in Philip S. Foner, ed., *The Complete Writings of Thomas Paine* (New York: The Citadel, 1969), I: 430.

employment and affirmed a modern conception of the right to education.[42]

Although Paine's view of the right to work was rooted in a classical liberal perspective that focused on the repeal of mercantilist restrictions on economic activity, he offered anomalous proposals based on collectivist notions of state responsibility. Paine promised in *The Rights of Man*, Volume II, "Employment, at all times, for the casual poor in the cities of London and Westminster."[43] Four years later, William Pitt, the Younger, offered Parliament a comprehensive poor law reform that would establish relief as a "right and an honour."[44] Although this proposal was quickly withdrawn from parliamentary scrutiny, it testified to the pressures in England as well as in France during the late 1790s to address social needs as well as political reform with reference to the rights of man.

Yet it was left to Louis Blanc, journalist, historian, and member of the 1848–49 French Provisional Government, to be the principal pioneer of the right to employment. Loubere goes further by claiming for Blanc and his colleagues at the daily Reforme "the kernel from which the principle of social security grew."[45]

Blanc himself delineates how his conception of the right to labor differed from those of Turgot, Paine, and others, arguing in his *History of the French Revolution of 1789*:

Do not be deceived, however. Turgot never went so far as to recognize the right to labor. He wished the poor to be left to develop their faculties freely, but he did not admit that society owed them the means of attaining it. . . . In a word, it was a right of laboring, and not the right to labor, which he admitted.[46]

Blanc was not always enamored of the concept of rights. He repeatedly compared the idea of having a right disparagingly with having the *power* to avail oneself of a right.[47] He foreshadowed the attitude of many twentieth-century commentators on human rights when he cas-

---

42. Thomas Paine, "Plan of a Declaration of the National, Civil and Political Rights of Man," in Foner, *Complete Writings of Paine*, Vol. II, pp. 559–560. Part II was published in London in 1792. George Lichtheim credits Paine with having "sketched the outline of the modern welfare state." Lichtheim, *Origins of Socialism*, p. 104.

43. Foner, *Writings of Thomas Paine*, II: 431.

44. Himmelfarb, *Idea of Poverty*, p. 74.

45. Loubere, *Louis Blanc*, p. 57.

46. Louis Blanc, *History of the French Revolution of 1789* (Philadelphia: Lea & Blanchard, 1848), I: 297.

47. Louis Blanc, *The Evils of Capitalism*, Bride Lane Reprints, No. 1 (London: Bride Lane, n.d.), pp. 14–15.

tigated rights "pompously proclaimed in sterile charters."[48] He defended the 1848–49 French Provisional Government's policies on the provision of work by endorsing John Stuart Mill's view that the revolutionary government had contemplated no right of individuals to demand work and had given no pledge that work would be found or created for each applicant.[49]

Nonetheless, no nineteenth century figure is more closely identified with the right to employment than Blanc. The key is his unqualified position favoring state responsibility to ensure full employment. As phrased in his leading work, *Organisation du Travail*, written in 1840: "It is necessary to use the whole power of the state and this is certainly not too great an undertaking for so great a need. That which the proletarians lack to free themselves are the tools of labor; these the government must furnish them."[50] Blanc utilized this volume to advocate that government should fund and found social workshops that would put essentially all unemployed persons to work and direct such projects until self-governing production cooperatives could evolve. The state would also aid every industry "which has suffered through extraordinary and unforseen circumstances."[51]

The revolutionary events of 1848 placed Blanc in a position to influence, but not directly shape, the partial implementation of his proposals. Blanc was brought into the Provisional Government but was not given a ministry. The Luxembourg Commission that he chaired, established by his colleagues to study and recommend labor policies, served as a political sop to deflect demands for a Ministry of Work.

In the heady revolutionary days of early 1848 the official proclamation of the right to work seemed to some a small political concession to massed Parisian workers. Yet the revolutionary constitution went no further than the 1793 Declaration of the Rights of Man regarding guarantees of work or subsistence. A decree of February 25, 1848 stated that "The provisional government of the French Republic undertakes to guarantee the worker's livelihood through work."[52]

Although expectations were raised for a program of national workshops that would fulfill the decree, these were neither established according to Blanc's criteria nor controlled by supporters of his plan.

48. Ibid., p. 14.
49. Louis Blanc, *1848: Historical Revelations* (London: Chapman and Hall, 1858), p. 84.
50. Louis Blanc, *Organization of Work* 7, trans. Marie Paula Dickore, University of Cincinnati Studies, Series II (Cincinnati, OH: University of Cincinnati, 1911), p. 46.
51. Ibid., p. 55.
52. Roger Price, *1848 in France* (Ithaca, NY: Cornell University Press, 1975), p. 68.

Instead the massive provision of work through state-funded work-shops was given a shabby and short-lived trial that largely discredited such programs for many decades thereafter. During this revolutionary period the right to work was extolled by workers' advocates as never before, the Comité-Démocrate Socialiste declaring, "The right to work is the first of all rights. It is the right to live."[53]

Its advocates were soon discredited in the wake of violence and revelations of high costs and waste. Blanc was left to argue after the fact that the workshops of 1848 had been a far cry from his earlier pro-posals. Nonetheless, history could record a precedent for large-scale funding of workshops primarily designed to provide jobs and subsis-tence to the victims of economic and political crisis.

The Socialist Tradition

Although socialism did not emerge whole cloth in nineteenth-century Europe, it developed into a major intellectual and political force in that period. Contributions of numerous advocates of socialism to the causes of socioeconomic rights in general, and the right to work in particular, are of fundamental importance. Yet the distance of socialists from governmental authority throughout the century, their frequent prefer-ences for utopian experimentation and wholesale revolution, and their concerns that reforms could block the coming of socialism all limited their contributions to the effective expansion of socioeconomic rights and the welfare state.

Perhaps the greatest contribution of nineteenth-century socialism to the cause of socioeconomic rights was its analysis of changing indus-trial relations and the overall condition of workers and their families. Various socialist theorists focused on plans to eliminate or ameliorate unemployment and underemployment, exploring such needs as edu-cation and training programs (Robert Owen)[54] and meaningful public employment (Owen, Claude Henri de Saint-Simon).[55] Many socialists never rejected the possibility of such amelioration, to be accomplished within a structure of free trade union activity, parliamentary involve-ment, public education, and coalitions with diverse forces on behalf of

---

53. *La Reforme*, April 20, 1849, cited in Price, *1848 in France*, p. 134.

54. Robert Owen, "Essays on the Formation of Character," in *The Life of Robert Owen Written by Himself* (London: Effinsham Wilson, Royal Exchange, 1857; rpt. Augustus M. Kelley, 1967), 1: 317.

55. Owen, *Life of Owen*, 1: 213; Ghita Ionescu, ed., *The Political Thought of Saint-Simon* (London: Oxford University Press, 1976), pp. 147–148.

particular political goals. Yet even socialists interested in non-revolu-
tionary approaches rejected many paternalistic legislative efforts, perceiving them as undercutting potential mass support for trade union-
ism and socialism by reducing union administration of workers' welfare
programs and by eroding the class-based consciousness of the majority
of workers.

Although not a socialist invention,[56] the right to work was given
considerable theoretical and popular advancement by various socialists, among them Charles Fourier. This French utopian also did much
to broaden the conception of the importance of work to the human
experience, emphasizing the ways in which labor could be made "attractive."[57] Fourier advanced a view of the sources of the right to labor,
relating it to the "the four cardinal rights: the chase, fishing, gathering
and pasturage."[58] The eclectic nature of the sources of socioeconomic
rights is underlined by the irony of Fourier's reference to work as an
apparently divine right: "God has condemned man to earn his bread
by the sweat of his brow; but he did not condemn us to be deprived of
the labor upon which our subsistence depends."[59] Fourier could not
have been more emphatic in his assertion of the centrality of this right:
"We have, then spent centuries in wrangling over the rights of man,
without thinking of recognizing the one which is the most essential,
that of labour, without which the others are nothing."[60] Fourier affirmed the need for "le regime garantist," which would assure work or
subsistence to all.[61]

The limits of the socialist contribution to socioeconomic rights loom
large despite such rhetoric. Fourier epitomized the emphasis on utopian experimentation that brought contempt from later advocates of
the transformation of capitalism. The first Socialist party able to have a
major impact on national legislation, that of Germany, was for decades
forced into a generally negative posture concerning major social policies by Bismarck and other enemies of socialism.

Whereas Karl Marx now looms as the leading socialist theorist of the

56. Samuel Zivs credits Johann Gottlieb Fichte for creating the "slogan" of the right to
work. Zivs, *Human Rights: Continuing the Discussion* (Moscow: Progress Publishers, 1980),
p. 39.
    57. Charles Gide, ed., *Selections from the Works of Fourier* (London: Swan Sonnenschein,
1901), pp. 163–170.
    58. Ibid., p. 191.
    59. Ibid., p. 190.
    60. Ibid., p. 191.
    61. Alexander Gray, ed., *The Socialist Tradition: Moses to Lenin* (London: Longmans,
Green, 1946), p. 188.

1800s, this was not evident for much of that century. Marx, even when condemning many proposals from various schools of socialist thought, blended elements of revolutionary communism and utopian socialism with economic analysis adapted from classical liberals.

Marx refused to consider the possibility of the right to work and other critical aspects of human rights within a capitalist framework. Although it has appropriately been said of Marx that "the entire body of his writings is one long analysis of what violates human dignity and human rights,"[62] the right to work could have little meaning for Marx within a system that he identified with forced labor and wage slavery. He stressed the absence of basic labor rights under capitalist law and viewed capitalism as increasingly incapable of providing the life-fulfilling benefits of work. As expressed by Marx in *The Class Struggles in France, 1848–50*, "the right to work is, in the bourgeois sense, an absurdity, a miserable pious wish."[63] This right would come only with "the appropriation of the means of production, their subjection to the associated working class, and therefore the abolition of wage labor, of capital, and of their mutual relations."[64] Without such a revolution, and the end of a system based on private property, under capitalism the right to work could mean no more or less than universal forced labor.

Marx was estranged from conceptions of human rights that were based exclusively on concern for individuals (as opposed to society) or that were deemed applicable to diverse social systems and various historical circumstances. He did suggest that there would be a right to work in the future socialist and communist societies, though he was just as emphatic concerning the obligation to work in such systems.[65]

Marx went beyond the critique of nineteenth-century industrial conditions expressed by other political figures and writers discussed in this chapter. His writings on alienation, the dissolution of traditional family patterns, and threats to the ability of workers to continue to provide for their own subsistence are major contributions that eventually influenced observers occupying a broad range of ideological positions.

Yet the major underlying contribution of Marxism to socioeconomic

62. John C. Haughey, S.J., "Individualism and Rights in Karl Marx," in Alfred Henelly and John Lensan, eds., *Human Rights in the Americas: The Struggle for Consensus* (Washington, DC: Georgetown University Press, 1982), p. 102.

63. Karl Marx, "The Class Struggles in France, 1848–50," in Saul K. Padover, ed., *Karl Marx: On Revolution* (New York: McGraw-Hill, 1971), p. 181.

64. Ibid.

65. See Bertell Ollman, "Marx's Vision of Communism: A Reconstruction," in Seweryn Bialer, ed., *Radicalism in the Contemporary Age* II (Boulder, CO: Westview Press, 1977), p. 44.

human rights was a strong commitment to an equality transcending
what he termed bourgeois right.[66] Marx focused attention on abstract
and utopian conceptions of equality—as with the borrowing from
others of the "to each according to his needs" slogan—instead of
contributing to particular public policy changes in support of equality
or social justice achievable in a capitalist or socialist setting. Marx
indicated, as in his *Critique of the Gotha Programme*, tactical interest in
certain reform measures relating to education and work that had been
proposed by other socialists.[67] Yet he provided few clear directions for
the extension of socioeconomic rights, offering instead penetrating
critiques of capitalist practices in these or other spheres. Marx has been
described as having "treated the subject [of unemployment] in such a
way as to discourage efforts to understand how it might be reduced or
eliminated."[68] Marxist contributions to the European welfare state
were limited until reformist disciples in Germany and elsewhere redirected socialism toward the social democratic modification of capitalism. Nonetheless, Marxist-Leninists pioneered the advocacy and implementation of the right to employment in the twentieth century.

The State and Full Employment: Emperor Napoleon III

The extraordinary variety of French nineteenth-century political experience shaped an experimental prototype for twentieth-century states
dedicated to maximizing employment through subsidies to private
corporations and other measures aimed at priming capitalist economies. Such an approach, identified with the Second Empire (1852–71)
of Napoleon III, advanced the legitimacy of state commitments to full
employment (though not the right to employment per se).

The French tradition of active state involvement in public works and
other economic development projects has deep roots, and was advanced in the 1820s by the drawing up of the Bexquey Plan, termed
"the first great public works program in the nineteenth century."[69]
Indeed, long before the events of 1848, France had a Ministry of Public
Works advancing systems of roads, canals, and railroads.

Emperor Napoleon III, who first took office as President Louis

---

66. Karl Marx, "Critique of the Gotha programme" (1875), in Karl Marx and Friedrich Engels, *Selected Works* (New York: International Publishers, 1970), p. 324.

67. Ibid., pp. 332–335.

68. Garraty, *Unemployment in History*, p. 104.

69. François Caron, *An Economic History of Modern France*, trans. Barbara Bray (New
York: Columbia University Press, 1979), p. 40.

Napoleon in 1848, is at least as difficult as Paine and Blanc to categorize in ideological terms. As summarized by Alain Plessis:

In the economic and social spheres, it would be vain to "classify" the emperor, to make him the disciple of any given school. He appears in turn as a man influenced by English liberals, as a "Saint-Simonian" Caesar, or at times as a socialist. He was above all an eclectic who borrowed from every doctrine whatever if his view could better the lot of the people.[70]

The highly authoritarian Napoleon III was far from consistently progressive in his social policies, and is identified with few concrete steps that advanced the French welfare state.[71] Yet he is important for the major place that the provision of employment played in his massive programs of public works and industrial development, as well as for his expansion of large-scale borrowing, loan guarantees, direct subsidies, and other measures to advance such "investments" in the public interest as railroads and urban redevelopment.[72] The savings of France were tapped by the state as never before, and the structure of the nation's banking and company law was firmly established.

Although the scale of the Second Empire's direct spending and accumulation of debt was remarkable only in contrast with certain preceding regimes,[73] Charles Kindleberger asserted that "not until 1944 and 1945 with the Monnet Plan did positive governmental intervention for growth assume the proportions of the Second Empire."[74] Napoleon III was constrained by his own conflicting beliefs and goals, and even more by his dependence on political elements that did not share his sympathies for the working classes. The emperor who had once authored *L'Extinction du Pauperisme*[75] had less than mixed results in advancing his version of the war on poverty. Yet a century later

70. Alain Plessis, *The Rise and Fall of the Second Empire, 1852–1871*, trans. Jonathan Mandelbaum (Cambridge: Cambridge University Press, 1985), p. 10.

71. One of the few was his regime's program for providing legal representation to poor workers. It also took various steps to legalize and tolerate the organization of labor. W. H. C. Smith, *Napoleon III* (New York: St. Martin's Press, 1972), p. 109.

72. See David H. Pinkney, *Napoleon III and the Rebuilding of Paris* (Princeton, NJ: Princeton University Press, 1958). Of course Emperor Napoleon III was not the only nineteenth-century political leader with an orientation toward public works and employment provision. Such a reputation was also earned, for example, by Joseph Chamberlain, later a long-term member of the British cabinet, during his tenure as mayor of Birmingham between 1873 and 1876.

73. Plessis, *Rise and Fall of the Second Empire*, pp. 64–65.

74. Charles Kindleberger, *Economic Growth in France and Britain, 1851–1950* (Cambridge, MA: Harvard University Press, 1964), p. 188.

75. A work of Louis Napoleon, circulated in 1844.

diverse historians were expressing appreciation for his innovative advocacy of governmental responsibility for employment.

Chancellor Otto von Bismarck and the Modern Welfare State

Although Bismarck must be included in any study of the development of socioeconomic rights in the nineteenth century, we need consider the limits as well as the extent of his legislative and administrative contributions. Although this man who dominated German affairs for more than twenty-five years thought little of the rights of workers, he acted boldly on their behalf regarding social insurance. He viewed such state sponsored programs as politically astute as well as the appropriate paternalistic duty of the German state.

Although each of the nineteenth century European figures discussed here embodied sharp contradictions in their social policies and viewpoints, this was especially true of Bismarck. The Iron Chancellor fostered classical liberal measures that included freer trade and trade union association and challenged the emerging Socialist movement with proposals for a broad program of social insurance. Notably, he resigned from office largely because he refused to go as far as his emperor in extending social legislation or promoting international cooperation regarding the protection of labor.

Although Bismarck's relationships with German political parties were eclectic, he is best understood as the heir to the aristocratic German landowners' tradition of public service and paternalism in domestic policy. As phrased by Hans Rothfels,

> He was a man of the traditional order of things and of Luther's social conception; he wished to maintain an adequate standard for the craftsman protected by his guild, and the personal relationship between worker and work.[76]

Yet he was not so dedicated to such a tradition as to reject all perceived legitimate arguments of liberals and socialists. Further, bold policy steps were taken to meet immediate political exigencies or as part of long-term strategies designed to outflank opponents and broaden constituencies.

Although Bismarck largely instigated Germany's *Kulturkampf*, the sharp confrontation between the State and the Catholic Church that developed during the 1870s, he subsequently depended greatly on the

---

76. Hans Rothfels, "Bismarck's Social Policy and the Problem of State Socialism in Germany," *Sociological Review*, Part I, 30, 1 (January 1938): 87.

Catholic Centre party to help secure Reichstag approval of his path-breaking social insurance programs. While not himself the direct inheritor of the political forces instigated by Bishop Wilhelm von Ketteler and other German founders of Social Catholicism,[77] he was able to reap benefits from their political legacy.[78]

Equally significant for the promotion of Bismarck's social policies was his ability to prevent a middle class takeover of the political system. He blocked this with such means as universal suffrage, parliamentary gerrymandering, selective cooptation of industrialists' families into the aristocracy, the forcing of liberal politicians into difficult parliamentary corners, and the delivery of very real state support for legitimate interests of German industry. Bismarck benefited greatly from the near collapse of German liberalism in the wake of the political debates of the late 1870s that challenged free trade and inaugurated repressive measures aimed at the Socialist left.[79] During the critical Reichstag considerations of social insurance in the 1880s the divided liberals could modify but not prevent the pioneering Bismarckian measures.[80]

Bismarck explored, during his first years in office, the possibility of a political alliance with the representatives of industrial labor, going as far as to confer with Ferdinand Lassalle on possible common objectives. Yet the Chancellor subsequently regarded the Socialists as the main threat to the German state.[81] To win the struggle against the Left, Bismarck utilized social insurance and other initiatives to bind the working class closer to the state. His social program mixed active repression of Socialist activists with measures that Bismarck himself

77. Alan Palmer, *Bismarck* (New York: Scribner's, 1976), pp. 205–206.

78. After contesting Bismarck for years over church-state issues, the Centre Party held one hundred Reichstag seats in 1881. William Carr, *A History of Germany, 1815–1945* (New York: St. Martin's Press, 1969), pp. 146, 159. See also Hartmut Lehmann, "Bodelschwinsh und Bismarck: Christlich-Konservative Sozialpolitik im Kaiserreich," *Historische Zeitschrift* 208, 3 (1969): 606–626.

79. A. J. P. Taylor and Marvin Rintala both embrace the view that there had been a "Junker defeat of the German middle class" engineered between 1862 and 1871, resulting in part from conservative adoption of key interests of middle class liberals during that period. See Marvin Rintala, "Two Compromises: Victorian and Bismarckian," *Government and Opposition* III, 2 (1968): 217–218; A. J. P. Taylor, *The Course of German History: A Survey of the Development of Germany Since 1815* (London: H.Hamilton, 1945), p. 108.

80. There was significant support from reform-oriented liberals such as those who helped constitute in 1872 the Verein für Sozialpolitik, designed to foster progressive social politics. In the 1880s Bismarck received support for his social insurance programs from a small but well-organized group of industrialists. Hans-Peter Ullman, "Industrielle Interessen und die Entstehung der Deutschen Sozialsicherung 1880–1889," *Historische Zeitschrift* 229, 3 (1979): 574–610.

81. Theodore Hamerow, *The Social Foundations of German Unification, 1858–1871* (Princeton, NJ: Princeton University Press, 1972), pp. 202–205.

identified with "state socialism."[82] Parliamentary Socialists, alert to the larger political war being fought, opposed the Chancellor's program for social insurance for more than a decade.

In economic terms, the German welfare state took off during "an extended period of depression and stagnation,"[83] an era marked by slower growth between two periods of rapid industrialization and more gradual advances for workers than for others. These conditions put classical liberalism—or its closest German equivalents—on the defensive and offered fertile ground for conservative proposals for social protection that were rooted in traditional German patterns of social policy and administration.

Despite Frederick the Great's 1794 Civil Code guarantee of work or subsistence, such traditional programs had not effectively included major state-sponsored employment programs. Bismarck dabbled in the promotion of employment, advocating in the 1860s a street-paving program for Berlin and state subsidies for struggling producer cooperatives.[84] Although he reportedly identified the right to work as part of the immemorial law of Germany on at least one occasion,[85] employment creation programs never constituted a major part of his social policy.

Consistent with this limited approach to the needs of most unemployed workers, Bismarck never offered a plan for unemployment insurance. Such programs first received government support in Switzerland in 1892, and spread to various continental cities before being adopted in various forms by Norway, Denmark, and Britain between 1904 and 1911.[86] Yet Bismarck's social insurance programs constituted widely studied models that were later adapted to unemployment by other governments.[87] It was not necessary for Germany to have state-sponsored unemployment insurance for it to help promote this crucial twentieth-century program elsewhere. Certain public policy developments are adapted from source concepts through what is termed "branching." As described by Grover Starling, "the development of public policy is not unlike the growth of a tree: branching out from a

82. William Dawson, *Social Insurance in Germany, 1883–1911* (Westport, CT: Greenwood Press, 1979), pp. 13–14 (orig. pub. London: T. Fisher Unwin, 1912).

83. Eda Sagarra, *A Social History of Germany, 1648–1914* (New York: Holmes and Meier, 1977), p. 425.

84. Hamerow, *Social Foundations of German Unification*, pp. 213–217.

85. Dawson, *Social Insurance in Germany*, pp. 2–3.

86. Hugh Heclo, *Modern Social Politics*, pp. 69–70; Garraty, *Unemployment in History*, p. 134.

87. Notable visits to Germany focusing on social insurance included that by then British Chancellor of the Exchequer Lloyd George in 1908.

few seminal ideas or themes are multifarious variations that lead to further variations."[88]

Bismarck's Germany offered the legislation and the record of implementation that encouraged much of the rest of Europe to plunge into social insurance on ever larger scales. It was demonstrated that social insurance could be administered efficiently, maintain strong political support from employers and workers alike, and not prove notably detrimental to national economic growth. The Chancellor provided income maintenance for such risks and inevitabilities as sickness, accidents, invalidity, and old age. Further, Germany's governmentally supported labor exchanges became a model for Europe.

Roman Catholicism and the Right to Employment: Pope Leo XIII and His Successors

The prescription of the right to work in post-1945 international human rights instruments depended in large part on its endorsement by strongly Roman Catholic countries in Europe and Latin America. Intellectuals and leaders of such states have periodically drawn on papal and other Catholic teachings to help justify their support for the promotion of rights in national constitutions as well as at intergovernmental forums.

Much contemporary social history understates the role played by the Roman Catholic Church, including its principal lay and religious spokespersons, in educating a broad public about social problems and preferred solutions in the nineteenth and twentieth centuries. Yet few, if any, scholars or politicians have the global audience of a pope, and none have their essays published in the world's leading newspapers as well as read to followers in churches throughout the world. As a force in transnational public policy debate, the Roman Catholic Church has few peers. Catholic alternatives to liberalism and socialism have had significant impacts on social policies affecting employment through such mechanisms as Christian Democratic parties, Catholic trade unions, and various other Catholic-related organizations promoting direct assistance to workers as well as other public policy viewpoints.[89]

The foundation for the evolution of Roman Catholic recognition of the need for new approaches to social protection is Pope Leo XIII's

88. Grover Starling, *The Politics and Economics of Public Policy* (Homewood, IL: Dorsey, 1979), p. 211.

89. Joseph A. Schumpeter, *History of Economic Analysis* (New York: Oxford University Press, 1954), pp. 764–765. I refer here to such organizations as the U.S. Knights of Labor, the Italian Salesian Order, and the French worker priest movement.

Rerum Novarum (The Condition of Labor), the 1891 encyclical which was written in the context of economic crisis and a rising socialist challenge in much of Western Europe. The seeds of Roman Catholic concern with the laborer's plight in the wake of the spreading industrial revolution had been sewn before and during Leo's papacy by such figures as Wilhelm von Ketteler, the Bishop of Mainz and theorist of German Social Catholicism, as well as the "Roman Committee for Social Studies" appointed by Leo.

Building on such work, Leo XIII (1878–1903) emerged as the primary authority for a part of Catholic thought that embraced the right to employment together with other basic aspects of the welfare state.[90] He labeled various rights of workers as natural rights while also strongly supporting a natural right to private property. Such workers' rights as freedom of association and the right to strike were also explicitly endorsed in *Rerum Novarum*. The right to employment was supported implicitly by Pope Leo in the following passage:

The Preservation of life is the bounden duty of each and all, and to fail therein is a crime. It follows that each one has a right to procure what is required in order to live; and the poor can procure it in no other way than by work and wages.[91]

Further, Leo XIII explicitly related the concept of distributive justice to industrial relations and offered significant, if grudging, acknowledgment of a substantial state role in assuring rights and social justice in that area. As viewed by Pope Pius XII fifty years later: "Leo XIII admonished [the State] that it had also the duty to interest itself in social welfare, taking care of the entire people and of all its members, especially the weak and the dispossessed, through a generous social program and the creation of a labor code."[92] Pope Leo's perspective was clearly traditional and paternalistic, evidenced by his admiring references to medieval guilds, his insistence on Christian worker and mixed employer-employee organizations, and

90. Michael Novak, *Freedom with Justice* (San Francisco: Harper and Row, 1984), pp. 61–69; Moody, "Leo XIII and the Social Crisis," pp. 72–78.
91. Pope Leo XIII, *Rerum Novarum* (The Condition of Labor), in William J. Gibbons and Gerald C. Treacy, eds., *Seven Great Encyclicals* (Glen Rock, NJ: Paulist Press, 1963), p. 21.
92. "Text of Pope Pius' Broadcast on the Fiftieth Anniversary of Leo XIII's Encyclical," *New York Times*, June 2, 1941, p. 4. For amplification of the Roman Catholic tradition concerning social and distributive justice see Jean-Yves Calvez and Jacques Perrin, *The Church and Social Justice* (Chicago: Henry Regnery, 1961), pp. 133–161.

his contempt for classical liberal as well as socialist solutions to the perceived social crises. Yet his enormous contributions to progressive Catholic social thought continue to the present, partly as a result of the papal tradition of commemorating and expanding on *Rerum Novarum* on each decennial anniversary.

The impact of papal and other Catholic pronouncements on work and social protection after *Rerum Novarum* was assured by their concentration on industrial relations and their contention that the situation of the worker was the essence of the social issue in Europe. Although geographically provincial, papal concerns focused on issues critical to industrial workers that required secular as well as clerical responses throughout the world. This tradition was probably unduly open to corporatist solutions to the organization and control of labor, and was reluctant to endorse some welfare state innovations or the direct participation of religious Catholics in the politics of the various nations. Yet it did provide a frame of reference that was sympathetic to a wide range of progressive proposals concerning social insurance, health and safety measures, more adequate wages, and additional time for leisure.

Roman Catholic support for the right to work that is more explicit than that offered by Leo XIII is identified with, among others, Heinrich Pesch (1854–1926), a disciple of Bishop von Ketteler and a link between the social writings of Leo XIII and subsequent progressive popes. Pesch contended that "Men have . . . as men in themselves, natural tasks and goals and, consequently, natural rights: the right to exist, the right to work, to acquire property, to activate their personal capabilities, the right to found a family, etc."[93]

Each decennial commemoration of *Rerum Novarum* helped sustain the widespread acceptance by Catholic nations of the international prescription of social and economic rights in general and the right to work in particular. During one such observance, a radio broadcast in the midst of World War II, Pius XII directly endorsed the idea that labor was both a duty and a right of every human being.[94] In his subtle 1941 presentation, Pius XII insisted on the natural rights origin of the right to work while rejecting the Marxist-Leninist and Fascist conceptions of such a right awarded by society, "as if man were nothing more than a mere slave or official of the community."[95] He spoke affir-

93. Heinrich Pesch, *Lehrbuch der Nationalekonomie*, rev. ed., (Freibert im Br., Germany: Herder, 1920–26), 1: 440, as quoted in Novak, *Freedom with Justice*, pp. 76–77.
94. "Text," *New York Times*, June 2, 1941, p. 4.
95. Ibid.

matively of "the right to reasonable liberty in the choice of a state of life and the fulfillment of a true vocation."[96] As such, Pius XII anticipated aspects of the liberal position in the postwar debates concerning the right to work.

Conclusion

The contemporary welfare state and the idea of a right to employment derive much of their strength from the ideological pluralism of their sponsors. In the case of social insurance, generally similar laws and systems emerged from divergent sources, its core elements later promoted by such international agencies as the ILO. The right to employment, in contrast, took on several distinct meanings, these rooted in the varying ideological sources. As a result, representatives of distinct ideological and religious traditions came to endorse the right to work after World War II without sharing a consensus about how this related to the obligations of national governments or the rights and duties of individuals.

The degree of consensus that existed in the middle of the twentieth century regarding socioeconomic rights was somewhat greater regarding the duties of states than the rights of individuals. This was largely because various strains of conservatism, liberalism, and socialism had been moving for over a century toward certain common perceptions about the appropriate duties of the state toward workers, the poor and other residents and citizens in the face of dislocations brought on by industrialization. Socialists and radicals articulated expanded conceptions of state duty and individual rights earlier in the nineteenth century than did those to their right on the political spectrum. Yet conservatives frequently pioneered major welfare state programs, sometimes seeking to head off Socialist political gains.

Nonetheless, few of the components of the contemporary welfare state have ever become firmly established as human rights, even in the most advanced welfare states. Rather, such programs have evolved primarily as extensions of old ideas about state duties and as contracts, sometimes provisional ones, between government and the governed. As noted by Gaston Rimlinger:

The modern welfare state has eliminated the punitive intent and established claims to benefits and services as a matter of individual right. But that right is

96. Ibid.

defined by rules of coverage and eligibility, and often by source of risk, and historically it has undergone important changes.[97]

Limitations to welfare rights are more evident in regard to public assistance, social services and state-provided employment than for social insurance, and the punitive and control functions of social protection have never been terminated. Each part of the welfare state has been vulnerable to periodic pressures to limit and reduce, as well as to expand, benefits and eligibility.

The duty of the state to ensure social protection is not the product of any particular social doctrine. Often the ideological divisions between left and right have centered on secondary issues, with various ideologies reinforcing consensus about state social duties. This has allowed major extensions of social protection, particularly in the European context, when socioeconomic and political conditions generated appropriate opportunities and demands for programs.

The sources of such social programs as social security have been explored during the past several decades by a myriad of historians and social scientists, some utilizing quantitative analysis of public policy determinants and outputs. Their findings concerning determinants of policy have centered on factors ranging from the growth of national income to the timely development of civil servants with capacities for social learning.[98] My research has led me to emphasize the impacts of great wars and major economic depressions as stimuli for new conceptions of the duties of states and their realization as new and expanded social programs.[99] Political revolutions have also played important roles, but they have contributed more to the legitimacy of new conceptions of rights and duties than to the promotion of effective and tangi-

97. Gaston V. Rimlinger, "The Historical Analysis of National Welfare Systems," in Roger L. Ransom et al., eds., *Explorations in the New Economic History* (New York: Academic Press, 1982), p. 162.

98. See Harold L. Wilensky, *The Welfare State and Equality: Structural and Ideological Roots of Public Expenditures* (Berkeley: University of California Press, 1975) and Hugh Heclo, *Modern Social Politics*. See also Douglas E. Ashford, ed., *History and Context in Comparative Public Policy* (Pittsburgh: University of Pittsburgh Press, 1992); Gösta Esping-Andersen, *The Three Worlds of Welfare Capitalism* (Princeton, NJ: Princeton University Press, 1990); and Meinolf Dierkes, Hans N. Weiler, and Ariane Berthoin Antal, *Comparative Policy Research: Learning from Experience* (New York: St. Martin's Press), 1987.

99. See Bruce, *Coming of the Welfare State*, esp. pp. 291–325; Richard L. Siegel and Leonard B. Weinberg, *Comparing Public Policies: United States, Soviet Union and Europe* (Homewood, IL: Dorsey, 1977), esp. pp. 55–64; Wilensky, *Welfare State and Equality*, pp. 70–85.

ble social programs in the near-term. In contrast, certain major wars and economic crises have both legitimized particular conceptions of social rights and provided the political environments that enabled ideas and programs to be implemented. Such widely shared experiences make inequality and destitution more visible and threaten the political stability of the state in ways that broaden political support for major advances of social rights. They have convinced establishment forces to accept the need for new conceptions of state duties regarding social protection. This has been true from the England of the 1640s to Germany in the 1880s,[100] and from much of Europe in the 1890s to the American experience with the Great Depression in the 1930s.[101]

European state paternalism faced a major challenge from classical liberalism in the course of the nineteenth century. It is notable that the extraordinary development of state responsibility for social protection in the twentieth century, particularly in the quarter century following World War II, has been followed by a new ideological and political challenge derived from classical liberalism. Will this challenge have a long-term impact on social policy in the 1990s and beyond?

My own skepticism about the staying power of the current classical liberal challenge as an approach to social issues is rooted in the historical evidence. One lesson is that additional social protection appears to be a highly predictable response to the evident abuse of certain workers and the poor during certain phases of capitalist development. This supports expectations of enlarged welfare and labor market programs in countries termed newly industrialized. A second is that particular social crises, especially major wars and depressions, frequently generate additional social protection in the name of national solidarity and in the interest of the political survival of governments of various ideological persuasions. New demands for social protection are also generated by new political movements in advanced industrial countries that are centered on gender, subnational, immigrant, and other kinds of group identity.

The efforts of the 1980s to limit the extension and selectively roll back American and Western European conceptions of the welfare state achieved substantial momentum, and current strains on national budgets preclude most efforts to resume significant expansion of the wel-

---

100. Christopher Hill, *The World Turned Upside Down: Radical Ideas During the English Revolution* (New York: Viking Press, 1972), p. 87; Arnold J. Heidenheimer, Hugh Heclo, and Carolyn Teich Adams, *Comparative Public Policy: The Politics of Social Choice in Europe and America*, 2nd ed. (New York: St. Martin's Press, 1983), pp. 214–215.

101. Heclo, *Modern Social Politics*, p. 79; Martha Derthick, *Policymaking for Social Security* (Washington, DC: Brookings Institution, 1979), p. 11.

fare state. Momentum for market-oriented structural reform continues in Eastern Europe and in various parts of Asia, Africa and Latin America. Pressure created by massive fiscal deficits and debt obligations propel trends in numerous countries that are contrary to the historical course outlined in this chapter. Yet analysis of contemporary trends in the European Community, the United States, and elsewhere in later parts of this book reveals renewed political pressures in the 1990s to attend to certain neglected welfare and labor market needs. And socioeconomic strains resulting from structural adjustment are prompting renewed attention to older traditions of distributive justice and paternalism in such regions as Latin America and Eastern Europe. The neglect of the human costs of structural adjustment can be expected to create problems for the reemergence of political forces that ignore basic human needs such as employment and the assurance of subsistence. Without historical analysis such statements would be defiant cries against apparent current trends. Yet it is those who imagine that the current situation is the end of history, or are confident that they are enjoying the beginning of a long era of global, market-oriented, free enterprise liberalism who have failed to observe certain long-term tendencies.

This chapter has analyzed the evolution of support for the right to work and for conceptions of the welfare state that reflect concern for the unemployed. Yet these developments constituted only a modest foundation for the later national and international recognition of full employment goals and the association of such state responsibilities with human rights. The present status of the right to employment and full employment is accounted for far more directly by the twentieth century events and strands of social and economic thought that are explored in the following chapter.

Chapter 3
Initiating International Involvement: The Right to Work and Full Employment Policies, 1900–1966

Much as horrendous war casualties have mocked periodic talk of peace in our time, record levels of unemployment have repeatedly accompanied ringing national and international endorsements of full employment and the right to work during the twentieth century. Unemployment continues to rival inflation as a great socioeconomic scourge of the industrialized and developing world, and can be compared with poverty and disease as a primary source of distress in many developing countries.

The continuing attraction of the right to work and the emergence of full employment goals and policies in the present century are discussed in this chapter. While both the right to work and full employment concepts retain to this day aspects of their utopian intellectual and historical origins, they have contributed to the generation of useful public policies as well as to disillusionment.

The historical and theoretical developments described in the previous chapter reflect early efforts to respond to the social dislocations of the accelerating industrial revolution. Proponents of various ideologies often came to differ largely in degree in their readiness to adopt old and new measures for the alleviation of poverty, the improvement of factory conditions, and the provision of increased work opportunities. Even as socialists of various stripes struggled to offer programs relevant to capitalist societies, various conservatives and liberals advocated measures that could be characterized at least in part as paternalistic humanitarianism.

The momentum for prescribing the right to employment and advocating full employment goals ebbed and flowed several times in the present century, apparently peaking during the quarter century following the Great Depression and World War II. Such support built on the socioeconomic experience, writings, and governmental programs discussed in the previous chapter as well as on the momentous developments of the first half of the twentieth century. Even between 1944 and 1966, when various major documents were developed, not all schools of political thought were enthusiastic about prescribing work as a human right. Yet exponents of diverse ideologies were then prepared to vote in various international forums for one or another version of such a right. Although the convergence of ideological and public policy positions was insufficient to shape a substantial consensus in that era about the precise nature of the right to work or the most appropriate methods for its implementation, it is significant that advocates of diverse ideologies and political systems supported the inclusion of employment in major international human rights documents.

In the last analysis it would be the refinement of particular macro- and microeconomic and social programs and policies, rather than the invocation of slogans or rights, that would most directly affect workers in socialist and market economies. Yet the right to work and full employment movements raised the salience of unemployment as a national and international problem, and thereby put pressure on governments to place greater stress on employment as a political end (though not an overriding one) when locked in conflict with such goals as price stability and balanced national budgets.

The relationship between slogan or concept on the one hand, and policy on the other, has been complex. At times promises of the right to work and full employment have substituted for public policies plausibly designed to expand employment. On other occasions these concepts have stimulated sincere national and intergovernmental efforts to develop new policies designed to promote employment.[1]

Although unemployment is now widely recognized as a major global economic and social problem, it is still not frequently viewed as a human rights issue. This fact reflects in part the failure of major international organizations and national governments to move from

1. A leading Japanese legal scholar noted in 1981 that his government "finds the International Labor Organization's Convention, 1964 (No. 122) difficult to ratify because of the far-reaching implications of the 'active policy designed to promote full, productive and freely chosen employment required by Article 1.'" Tadashi Hanami, "The Influence of ILO Standards on Law and Practice in Japan," *International Labour Review* 120 (Nov.–Dec. 1981): 776. This is testimony to both the then advanced policy orientation of the Convention and the seriousness with which many governments viewed their obligations under ILO conventions. As of December 31, 1991 some 74 states had ratified ILO Convention No. 122.

the formal prescription of a right to employment or work to actions that meaningfully foster fulfillment of that human need. In recent years the idea of a right to employment has failed to generate substantial additional support despite the existence of extraordinary levels of unemployment in many developed and developing countries. There continues to be great resistance to the acceptance of employment as a "fundamental human right" and of full employment as an overriding national or international goal.

This chapter concentrates on the evolution of the concept of the right to employment in the present century. It traces its wider acceptance in the wake of the Great Depression and two world wars, analyzes the struggles to define the concept in international instruments, reviews the scholarly debates about the legitimacy of employment as a human right in the aftermath of its acceptance by international organizations and, finally, notes certain new justifications of this right offered by contemporary scholars and officials.

This complex subject has been shaped by often conflicting contributions of numerous academic disciplines, reflecting various mixtures of idealism and pragmatism. At every stage the debate has been heavily infused by ideological struggle linked to perceptions of how national and organizational interests could be affected by various formulations of the right to work.

Although prescription of a right cannot be wholly divorced from its implementation, the present chapter focuses on the former. International prescription has been defined as a process in which governments cooperate with one another to formulate and undertake commitments.[2] The origins of new prescriptions often lie in previously developed ones, because governments feel freer to accept in new international instruments variations on commitments that their own state accepted earlier in national statutes or constitutions or in previous international instruments. The relationship between prescription and implementation is complex. Policymaking, a dynamic process, normally involves reconsidering earlier prescribed policy in the light of both the problems encountered during implementation and the overall development of the situation that first invited a public policy response.

The prescription of the right to work has been an exercise in extensive social learning by the various parties involved. When the initial decisions were made in the 1940s to include the right to work in major international instruments, few advocates were able to confidently state

---

2. Myres S. McDougal, Harold D. Lasswell, and Lung-chu Chen, *Human Rights and World Public Order* (New Haven, CT: Yale University Press, 1980), p. 265.

the basis or content of such a right. It was not clear then whether such a prescribed right would essentially seek to promote action by governments on behalf of full employment or would, instead or additionally, reinforce legal rights to particular jobs with national governments as the employers of last resort. It was also unclear how the right to work would relate to such issues as job security, equal opportunity for various groups, and income maintenance. Questions of forced labor and the duty to work also greatly complicated discussion of such a right. These were only a few of the issues that have faced the major national governments and international agencies responsible for prescribing this right during the past forty five years.

In time the perceived imperative to achieve a measure of global consensus partially overcame the enormous differences among governments and other interested parties regarding such questions. As a result, the right to work was repeatedly included in international human rights documents, these including the United Nations Universal Declaration of Human Rights (adopted in 1948) and International Covenant on Economic, Social and Cultural Rights (adopted in 1966), the Council of Europe European Social Charter (adopted in 1961), the Organization of American States American Declaration of Rights and Duties of Man (adopted in 1948), and the Organization of African Unity Africa [Banjul] Charter on Human and Peoples' Rights (adopted in 1981).[3]

The reader will find in the remainder of this chapter a presentation of the trends in ideas and policy that set the stage for the explicit international recognition during and soon after World War II of the right to work and the policy goal of full employment. The first half of the present century included extraordinary developments that included two world wars and the most severe and widespread economic depression in modern history. Such events were catalysts for ideas and programs that had roots in earlier centuries but that required the sense of social solidarity that such events engendered.

---

3. Universal Declaration of Human Rights, adopted December 10, 1948, G.A. res. 271A(III), U.N. Doc. A/810, at 71(1948); International Covenant on Economic, Social and Cultural Rights, opened for signature December 16, 1966, entered into force Jan. 3, 1976 (Appendix IV, this volume); European Social Charter, signed October 18, 1961, entered into force February 26, 1965 (Appendix III, this volume); American Declaration on the Rights and Duties of Man, adopted May 2, 1948 by the Ninth International American Conference, Bogotà, *Novena Conferencia Internacional Americana: Actas y Documentos*, VI (Bogotà: Colombia Ministry of Foreign Relations, 1953): 297–302, OAS Off. Rec. OEA Ser. L/V/I.4 Rev. (1965); African [Banjul] Charter on Human and Peoples' Rights, OAU Doc. CAB/LEG/67/3 rev. 5, 21 I.L.M. 58 (1982), entered into force Oct. 21, 1986.

Experiments and Debates, 1900–1928

Recognition grew from the 1880s to after World War I that European governments must meet at least some of the needs of their unemployed, using such programs and devices as labor exchanges, counter-cyclical public works, and unemployment insurance. This changing awareness of the nature of this problem, and the scope of possible palliatives and preventatives, was accelerated by the economic distress affecting much of Europe in such periods as 1893–1895 and 1904–1905.

The distress engendered by financial panics and economic depressions, compounded in Britain by the effects of the Boer War, intensified the growing movement to create study groups and other structures designed to reconsider basic premises and policy options. Such groups utilized civil servants, academics, and social service providers, among others, and helped move various countries to adopt major reforms.

An embryonic international structure for communication and education in areas related to social security and labor legislation also emerged before 1914. Central to the political processes of the era immediately preceding World War I was the empirical investigation and discussion of options for preventing unemployment or ameliorating its effects on individuals and communities. It was also a time for unprecedented consideration of other countries' programs, sometimes through study missions to pioneering countries and municipalities.

In Britain, empirical liberals and canny socialists linked up between 1904 and 1914 to emulate German and other experience with labor exchanges, promote locally based public works, and embark on the world's first national system of unemployment insurance. However, the pace of reform varied widely even among European countries. Progress in Britain and Sweden before 1914 contrasted with very limited change in France.

One of the major features of public policy discussion about unemployment in the first quarter of the twentieth century was the fuller emergence of sectors of European and American liberalism as forces for social reform. Substantial redirection of liberalism was required toward the acceptance of state responsibility for public welfare as well as liberal involvement with empirical studies and committee work bearing on this subject.[4] While redirection was most evident in the legislation promoted by Britain's Liberal Party between 1905 and 1914, it had

4. See Anthony Arblaster, *The Rise and Decline of Western Liberalism* (Oxford: Basil Blackwell, 1984), esp. pp. 284–291.

contemporary echoes in American Progressivism and French Radicalism.[5]

Thus a major part of the foundation of the twentieth century public policy agenda for dealing with unemployment was put into place early in the century in Western Europe. In this period advocacy of a right to work principally constituted background political propaganda—and implicit threats to social order—from such forces still without governmental power as the new British Labour Party.[6] Yet by 1917–18 the right to work reemerged forcefully as a revolutionary and constitutional slogan from Soviet Russia to Weimar Germany.

Pre-1929 national economic policies rarely included constructive approaches to fiscal or monetary policy designed to affect business cycles or unemployment. Donald Winch notes that the Unemployed Workman's Act of 1905 and the Development and Road Fund Act of 1909 "made Britain the first country to make nominal provision at least for forward planning of contra-cyclical public expenditures."[7] Yet such policies did little more than affect the timing of overall public spending, and did not go far to expand the scale of public works or to anticipate Keynesian fiscal policy. Although a strong public works approach was advocated in Britain by Beatrice and Sidney Webb between 1904 and 1911,[8] this part of their program had only limited impact on government policy there.

The principal lesson of the first three decades of the century—one that would become fully evident with the coming of the Great Depression—was that the public policies put into place dealt very ineffectively with continuing business cycles and economic dislocations despite the emergence of increasingly sophisticated analyses of those developments. By 1929 labor exchanges and state-subsidized unemployment insurance were widely in place in Western Europe,[9] and in some countries such coverage of workers was already quite broad.[10] Yet unem-

5. On French developments see Judith F. Stone, *The Search for Social Peace: Reform Legislation in France, 1890–1914* (Albany: State University of New York Press, 1985).

6. J. R. Hay, *The Origins of the Liberal Welfare Reforms, 1906–1914* (London: Macmillan, 1975), p. 49; José Harris, *William Beveridge: A Biography* (Oxford: Clarendon Press, 1977), p. 153.

7. Donald Winch, *Economics and Policy: A Historical Study* (London: Hodder and Stoughton, 1969), p. 55.

8. See Beatrice and Sidney Webb, *The Prevention of Destitution* (London: Longmans, Green, 1911).

9. By 1925 there were twenty-five nations with unemployment insurance programs. Those without such programs included France and the United States. John Garraty, *Unemployment in History: Economic Thought and Public Policy*, p. 147.

10. See Joseph A. Schumpeter, *Theories der Wirtshaftlichen Entwicklung* (1912), and

ployment insurance programs proved to be weak palliatives, burdening national budgets and often being transformed into welfare grant programs. Labor exchanges, assisting some workers to find available jobs, could only help grease systems subject to periodic crises.

The themes of a right to work and full employment were expressed rather forthrightly at various points during those three decades, particularly as part of the wartime calls for social solidarity. Yet they were not proclaimed universally or translated into effective economic programs. The International Labor Organization addressed unemployment beginning in 1919, but was slow to become a major source of influence concerning relevant public policy. Tolerance of historically high levels of unemployment marked the 1920s in Britain, the United States and elsewhere, and macroeconomic orthodoxy held firm until the Great Depression forced its retreat.

Ideology and Events, 1929–1950

Support for the right to work grew substantially between 1929 and 1945, the years of the Great Depression and World War II. These events and experiences brought the perspectives of North America and much of Western Europe somewhat closer to each other and to those of the Soviet Union respecting the obligations of the state to ensure full employment.

The Great Depression of the 1930s shattered what was left of the ambivalence and negativism felt by many Western economists, political leaders, and broader publics regarding the state's responsibility to the unemployed. It brought a public policy response in various Western European countries that was infused by the first acceptances of the principles of Keynesian macroeconomic stimulus.[11] In the United States, which suffered longer and deeper from the Great Depression than virtually any European country, the experience stimulated the first federally sponsored social security program since the Civil War pension program as well as massive work relief. These policy developments became sources of pride for a New Deal administration (including its First Lady) that later contributed much to the international human rights prescriptions of the 1940s.

Although World War II had a direct effect on employment in West-

---

W. C. Mitchell, *Business Cycles* (1913), both cited in Garraty, *Unemployment in History*, p. 147.

11. See Garraty, *Unemployment in History*, pp. 188–215; Charles P. Kindleberger, *The World in Depression, 1929–1939* (London: Allen Lane, 1973); Peter A. Gourevitch, *Politics in Hard Times* (Ithaca, NY: Cornell University Press, 1986), pp. 124–180.

ern Europe and North America opposite to that of the Great Depression, it infused various countries with the solidarity necessary to shape national commitments to avoid future employment blights. Further, wartime fiscal deficits on both sides of the Atlantic constituted successful experiments in large-scale Keynesian stimulation to achieve full employment. The Holocaust and the massive flows of refugees created by the war directly stimulated commitments expressed in the 1948 Universal Declaration. Finally, the social justice issues that are at the heart of socioeconomic rights served as ideal rallying cries for the leaders of the Allied powers in their statements on war aims.

National commitments to full employment in the peak years of national concern for employment, 1943–46, including the 1944 British government White Paper on Employment Policy, Franklin Roosevelt's 1945 State of the Union Address, and the 1946 U.S. Employment Act, were significant despite the inevitable watering down that characterized their formulation and implementation.[12] Numerous other governments also formally proclaimed full employment goals in the wake of emerging confidence that Keynesian economic management policies could keep unemployment levels at permanently low levels.[13]

Various international meetings and declarations of the 1940s echoed these national experiences. The lesson had been learned in the most difficult possible way that massive unemployment could be caused and aggravated by the absence of enlightened internationalism in social and economic policies. One of the most significant forums for the expression of this consensus was the 1944 General Conference of the International Labor Organization, held in Philadelphia. At that conference U.S. Secretary of Labor Frances Perkins took the following remarkable position on national government roles regarding unemployment:

We know that long-term mass unemployment can be prevented in any modern society. It must be accepted as a fundamental labour standard that steady and regular jobs will be available for all who are able to accept work discipline and to achieve some minimum of skill and efficiency.[14]

---

12. See Stephen K. Bailey, *Congress Makes Law: The Story Behind the Employment Act of 1946* (New York: Columbia University Press, 1950). On January 6, 1945, Franklin D. Roosevelt referred to "the right to a useful and renumerative job" as "the most fundamental" and pledged to maintain full employment after the war. Roosevelt, "The State of the Union," *Vital Speeches of the Day* 11, 7 (January 15, 1945): 194–200.

13. Garraty, *Unemployment in History*, pp. 228–232; Winch, *Economics and Policy*, pp. 255–277.

14. International Labour Conference, 26th Sess., *Record of Proceedings* (Montreal: ILO, 1944), p. 22.

This U.S. view, widely shared at this conference, expressed confidence in the efficacy of economic stabilization and management policies that only a few countries had yet demonstrated to be effective in peacetime. The "Declaration of Philadelphia" expressed the confidence of the majority of the conference representatives "that the fuller and broader utilization of the world's productive resources necessary for the achievement of the objectives set forth in this Declaration can be secured by effective international and national action."[15]

Such optimistic responses to national and international developments blended well with the development and expression of Catholic social thought supportive of workers' rights. Evolving Roman Catholic doctrine had considerable influence on Latin American and Western European sentiment regarding the right to work during this critical era of international prescription. Continuing the anniversary reaffirmations of and elaborations on Leo XIII's *Rerum Novarum*, Pius XI's *Quadragesimo Anno* (Reconstructing the Social Order, 1931) and other papal works straddled many critical social issues but continued to elaborate a Catholic response to unemployment and industrial exploitation. Pius XII contended in a 1941 radio broadcast that labor was both a duty and a right of every human being.[16] However, mainstream Catholic social doctrine was still tempered in mid-century by an ambivalence toward dependence on the state for the delivery of benefits to workers.

Related attitudes and traditions reinforced support for the right to work in Catholic Europe and Latin America. These included civil law conceptions of workers' status and corporate rights, reinforced in Latin America by expressions of egalitarian anti-imperialism.[17] Although the socioeconomic experiences of most Latin American countries were quite different from those of most industrialized European countries, various of the former were increasingly disposed to include right to employment provisions in their national constitutions and to support such sentiments in international forums. Furthermore, between 1945 and the early 1960s Latin American states had disproportionately strong representation in the United Nations.

15. Ibid., p. 623.

16. See discussion of this broadcast in Pope John XXII, *Mater et Magistra* (Christianity and Social Progress), May 15, 1961, in William J. Gibbons and Gerald C. Treacy, eds., *Seven Great Encyclicals* (Glen Rock, NJ: Paulist Press, 1963), p. 44.

17. On corporate group rights in Latin America see Howard Wiarda, "Democracy and Human Rights in Latin America," in Wiarda, ed., *Human Rights and United States Human Rights Policy* (Washington, DC: American Enterprise Institute, 1982), p. 45. See also John P. Humphrey, *Human Rights and the United Nations: A Great Adventure* (Dobbs Ferry, NY: Transnational, 1984), p. 66.

In the decade after 1945, strong proclamations of the state's obliga-tion to ensure the right to work also could be found in the constitu-tions, statutes, and other leading statements of various Communist-ruled states. The 1936 Soviet Constitution pioneered the idea of consti-tutionally mandated "guaranteed employment." Each new "people's republic" also "guaranteed" or "ensured" the right to work in constitu-tions adopted between 1948 and 1952. They augmented their guaran-tees with language adapted from Article 118 of the Soviet Constitution of 1936: "The right to work is ensured by the socialist organization of the national economy, the steady growth of the productive forces of Soviet society, the elimination of the possibility of economic crises, and the abolition of unemployment." As noted by Arvid Brodersen, "Few pieces of Stalinist law have been more amply commented on by Soviet legal experts or more enthusiastically hailed as a great revolutionary innovation than the right-to-work statute."[18] The main innovation was the concept of a state guarantee, which contributed greatly to the self-image of each Communist-ruled state from 1936 to the mid-eighties.

The idea of a state-guaranteed right to work had spread beyond the Eastern bloc before and during the period that United Nations organs debated this concept. It could be found in the constitutions of such diverse nation-states as Nationalist China (1947), Luxembourg (1948), Syria (1950), Jordan (1951), and Cuba (1952). Obviously, no single ideology or pattern of national experience explains such diversity.

Yet most of the non-Communist states that affirmed the right to work in their post-1945 constitutions preferred not to offer state guar-antees in such clauses. Some countries adopted a middle position. The 1947 Venezuelan Constitution proclaimed that "the state should take steps to enable every person to obtain his livelihood through work."[19] Italy committed itself in 1947 to "promote conditions that render this right effective," and the government of the Western sectors of Berlin pledged in 1950 to make the right to work effective "by means of a policy aiming at full employment and economic planning."[20]

Although socioeconomic forces propelled the movement to legislate a right to employment, certain towering thinkers played critical roles as

18. Arvid Brodersen, *The Soviet Worker* (New York: Random House, 1966), p. 47.

19. United Nations, *Yearbook on Human Rights* (New York: United Nations, 1948), p. 354. For an updated summary of national clauses see Jean Mayer, "The Concept of the Right to Work in International Standards and the Legislation of ILO Member States," *International Labour Review* 124 (1985): 225–242.

20. United Nations, *Yearbook on Human Rights for 1947* (New York: United Nations, 1947), p. 163; United Nations, *Yearbook on Human Rights for 1950* (New York: United Nations, 1950), p. 106.

intermediaries. Among the most significant were the British and Swedish social thinkers and economists noted below.

Intellectual Godfathers: New British Perspectives

Several British scholar-statesmen, including John Maynard Keynes, T. H. Marshall, and William Beveridge, had major impacts on the understanding of the right to employment and governmental responsibilities toward full employment in their own as well as in many other countries. The influence of Keynes on employment policies spread widely beginning in the 1930s. A transnational school of Keynesian economics emerged, devoted in part to the use of fiscal policy to create and maintain full employment. Although Keynesian prescriptions were still "the monopoly of reformers and radicals during the 1930s and 1940s"[21] (with the exception of a few countries), by 1945 various industrialized countries had incorporated into their national politics the idea that political survival depended in no small way on government's ability to limit unemployment.

The alleged permanence of this change may well be questioned in the light of certain recent developments. Yet there can be no doubt that support for a universal right to work was greatly stimulated by Keynes's view that unemployment and depression were the consequences of deficient demand for goods and services and by his prescription of government stimulation of the necessary demand through government deficit spending and/or reduced taxes.

The contributions of T. H. Marshall were far less direct than those of Keynes. In fact this leading sociologist viewed work more as a duty than a right and worried about the impact of other welfare state benefits on the fulfillment of this duty of citizenship. Marshall's major contribution to the concept of the right to employment is found in his 1949 formulation of how rights expand, based on his schema concerning the evolution of citizenship. For Marshall, British "social rights" of the twentieth century followed logically from the civil rights of the eighteenth century and the political rights of the nineteenth. The aim of social rights was viewed as the shaping of equality of status among citizens.[22] Despite Marshall's rejection of a right to work, his legitimization of social rights arguably contributed to the movement to include socioeconomic rights when human rights were prescribed in the decades following World War II. The rights of citizens and human rights blurred in an era

21. Robert Lekachman, *The Age of Keynes* (New York: Random House, 1966), p. 270.
22. The 1949 Alfred Marshall lectures, in T. H. Marshall, *Class, Citizenship, and Social Development* (Garden City, NY: Doubleday, 1964), p. 113.

in which a broad range of welfare state benefits were promoted as human rights.

Beveridge, while lacking such a historical conception, integrated at a crucial time the concept of full employment with his own earlier version of an expanded British welfare state. His major work of the 1940s, *Full Employment in a Free Society*, was quickly translated and distributed throughout much of the world.[23] Although some criticized it as repeating Beveridge's own early work on employment,[24] he was indisputably in the right place at the right time with the synthesis that people sought and won credit as the father of the post-World War II British welfare state. It followed by two years Beveridge's highly influential "Report on Social Insurance and Allied Services," and was presented as a sequel to that study. In *Full Employment* Beveridge emphasized that "idleness" is "a positive separate evil from which men do not escape by having an income," and developed the view that social security and full employment policies were reciprocally beneficial.[25] As stated by José Harris, Beveridge "linked Keynesian economics with an overall strategy for post-war social planning."[26]

A link between the three men, the social theorist, the economist, and the civil servant, and the reincarnation of the right to work concept was historian and science fiction writer H. G. Wells. Wells dedicated much of the period between 1939 and 1943 to the elaboration and promotion of a "Declaration of the Rights of Man." Versions of this document reportedly influenced the 1941 Atlantic Charter.[27] Wells's conception of the "right to work" identified it as each individual's entitlement without directly addressing the issue of the duties of the state to ensure it. His proposed prohibition of "work for the sole object of profit-making" represented a radical twist on the concept.[28]

Swedish Contributions

Keynesian approaches to unemployment were both anticipated and adapted by various leaders of the minority Social Democratic government that came to power in Sweden in 1932. Major contributors to the self-consciously counter-cyclical Swedish budget policies of that period

23. William H. Beveridge, *Full Employment in a Free Society* (New York: W. W. Norton, 1945).

24. Garraty, *Unemployment in History*, pp. 229–230.

25. Beveridge, *Full Employment*, p. 18.

26. Harris, *William Beveridge*, p. 439.

27. David C. Smith, *H. G. Wells: Desperately Mortal* (New Haven, CT: Yale University Press, 1986), p. 604n.

28. Ibid., p. 491.29.

included Ernst Wigforss, Gunnar Myrdal, and Dag Hammarskjöld.[29] However, the most persistent Swedish contributor to the world's perception of the state's ability to contribute to the right to work has been labor economist Gösta Rehn. Beginning in the 1940s, Rehn sought to shift the primary focus of government policy away from stimulation of aggregate demand and toward selective job-creating measures.[30] Although Rehn's perspective had limited impact beyond Scandinavia before the 1960s, in that decade few economists matched his contributions to the transnational dialogue concerning particular national government programs designed to achieve and maintain full employment. Rehn, like Keynes and Beveridge, sought to advance full employment without directly promoting work as a basic human right. Emphasis on approaches not based on rights later made it easier for others to abandon the goal of full employment as stagflation spread through much of Western Europe and North America after 1973.

Overview: Historical Experience and Intellectual Contributions

Various shared historical experiences of the 1930s and 1940s, together with the movement in the West toward a feasible economics of full employment, made it possible for representatives of diverse economic and political systems to find areas of agreement when the United Nations sought to prescribe the right to employment beginning in 1947. After 1945, intellectual thought and trends in public policy made it difficult for any Western government to take an essentially laissez-faire position concerning responsibility to the unemployed. However, these developments failed to create a consensus concerning the nature of the right to work, leaving more disagreement than agreement concerning the legitimate and appropriate roles of the state in relation to employment. Although the gap between Communist-ruled and Western states regarding such matters narrowed between 1930 and 1950, it remained wide and constituted a major subject for competing propaganda in the Cold War era.

The strong affirmation by Communists regarding the constitutional obligation of governments to guarantee full employment contrasted with the increasing hesitancy of various Western governments to make such legal commitments as the Great Depression and World War II

---

29. Assar Lindbeck, *Swedish Economic Policy* (Berkeley: University of California Press, 1974), pp. 82–83.

30. Gösta Rehn, "Recent Trends in Manpower Policy," *European Yearbook* XXI (1973): 93.

passed into history. These developments set the stage for sharp debates concerning the formulation of the right to work within various international organizations from 1947 to the collapse of European Communism. The results have reflected the changing balance of power in these organizations as well as the evolution of thinking about states' obligation regarding employment. The United Nations and International Labor Organization debates described in the following pages answered some questions concerning individual rights and governmental obligations regarding employment while leaving many others unresolved.

The United Nations Debate, 1947–1966

The early United Nations deliberations on the right to employment were strongly influenced by both the Cold War and the emergence of Third World countries as a force in its forums. Debates in the 1940s and 1950s helped to shape both the Universal Declaration of Human Rights and the International Covenant on Economic, Social and Cultural Rights. It was assumed that the latter document would offer detailed prescriptions that would entail a degree of national obligation. This would go beyond the mere statements of principle in the Universal Declaration.

The debates and formulations of the various U.N. organs that considered the right to employment raised many of the central questions concerning international involvement with such a right even in the absence of a clear sense of direction on this issue. The right to employment assumed a central place in the United Nation's consideration of economic and social rights, and the treatment of employment in the Economic and Social Covenant set patterns for the prescription of various other rights in that instrument.

Most officials involved in the U.N. process understood at an early stage that the Universal Declaration and the two covenants should be designed both to educate a major part of the world about areas of widespread consensus on rights and to guide subsequent national constitutional and statutory developments. However, the nature of the global consensus on employment was worked out only after sharp and prolonged confrontation. In some cases national representatives refused to support formulations similar or parallel to language in their own constitutions and statutes. This resulted from shifts to the right in the politics of major participating countries as well as Cold War opportunism. In other instances representatives sought to take political advantage of the appeal of guaranteed employment to win points in the larger East-West and North-South political contests.

The major decisions on the Economic and Social Covenant regarding the right to work were taken in the Commission on Human Rights (CHR) in 1951–52 and in the Third Committee (Social, Humanitarian and Cultural) of the General Assembly in 1956–57.[31] Although the 1956–57 Third Committee was more representative of Third World sentiment than the Commission had been through 1951–52, the resolution of the right to employment issue in the Covenant was only moderately affected by decolonization due to delays in admitting additional Third World states to the United Nations.

Between 1947 and 1952 the dominant personalities on the Commission tended to reflect and reinforce Western influence. They included Eleanor Roosevelt, the Commission's first chair, René Cassin of France, Charles Malik of Lebanon, and P. C. Chang of the Republic of China. During the Commission debate on the Universal Declaration and the Economic and Social Covenant, majority coalitions were formed by five Western European states plus the United States, Australia, Nationalist China, and two or more other members from Latin America or Asia. Although such majorities were not obtained on all important issues pertaining to the two documents discussed here, they were secured rather consistently in relation to the right to work article. However, even in this first phase it was necessary for Western representatives to develop compromise formulations in order to attract Latin American and Asian votes.

Reflecting their national constitutions and their sense of political and ideological advantage for their position, Communist delegates continuously sought to have the Economic and Social Covenant mandate "guarantees" by each ratifying state of their nationals' right to work. Failing to obtain majority support for such a formulation, they and some of the more socialist-oriented Third World Commission members then worked to include language fostering or requiring such particular governmental commitments as facilitative legislation and training programs.

In contrast, from an early point various Western delegates sought to develop majority support for formulations of the right to work that provided no binding obligation on states to guarantee jobs and that expressed government obligation only in general terms in a preamble

---

31. For discussions of the debates on the development of the Covenant on Economic, Social and Cultural Rights, see A. Glen Mower, Jr., *International Cooperation for Social Justice: Global and Regional Protection of Economic/Social Rights* (Westport, CT: Greenwood Press, 1985), pp. 7–46; Natalie Kaufman Hevener, "Drafting Human Rights Covenants," *World Affairs* 148, 4 (Spring 1986): 233–244; and Humphrey, *Human Rights and the United Nations*.

statement affecting all economic, social, and cultural rights. These Western delegates also sought to counter the Communist advantage regarding the rhetoric of guaranteed employment with pointed references to forced labor and totalitarian control of economics, reflected in proposed language designed to protect individuals from compulsory labor and to minimize the obligations of states with limited governmental control of labor markets.

However, the Western group had some difficulty maintaining the necessary degree of unity. This reflected the uneven and incomplete nature of the historical and intellectual reconsideration of unemployment in Western Europe and North America between 1930 and 1950 and the short life of the spirit of the Declaration of Philadelphia. Despite the country's pivotal intellectual role described above, the United Kingdom took an especially restrictive approach at the United Nations on the matter of state obligations to the unemployed. In contrast, Denmark in 1951 endorsed inclusion in the Economic and Social Covenant of a pledge by ratifying states to "promote" the right to work for "all its nationals."[32] With U.S. leadership, a majority coalition accepted language along the lines of the Danish position. Some reluctant developing countries were brought into the majority coalition as a result of language that recognized the inability of certain states to immediately assure various economic and social rights.

The U.N. debate was influenced considerably by various representatives of labor organizations who were given regular access to Commission deliberations. Although the views of these organizations were almost as diverse as those of the national government representatives, the dominant Western-oriented international labor union federations tended to reiterate and reinforce the anti-Communist rhetoric of Western governments, and often gave more emphasis to their opposition to forced labor than to the urging of greater state obligations to guarantee employment. The ILO, with representatives of each of its tripartite elements as well as its Office, emphasized concerns about retaining ILO control over international labor standards. In May 1952, the Swedish representative to the Commission referred to ILO support for "a declaration rather than an article with legally binding obligations."[33] Until 1964 ILO representatives were handicapped by their organization's failure to develop an updated position on government obligations to the unemployed. It is likely that the organization's representa-

32. U.N. Commission on Human Rights, *Official Records*, Seventh Sess., April 21 and 27, 1951 (E/CN.4/AC14/SR2, p. 6; E/CN.4A/AC15/SR3, p. 12).

33. U.N. Commission on Human Rights, *Official Records*, 227th Sess., May 5, 1952 (E/CN.4/AC15/SR277, p. 3).

tives would have taken a more positive position on the question of state responsibilities if the ILO's Employment Policy Convention had been adopted earlier. Without such guidance even the representative of the ILO Workers' Group expressed a desire to see in the Covenant merely a "proclamation of general principles," and identified states' obligations in terms of labor training rather than the provision of work.[34]

Other factors influencing the Human Rights Commission's formulation of the right to work included the attitudes of the U.N. Secretariat, the particular rules, norms, and practices of the Commission, and the ability of Commission members as well as non-member governments to secure certain guiding resolutions from the parent Economic and Social Council and the General Assembly. Each factor contributed to the highly political context of the drafting process.

When the discussion of the right to work shifted from the Commission to the Third Committee of the General Assembly in 1956, the political environment changed markedly. In contrast to the eighteen Commission members, the Third Committee had seventy-nine. The United States, having indicated earlier that it would not ratify the two covenants, had relatively little influence on the deliberations during this phase.

The Soviet bloc was able to win a symbolic victory regarding state obligations in the Third Committee when a Polish amendment, accepted by a very narrow vote, added to the draft Covenant's right to employment article (Article 6) the obligation of every state party to "take appropriate steps to safeguard this right."[35] The Third Committee also forced Britain to withdraw an amendment that would have removed the Commission's formulation of the kinds of steps that states should take in the interest of full employment. Although the Commission's version of Article 6 was not fundamentally changed by the Third Committee, the Communist-ruled states and some of the more radical Third World countries felt vindicated and voted in favor of the right to work article. In response, a significant number of Western industrialized states abstained, directly reversing the lineup of supporters and abstainers in the final Commission on Human Rights vote formulating the right to employment.

34. U.N. Commission on Human Rights, *Summary Record of the First Meeting of the Working Group on Economic, Social, and Cultural Rights*, Geneva, 26 April 1951 (E/CN.4/AC14/SR1, p. 12), E/CN.4/AC14/SR3, p. 16). For a strong argument that the ILO positions were based mostly on jurisdictional grounds see Humphrey, *Human Rights and the United Nations*, pp. 141–143.

35. This contrasts with the acceptance in Article 2 of the term "guarantee" regarding non-discrimination in all spheres of rights noted in the Covenant on Economic, Social and Cultural Rights.

The Critical Questions at the United Nations

With divisions exacerbated by East-West and North-South rivalries, the formulation of the right to work in the adopted International Covenant on Economic, Social and Cultural Rights rather accurately reflected the limited U.N. consensus on this issue in the 1950s. Although the specific language was negatively affected by a somewhat hasty final vote in January 1957, the adoption of Article 6 culminated a prolonged process of social learning on the subject of the right to work. Many questions should have been answered or, at least, addressed squarely. To what is the individual entitled? Who has the right to work? To what degree is the state obligated to assure this right? What particular steps should states be obligated to take? Should individuals or foreign governments be able to invoke any international legal right in national courts or in international forums? Should this right be deemed to exist immediately in relation to all ratifying states, or is it one that could be allowed to develop progressively? How does the right to work relate to social insurance and equal employment opportunity? Can states be allowed to "promote" the right to work through forced labor, strike-breaking, or other measures that relate to a supposedly parallel duty to work? Should the right to work be stated as a principle or as a rule?

Article 6 of the Economic and Social Covenant is the product of prolonged debates on each of these questions. Although the final version failed to secure strong support from North America and Western Europe for ideological reasons, it was limited in various respects by what most of these states and many Third World countries were not prepared to accept regarding such matters.

The idea of a state guarantee of either full employment or an individual's right to appropriate work was flatly rejected. It was a victim of its Communist sponsorship as well as the widespread belief that such a guarantee was beyond the ability of most states to provide. Instead, each ratifying state would accept the commitment to "take appropriate steps," in other words to act in good faith to maximize employment through macro- and microeconomic and other policies in the context of its overall efforts to develop and stabilize its economy.

The beneficiaries of the right to work are to be "everyone," presumably all legal residents, though U.N. discussions dealing with such possible limiting factors as age and nationality accurately reflected contemporary inequalities. The major reservation relevant to this clause appears in Article 2, which freed "developing countries" to determine to what extent they would guarantee any of the stated economic rights to non-nationals. The same article provides that all listed economic, social, and cultural rights could be achieved progressively and "to the maximum of [each state's] available resources," there-fore not setting immediate obligations for those states.

The United Nations accepted the right to work as an entitlement separate from social insurance, equal opportunity for various groups, and relief from hunger. In positive terms this reflected a consensus that work was more than a means of subsistence, as reflected in the Com-mission's formulation that work was "the basis of all human endeav-or."[36] The holder of this right is explicitly endowed with "opportunity to gain his living by work which he freely chooses or accepts." Although some may read into this formulation an implicit right to a job, the explicit entitlement is limited to "opportunity" to be promoted by "technical and vocational guidance and training" and other legislated measures. Nowhere is it stated or implied that any given individual is entitled to access to such programs or to a job.

Both the Commission and the Third Committee insisted on retain-ing language designed to protect workers from forms of forced labor organized by states in the name of full employment or the duty to work. Various speakers associated forced labor with regimes that took credit for full and guaranteed employment. Forced labor in the Soviet bloc and elsewhere was frequently on the ILO agenda in that era, providing a rallying point for Western-led political pressure on coun-tries accused of such policies. Yet the U.N. debate was complicated by widespread support for the idea that work was a duty as well as a right. The somewhat stronger attachment to this concept among the mem-bers of the broader-based Third Committee, as compared with the early CHR, led to weakened injunctions against forced labor in the final version of the right to work article. However, the Third Commit-tee's version still registered concern for this issue through clauses referring to work "freely chosen or accepted" as well as "conditions safeguarding fundamental political and economic freedoms to the individual." Representatives of various Western states considered these phrases to be among their major political accomplishments in the U.N. struggle over the formulation of the right to work.

In the end the United Nations turned away from invoking the right to employment as a rule, instead affirming it as principle and policy in a promotional instrument. Such rules were to be left to ILO conventions and other more specific and presumably more enforceable instru-ments. Such a principle, in Dworkin's view, is a standard that competes with other standards. However, a principle has the standing of "a

36. Although this particular phrase was dropped by the Third Committee, that body also entertained frequent statements that gave primacy to work among the various socioeconomic rights.

requirement of justice or fairness or some other dimension of morality."[37]

With an unparalleled opportunity to establish the early postwar global consensus concerning the meaning of the right to work, the approved U.N. prescription failed to greatly please or displease any side of the debate. It was a product of compromise, social learning, and fading confidence in the larger significance of the effort to codify human rights in a declaration and two covenants. Without question, the resulting formulation was clumsy, largely a patchwork of symbolic phrases.

37. For these distinctions see Ronald M. Dworkin, "The Model of Rules," *University of Chicago Law Review* 35 (1967): 23.

Chapter 4
Support and Reconsiderations: Beyond the Covenants

Although Susan Moller Okin may not be quite correct in stating that the Universal Declaration "started the controversy" about the legitimacy of economic and social rights as human rights, it is evident that a debate on this subject was greatly stimulated by that document as well as by the subsequent U.N. Covenant on such rights.[1] Failure to achieve greater consensus concerning various particular rights in debates and votes on the Declaration and covenants limited the legitimacy of those prescribed rights. Contemporary and subsequent academic and media criticisms often focused on the right to employment itself, but also targeted ancillary employment rights, other particular socioeconomic rights, and socioeconomic rights in general.

Much as the idea of a right to employment gained from such social and economic events as the Great Depression and World War II, other great forces and events tended to revive competing classical liberal themes during and subsequent to that period. In circumstances of mass unemployment and later wartime mobilization, many intellectual and governmental leaders in leading Western democracies supported such measures as industrial cooperation, corporatism, increased governmental planning, and expanded social security. This was true despite the existence of negative as well as positive models of each of these phenomena. Although it could be argued that the ends of national solidarity and socioeconomic stability required movement in the direction of social democracy, others set different priorities based on

---

1. Susan Moller Okin, "Liberty and Welfare: Some Issues in Human Rights Theory," in J. Roland Pennock and John W. Chapman, eds., *Human Rights/NOMOS XXIII* (New York: New York University Press, 1981), p. 239.

their own intense mid-century experiences. Revival of crucial elements of classical liberal social and economic policies were accelerated even before the U.N. debates of the late 1940s by the writings of Friedrich Hayek and others.

As William Beveridge advanced a new welfare state era in the 1940s, Hayek contemporaneously drew a line between the traditional role of the welfare state as provider of a floor of benefits for the truly needy and a concept of distributional justice that included a state obligation to assure employment to all. His challenge was not only to the methods of Keynes and others but also to the ends themselves. By 1944 Hayek had framed a broad attack on efforts to promote security of employment through state planning and controls, asserting, "There can be little doubt that it is largely a consequence of the striving for security by these means in the last decades that unemployment and thus insecurity for large sections of the population has so much increased."[2] He anticipated that "the fascination of vague but popular phrases like 'full employment' would lead to extremely shortsighted measures and even desperate expedients."[3] The preferred alternative, one that was to be fleshed out by his disciples in the 1970s and 1980s, was a strategy focused on the adaptation of workers and technologies in national and international economies prepared to sustain substantial transitional pain.

Hayek's free market economic prescriptions were linked to his identification of the right to work with Soviet-style and fascist coercion. He emphasized individual freedom to choose and change employment rather than to be assured of a state-chosen job, asserting that "the able worker" who is prepared to "sacrifice" could achieve his employment goal.[4]

Although Hayek's writings were viewed by many contemporaries as the last gasp of nineteenth-century free market liberalism, they turned out to be more of a new beginning for a slowly reviving classical liberal policy tradition. Thirty years later Robert Nozick cited Hayek approvingly while asserting that "no end-state principle or distributional patterned principle of justice can be continuously realized without continuous interference with people's lives."[5] From Hayek and Nozick to George Gilder, a renewed thrust was given to Western social thought that fundamentally challenged an apparently strong consensus sup-

---

2. Friedrich A. Hayek, *The Road to Serfdom* (Chicago: University of Chicago Press, 1944), p. 129.

3. Ibid., pp. 206, 208.

4. Ibid., p. 94.

5. Robert Nozick, *Anarchy, State, and Utopia* (New York: Basic Books, 1974), p. 163.

porting social and economic human rights dependent on positive state action and obligations.

Various Hayek arguments regarding the inadvisability of committing nation-states to full employment and the right to work were refined by others. Employment as a human right was closely linked to the confidence of such figures as Keynes, Beveridge, Frances Perkins, and Gösta Rehn in the availability of policies and programs adequate to assure full employment. In most of Western Europe confidence in the availability of the necessary economic tools to achieve full employment was rarely flatly rejected during the three decades following World War II. Instead, belief in the possibility of shaping full employment economies has been countered most often by arguments concerning alleged unacceptable trade-offs, especially higher inflation and the promotion of a duty to work, expected to result from programs and policies that accept full employment as the major priority.[6]

Nonetheless, a strong undercurrent of criticism has centered on the claim that the right to work is impractical and unworkable. One aspect of this concerns the difficulties involved in defining the right. Certainly the aimlessness of the United Nations effort to provide a definition helped suggest to Dutch jurist J. J. M. van der Ven that "the right to work must be more sharply defined to become workable."[7] Dahrendorf carries forward a version of the impracticality argument from the vantage point of 1988, viewing full employment as necessarily resulting from the creation of peripheral or dispensable jobs in inefficient economies.[8]

A variation on the impracticability argument is the non-enforceabil-

6. See *The Welfare State in Crisis*, Conference on Social Policies in the 1980s (Paris: OECD, 1981).

7. J. J. M. van der Ven, "The Right to Work as Human Right," *Howard Law Journal* 11 (1965): 409.

8. Ralf Dahrendorf, *The Modern Social Conflict: An Essay on the Politics of Liberty* (New York: Weidenfeld and Nicolson, 1988), p. 147. The practicality issues also arise repeatedly in public policy discussions that do not hinge directly on the standing of employment as a human right. While it is not critical to the legitimacy of the right to employment if a particular employment policy or program is criticized or rejected, the concept may be threatened if both the feasibility of government efforts and the basic responsibility of government to provide full employment are effectively challenged. These seem to be among George Gilder's goals in *Wealth and Poverty* (New York: Basic Books, 1981). The popularity in the early 1980s of Gilder's comments on the U.S. government's responsibilities is one further indicator of the pendulum nature of opinion on full employment during the last two centuries. Gilder quotes Alfred Marshall on behalf of pre-Keynesian notions of government restraint concerning employment. Although he attacks particular U.S. employment policies and programs, especially the Comprehensive Employment and Training Act of the 1970s, it is clear that Gilder is mainly offering a different conception of governmental responsibility relative to private industry.

ity theme. One version of this argument held that the Covenant on Economic, Social and Cultural Rights was vulnerable insofar as it pointed to goals as much as existing conditions, and also initially involved weaker implementation mechanisms than those provided for in the Covenant on Civil and Political Rights. The former covenant was challenged by some who asserted that rights could not be termed human rights if they needed to be achieved progressively and could not be prescribed in terms that involved effective national or international guarantees or implementation processes. Dahrendorf argued recently that the term "right" was being misused in regard to work because "no judge can force employers to hire unemployed people."[9] For philosopher Joel Feinberg, the failure of most socioeconomic rights to be treated as "grounds of any other people's duties" leaves them as "manifesto" rights that are merely "permanent possibilities of rights."[10]

Another major line of Western criticism focuses on the theme that employment is at most a citizenship right in certain states, and is not a universal right of all persons. Such a view links the positions of D. D. Raphael, Maurice Cranston, and Ernst Haas. Raphael emphasized the distinction between "rights as a member of a particular society" and the human rights each person has "simply as a member of the human race."[11] While Raphael endorsed the inclusion of such "rights of citizenship" as employment in international declarations of rights, he insisted that there is "a difference of principle" between "the rights of liberty" and all others. (It may be recalled that T. H. Marshall had not acknowledged any such difference of principle among the various rights that he combined under the heading of rights of citizens.)

Haas contended that advocacy of such welfare rights as employment is tantamount to suggesting that "the Scandinavian welfare state is to be the model for the world," insisting that this is clearly beyond the economic and administrative capacity of most states.[12] Cranston expanded on this theme by insisting that human rights need enjoy uni-

9. Dahrendorf, *Modern Social Conflict*, p. 148.

10. Joel Feinberg, *Rights, Justice, and the Bounds of Liberty: Essays in Social Policy* (Princeton, NJ: Princeton University Press, 1980), p. 153. The point about the absences of duties is made even more emphatically by Charles Frankel, who suggests that lack of clear duties regarding socioeconomic rights makes them something other than rights. See Charles Frankel, *Human Rights and Foreign Policy*, Headline Series No. 241 (New York: Foreign Policy Association, 1978), pp. 37–38.

11. D. D. Raphael, "Human Rights: Old and New," in Raphael, ed., *Political Theory and the Rights of Man* (Bloomington and London: Indiana University Press, 1967), p. 66.

12. Ernst B. Haas, *Global Evangelism Rides Again: How to Protest Human Rights Without Really Trying* (Berkeley, CA: Institute of International Studies, 1978), p. 8.

versal moral standing and also be "of paramount importance." He observed that such rights as social security and holidays with pay "belong to a totally different moral dimension" from such others as freedom of movement or life itself.[13] It seems clear that he placed employment rights in the category of such "inferior" rights.

Sociologist John Boli-Bennett builds on Hayek's effort to associate the advocacy of such rights as employment with a kind of conspiracy to aggrandize the modern state at the expense of the liberty of the citizen.[14] Attacking the welfare state itself, Boli-Bennett condemns socioeconomic rights and their guarantee by the state as incorporating the citizen into the state's programs, thereby further legitimizing the state's control over society. As such, socioeconomic rights are not merely lesser rights; they are seen as means by which true human rights are subverted. Dahrendorf picks up this theme when he suggests, "In terms of liberty, it is more important to establish the right not to work, so that governments cannot force people into a dependence which they want to escape."[15]

The arguments of these and other critics challenge the legitimacy of the right to employment together with or separately from other socioeconomic or welfare rights. In the following section we review how the legitimacy of the idea of employment as a human right has been defended and evaluate its prospects for increased acceptance as a right of all.

New Support for a Human Right to Employment

Broad acceptance of a human right to employment requires an adequate rationale as well as supporting developments in positive law and public policy. Various elements of the needed justification have sometimes developed in direct response to such criticisms as those noted above. As such, the case for the human right to employment is partly a refutation of objections offered on natural rights and other grounds. However, creative cases for the standing of employment as a human right have also emerged, some of these based on frontier concepts of philosophy, law, and related fields.

13. Maurice W. Cranston, *What Are Human Rights?* (London: Bodley Head, 1973), p. 68. This is the revised edition of the original work published as *Human Rights Today* by Ampersand in 1962.

14. John Boli-Bennett, "Human Rights or State Expansion? Cross-National Definition of Constitutional Rights," in Ved P. Nanda et al., eds., *Global Human Rights: Public Policies, Comparative Measures and NGO Strategies* (Boulder, CO: Westview Press, 1981), p. 176.

15. Dahrendorf, *Modern Social Conflict*, p. 148.

It was noted earlier in this study that the intellectual grounding for the right to employment was relatively undeveloped before and during the United Nations debates on that subject. Various advocates based their views more on their sense of the value or attainability of such a right than on theoretical conceptions of how employment related to any broad conception of human rights. Yet usefulness or achievability are not adequate foundations in themselves for a basic human right. Acceptance of something such as a right requires linkage to the great tradition of natural rights, to another historical source of human rights, or to respected emerging conceptions of the sources of such rights. The development of each of these possible sources for the right to employment is reviewed below.

The Natural Rights Case

For many Western-educated scholars the concept of natural rights provides the only true basis for a human right. To concede that employment cannot meet the tests of natural rights would be to concede a great deal in terms of legitimacy and standing for the right to employment. As the debate unfolded, various advocates of the human right to employment made no such concession. Instead, they rejected the host of objections leveled against employment and other socioeconomic rights on natural rights grounds, including the charges that such a right lacks practicality, enforceability, universality, fundamental importance, ability to generate duties, and moral dimension.

The proponents of the natural right status of employment rights generally seek to establish it as co-equal to major political and civil human rights, and as part of the panoply of basic rights. This is evident in the natural-rights-oriented defenses of the human right to employment offered by Carl Friedrich and Jack Donnelly.[16] However, James W. Nickel goes beyond this to identify employment as "the central means to many of the essential goals of life."[17] Proponents appeal to the readers' own presumed notions about the enormous value of employment and the prerequisites of natural rights. Some reject excessively comprehensive criteria for the existence of a natural right,

16. Carl J. Friedrich, "Rights, Liberties, Freedoms: A Reappraisal," *American Political Science Review* 57, 4 (December 1963): 841–854; Jack Donnelly, "Human Rights as Natural Rights," *Human Rights Quarterly* 4, 3 (Summer 1982): 404.

17. James W. Nickel, "Is There a Human Right to Employment?" *Philosophical Forum* 10 (1978–79): 158. Nickel's article combines an implicit defense of the natural rights status of the right to employment with additional justifications of that right based on the ideas of John Rawls.

explicitly objecting to the proposition that such a right need be immediately practicable or enforceable.[18]

Some challenges to those who reject employment as a natural right
have been very direct. Okin asserts that Cranston, in rejecting the
fundamental importance and moral dimension of socioeconomic
rights, has slanted his own argument "by comparing the most essential
liberty rights with the least essential economic rights."[19] Further, by
reminding her audience of Locke's concern for protection of rights
against private persons in the state of nature, Okin seeks to refute the
idea that natural rights are limited to spheres of governmental obligation to the individual.

What is the major significance of the natural rights case for a right to
employment? First, it provides support that is based on the most traditional, and probably most legitimate, Western frame of reference concerning rights. To the extent that the right to employment can be
related to classical authorities and various great historical documents
listing natural rights, it is less necessary to rely on newer and less widely
accepted bases for such a claim.

Secondly, the identity of the contemporary supporters of the natural
right to employment is significant. They include the late Carl Friedrich, a patriarch of political science with a strong reputation for concern with the "liberty" rights that he saw destroyed by "totalitarianism,"
as well as various scholars who are helping to set the agenda for current
research in this field. Notably, the inclusion of employment as a natural
right is supported in the highly influential *Pacem in Terris* of Pope John
XXIII and the *Laborem Exercens* of John Paul II.[20] As was true in the last
quarter of the nineteenth century, Rome was responding to increasing
concerns transmitted by national churches about employment and
related social issues. In the 1980s the Canadian and U.S. Catholic
bishops led the way with impassioned and detailed calls for full employment, linking this to such values as human dignity, increased social
solidarity, and self-reliance. Such significant authorities bolster the

18. Ibid., p. 168.
19. Okin, "Liberty and Welfare," p. 242.
20. Pope John XXIII, *Pacem in Terris* (Peace on Earth), April 11, 1963, in Joseph
Gramillion, *The Gospel of Peace and Justice* (Maryknoll, NY: Orbis Books, 1976), p. 205.
Pope John XXIII cites Pius XII's June 1, 1941 radio message as his authority. See also
references to the right to work in Pope John Paul II's encyclical *Laborem Exercens* (Performing Work), *National Catholic Reporter*, September 25, 1981, p. 23. Empirical evidence
to support the principle of the right to work was offered by the National Conference of
Catholic Bishops (U.S.) in their November 1986 pastoral letter, "Economic Justice for
All: Catholic Social Teaching and the U.S. Economy," *New York Times*, November 14,
1986, p. A14.

legitimacy of a claimed natural right to employment and can be invoked in debates inside and outside of international organizations. At the least, ridicule of the idea of a natural rights claim to employment has been blunted by authorities who share the same intellectual traditions as some of their challengers. Western voices have thereby helped to establish a natural rights justification of the right to employment, one that can stand alone or be combined with other rationales that have emerged.

Positive Law Basis

Increasing support for the right to employment and other socioeconomic rights appears in the varied sources of international law accepted by legal positivists. This is an age of proliferating sources of international and national law affecting human rights and employment, though much of the new international law is quite weak in terms of the sanctions that are central to positivist legal theory.[21] Of course, the Universal Declaration and covenants themselves fit into the positive law framework and are intended to be anchors for further development of sources ranging from multilateral treaties to national statutes. Yet the positivists can also point to other international legal instruments that more plainly embody rules, not just principles, and incorporate sanctions and compliance mechanisms that seek to meet tests of effectiveness.

A continuing array of resolutions, conventions, recommendations, and other intergovernmental instruments have proclaimed the right to work and the necessity of commitments to full employment. These will be enumerated and assessed in detail in the chapters of this book dealing with the international employment regime.

Most chroniclers of international labor law have accorded human rights standing to only some of the developments in their fields.[22] This reflects a refusal to extend the use of the term human rights beyond such civil liberties and civil rights issues as forced labor, non-discrimination and free trade union association. However, the conscious effort of Myres S. McDougal, Harold D. Lasswell, and Lung-chu Chen to integrate positivism with several other perspectives on human rights

21. Nicholas Greenwood Onuf, "Global Law-Making and Legal Thought," in Onuf, ed., *Law-Making in the Global Community* (Durham, NC: Carolina Academic Press, 1977), pp. 8–9.

22. See Nicolas X. Valticos, *International Labour Law* (Deventer, Netherlands: Kluwer, 1979), and James Avery Joyce, *World Labour Rights and Their Protection* (New York: St. Martin's Press, 1980).

suggests the possible future acceptance of other contributions of international labor law as socioeconomic human rights, including the right to work.

The importance of developments in international positive law is greatly augmented by its ability to promise a degree of compliance and sanctions. Certain recent developments within the European Community and the Council of Europe regarding the legal protection of socioeconomic rights represent institutional breakthroughs in this regard. These include the provision of effective recourse by individuals and other non-government actors to agency organs, the adoption of authoritative international legislation, active enforcement efforts by organization officials, and enforceable rulings by international courts. This is not to paint a picture of accelerating or rampant supranationalism. The Council of Europe brings relatively few complaints to its European Court of Human Rights. The European Community has faced periodical member state defiance of its legal judgments and successful efforts to reduce the supranational and federal pretensions of its administrative arm. Further, neither of these European organizations was created primarily to champion the human rights of workers; their efforts in this regard have been secondary to other organizational objectives. Nonetheless, additional forms of international authority have been developed, especially in the area of equal protection.

McDougal and his colleagues emphasize advancement of the right to employment through international promotion of equal protection and non-discrimination. The significant advances in the prescription of global and European rights of equal opportunity and treatment regarding employment are developed in sections of their work focusing on "claims for freedom from discrimination" on the basis of race, gender, religion, political opinion, language, age and alien status. However, their presentation of the considerable progress in prescribing equal protection rights is combined with the concession in 1980 that "the contemporary provisions for implementation and application of the vast body of transnational prescriptions designed to secure equality of women with men is even more primitive than that designed to minimize racial discrimination."[23]

I would build on this McDougal-Lasswell-Chen perspective to call attention to the contribution that international law based on the concept of equal protection has played and probably will continue to play in the development of the human right to employment. Equal protection and non-discrimination are among the most widely accepted and

23. Myres S. McDougal, Harold D. Lasswell, and Lung-chu Chen, *Human Rights and World Public Order* (New Haven, CT: Yale University Press, 1980), p. 650.

certainly among the most frequently prescribed human rights principles in the world today. Note the emphasis on opposition to discrimination in many U.N.-initiated human rights instruments of the past two
decades and the somewhat special treatment given to racial discrimination complaints in U.N. human rights review processes.[24] Employment
rights play a central role in international law aimed at discrimination,
with legal efforts seeking to reach such basic aspects of that right as
opportunity and remuneration. The employment rights of women
have been given special attention by the ILO and European Community.[25] Although no society has been cleansed of widespread employment discrimination based on gender, many European and North
American women, at least, have obtained meaningful rights of access
to training and non-traditional employment, as well as greater equality
of pay and working conditions. Many aliens in European Community
states have been able to enjoy individual rights to job retention despite
great pressures to resolve a major part of Europe's prolonged post-
1973 economic crises at their expense. And international efforts have
begun to focus on the employment rights of persons disabled by HIV
and other diseases and injuries.[26]

A second major area in which positive international law contributes
to the right to employment is that of termination of employment in the
face of arbitrary individual firings, large-scale plant closings, mergers,
and dissolution of firms. Due process and other issues raised in these
situations go to the heart of the job security dimension of the right to
employment. Such catastrophic situations became increasingly serious
public policy issues during the deep global recession of the early 1980s.
These pressures led to a plethora of proposed and enacted protective
legislation at the local, national, and international levels. The force
behind such legislation is the political view that, in times of shrinking
employment opportunity, governments need to emphasize the avoidance of unnecessary job losses and the provision of appropriate re-

24. United Nations, *United Nations Action in the Field of Human Rights* (New York:
United Nations, 1988), pp. 51–63.
25. See S. Mazey, "European Community Action on Behalf of Women," *Journal of
Common Market Studies* 27 (September 1988): 63–68.
26. A. H. J. Swart, "The Legal Status of Aliens: Clauses in Council of Europe
Instruments Relating to the Rights of Aliens," *Netherlands Yearbook of International Law* 11
(1980): 3–64; John Claydon, "International Protection of the Welfare of Migrant
Workers," in Ronald St. John Macdonald, Douglas M. Johnston, and Gerald L. Morris,
eds., *The International Law and Policy of Human Welfare* (Alphen aan den Rijn, Netherlands: Sijthoff & Nordhoff, 1978), pp. 347–372; Joseph Steiner, "The Right to Welfare:
Equality and Equity Under Community Law," *European Law Review* 10, 1 (February
1985): 21–42; and R. Cohen and L. Wiseberg, *Double Jeopardy: Discrimination Against
Persons with AIDS* (Cambridge, MA: Human Rights Internet, 1990), pp. 25–27.

training and other assistance for those affected by necessary economic adjustments.

With prodding from trade unions and other labor-oriented organizations various national governments and international organizations have cautiously but meaningfully challenged such basic concepts of managerial prerogative as "employment at will" during the past three decades. Steps have included ILO and OECD "codes of conduct" for multinational enterprises and the European Community directives on transfers of business units and "collective redundancies."[27] In 1982 the ILO completed its review of its 1963 recommendation on termination of employment and developed its first convention on individual and collective terminations.[28] Several studies indicated that the 1963 recommendations stimulated related national legislation.[29] The latter convention at least initially enjoyed substantial support from employers' organizations as well as from trade unions, and has had significant impacts even in states with relatively advanced approaches to such matters as notice, information, and consultation.

International acceptance of the ideas that workers have rights to their jobs, individually and collectively, largely depends on support for such an idea in various influential countries. Although the United States has acted strongly against numerous terminations resulting from discrimination, its national and state governments have been reluctant to develop protective legislation in relation to more typical individual dismissals or collective redundancies. This has reflected both the relative weakness of U.S. trade unions and their historical preference for employing collective bargaining to deal with such problems. Even the United States has recently begun to approve various state and federal statutory proposals for protection of workers in the face of large-scale closings and mergers, stressing the concept of notice.[30] Such measures, however, come decades after more comprehen-

27. Norbert Horn, "International Rules for Multinational Enterprises: The ICC, OECD, and the ILO Initiatives," *The American University Law Review* 30 (1981): 923–940; Leslie Allan Lugo, "Protecting Workers Faced with Job Loss Due to New Technology: The EEC Approach," *Comparative Labor Law* 8 (1987): 183–195.

28. Brian Napier, "Dismissals—the New ILO Standards," *Industrial Law Journal* 12, 1 (March 1983): 17–27.

29. Edward Yemin, "Job Security: Influence of ILO Standards and Recent Trends," *International Labour Review* 113 (1976): 17; Committee of Experts on the Application of Conventions and Recommendations, *Termination of Employment: General Survey,* International Labour Conference, 59th Sess., 1974, Report III, Part 4B (Geneva: ILO, 1974), para. 161.

30. By the end of 1984 plant closing laws had been adopted by Massachusetts, Wisconsin, Maine, and Connecticut. *Labor and Employment Law* (October 1984): 1. A limited requirement of notice to certain workers became federal law in 1988.

sive protective measures were adopted in various Western European states as well as in Canada.

More characteristic of the 1980s were modest roll-backs of such employment protection measures, this reflecting Thatcher-Reagan orientations to free enterprise. This is evident in the German Federal Republic's 1985 Employment Protection Law, which that country's trade unions charged "encroached on the established protection rights of employees."[31] Martin Vranken noted in 1986 a distinct trend toward deregulation in the social domain in Western Europe, involving "government efforts to reform or even to abolish major parts of basic social legislation molding employment relationships."[32]

Employment security in the industrialized world is being undercut both by the efforts of various national governments and intergovernmental organizations to promote "structural adjustment" globally and by the collapse of Marxist-Leninist regimes in Eastern Europe. The politics of the structural adjustment effort in such organizations as the OECD and International Monetary Fund in the 1980s, targeted at real as well as possibly dubious rigidities in labor markets, is traced in subsequent parts of this book. In the Soviet Union and the East-Central European countries, the sources of severe strains on employment security even before the political collapse of 1989–91 included unsustainable international debt and the loss of guaranteed markets for inferior industrial goods.[33] After 1989 some new regimes have proceeded with radical economic restructuring marked by "shock" methods that accept very high levels of unemployment and prices as a necessary short- or intermediate-term price to be paid for eventual recovery.

A third area of relevant positive law development relates to formal national commitments to the right to employment. This includes national constitutional guarantees and statutes as well as the continuing

31. *Report on Social Development, Year 1985* (Brussels: Commission of the European Communities, April 1986), Vol. 1, p. 8.

32. Martin Vranken, "Deregulating the Employment Relationship: Current Trends in Europe," *Comparative Labor Law* 7 (1986): 143.

33. For background see Blair A. Ruble, "Factory Unions and Workers' Rights," in Arcadius Kahan and Ruble, eds., *Industrial Labor in the USSR* (New York: Pergamon, 1979), pp. 59–79, and Anna-Jutta Pietsch and Heinrich Vogel, "Displacement by Technological Progress in the USSR," in Jan Adam, ed., *Employment Policies in the Soviet Union and Eastern Europe* (New York: St. Martin's Press, 1982). For more on recent developments see "Soviet Unemployment: Facing the Facts," *Pravda*, October 31, 1989, in *Current Digest of the Soviet Press* XLI, 44 (1989): 6–7; "Poles Stoically Face Rising Unemployment," *Soviet/East European Report* VII, 20 (March 1, 1990): 4; I. Adirim, "A Note on the Current Level, Pattern and Trends of Unemployment in the USSR," *Soviet Studies* XLI, 3 (July 1989): 449–461.

efforts to prescribe and advocate the right to employment through intergovernmental organizations. The number and type of nation-states that have declared a right to employment in their constitutions have increased, albeit only incrementally.[34]

Nonetheless, it is probable that the strength of efforts to promulgate the right to work continues to decline at the national level. A very disappointing turning point occurred during the 1975–78 U.S. debate over the proposed Humphrey-Hawkins Full Employment Act. Various drafts of the bill proposed a right to a job and a general statement calling for employment opportunity for all. However, its history mirrored that of the 1946 Employment Act in fundamental ways, and the final statute fell far short of its sponsors' hopes despite strong testimony from such advocates as Leon Keyserling, Lester Thurow, Sar Levitan, and Eli Ginzberg.[35] The passage of a statute that lacked specific provisions for job creation was followed by the Reagan administration's replacement of the Comprehensive Employment and Training Act (CETA) with a far less ambitious approach to employment training and governmentally sponsored employment.

The collapse of Marxist-Leninist regimes in Eastern and Central Europe has produced both a practical and ideological retreat from full employment and the right to employment. It was argued in *Pravda* in March 1988 that "Looking back at the false 'welfare' notions of social protections and full employment that prevailed in the period of stagnation and leveling, and that allowed a fair number of people to take life easy, will carry us backward to stagnation, shortages and hard times."[36]

The efforts of the past several decades to continue to prescribe a right to work or employment through intergovernmental organiza-

---

34. A 1985 ILO study found that thirty member states "recognize or mention the right to work" in their national constitutions. Of these, eighteen then had centrally planned economies and twelve had market economies (only two of the latter being developed states). Twenty-five of the thirty nations mentioned a guarantee of this right. Although various European countries that are abandoning centrally planned economies probably will formally abandon pledges of guaranteed employment in their constitutions, it is also likely that most will invoke weaker pledges of full employment in those documents. Jean Mayer, "The Concept of the Right to Work in Interntaional Standards and the Legislation of ILO Member States," *International Labour Review* 124 (1985): 225–242.

35. See David Ziskind, "U.S. Legislation toward Full Employment," *Comparative Labor Law* 2, 3 (1978): 167; Hubert Humphrey, "Guaranteed Jobs for Human Rights," *Annals of the American Academy of Political and Social Science* 418 (March 1975): 17–25; Eli Ginzberg, *Good Jobs, Bad Jobs, No Jobs* (Cambridge, MA: Harvard University Press, 1979), pp. 171, 184.

36. Commentary by V. Badov in *Pravda*, March 4, 1988, in *Current Digest of the Soviet Press* XL, 10 (1988): 8.

tions is discussed in the following chapters. This effort has not progressed significantly beyond the statements in the U.N. Covenants and may well have been effectively blunted by challenges made in the ILO arena in 1983–84. Nonetheless, the effort to codify in international legal and policy instruments such a right as well as the goal of full employment is quite likely to be revived in other times and circumstances given the history of persistent support for these causes.

Such developments reflect the various ways in which positive law addresses the employment rights agendas set by contemporary conditions and social forces. Such agendas are usually first dealt with experimentally and partially at the national level and then promoted at the international level in order to broaden and harmonize national trends. Necessary employment rights have been defined through political compromise and judicial edict. In some instances the system has helped to eliminate outrageous patterns of discrimination and arbitrary exercises of managerial prerogatives that are no longer generally accepted in most Western and certain other societies.

However, the greatest parts of such problems as discrimination, job insecurity, and mass unemployment are not being resolved through such international positive law prescriptions. Most intergovernmental formulations are marked by diplomatic vagueness and compromises that reflect the least common denominators of national law and international debates, even as critical employment rights issues are being addressed and some new flesh is being put on the previously skeletal right to work.

Frontier Concepts

The assertion of natural rights and the development of numerous positive law protections have promoted recognition and respect for the right to employment. However, these developments alone have not been sufficient to create a consensus for the idea that the right of all men and women to employment is worthy of effective national and international protection.

Additional conceptual underpinning is clearly needed to convince a greater proportion of intellectual leaders, governmental and intergovernmental administrators, and politicians that a human right to employment is more than a luxury relevant only to rich industrialized states or a right that can appropriately be ignored when nations face serious economic problems. Such a right can obtain greater weight through association with emerging conceptions of human rights that complement natural and positive rights and affirm new perspectives on social and economic justice. Such concepts that have been linked in recent decades to the right to employment include distributive justice, basic needs, the right to development, and new interpretations of the values of human dignity and self-respect.

Louis Henkin has written of the fusion of democratic-libertarian and socialist conceptions during the formative post-1945 stage of the prescription of universal rights.[37] Such a synthesis is already proceeding through another stage in an era in which the formulation of new concepts of international law and global reform are increasingly shaped by Third World advocates who recognize that unemployment and underemployment are among the most serious problems in developing as well as developed countries. As expressed in the Declaration of Principles of the 1976 ILO-sponsored Tripartite World Conference on Employment, Income Distribution and Social Progress, "Unemployment, underemployment and marginality are a universal concern and affect at least one-third of humanity at the present time."[38] This new emphasis on Third World unemployment has been reinforced by reports from the Brandt Commission on International Development Issues and other authoritative observers of the plight of developing countries.[39]

Such perceptions have given considerable impetus to human rights theorists who emphasize basic needs. The 1976 ILO Employment Conference Declaration asserted, "In all countries, freely chosen employment enters into basic-needs policy both as a means and an end."[40] Basic needs were elevated to a major category of human rights by numerous international resolutions and were even recognized authoritatively by the U.S. Carter administration.[41] Its standing has also been

---

37. Louis Henkin, *The Rights of Man Today* (Boulder, CO: Westview Press, 1978), p. 77.

38. Declaration of Principles and Programme of Action, adopted by the Conference in Geneva, June 4–17, 1976, in *Follow-Up of the World Employment Conference* (Geneva: ILO, 1979), pp. 124–145.

39. Willy Brandt notes, "An enormous challenge derives from the millions of unemployed in the North, but still more from the far greater number in the South." *North-South: A Programme for Survival*, Report of the Independent Commission on International Development Issues (Cambridge, MA: MIT Press, 1980), p. 21. This report calls attention to the fact that the majority of migrant workers were then from developing countries and argues that newly industrialized countries are not a threat to employment in advanced industrial states. See also the Brandt Commission on International Development Issues, *Common Crisis North-South: Cooperation for World Recovery* (Cambridge, MA: MIT Press, 1983).

40. *Follow-Up of the World Employment Conference*, p. 126.

41. Graciela Chichilnisky and H. S. D. Cole contend that "basic needs" and its widespread acceptance by the international community stems from Amilcar O. Herrera et al., *Catastrophe or New Society? A Latin American Model*, published by Fundación Bariloche

strengthened by the philosophical defense of the human right to "subsistence" developed by American philosopher Henry Shue and others.[42]

Before 1976 employment had generally not been included among the primary elements of the basic needs concept. Rather, the focus had been on such commodities and services needed for human physical survival as food, shelter, and health care. As such, the later inclusion of employment as a "basic need" involved broadening that concept, a step justified by the contribution made by employment to the obtaining of the means of subsistence as well as the direct role played by employment in human physical and psychological well-being. The latter perspective seems increasingly justified in the light of growing evidence that unemployment contributes significantly to levels of physical and mental illness and disability even in societies that provide substantial income maintenance. The International Labor Office has built its position regarding employment and basic needs on the connection between employment and poverty, stressing that hundreds of millions of unemployed or underemployed in the developing world constitute a very large part of the global poverty problem.[43]

The right to employment has also been linked in the past decade to an emerging right to development. It has been difficult to sell the idea of a right to development in the First World, in part because such a claimed right has been hard to define, has tended to be viewed as the right of nations rather than one enjoyed by individuals, and has few explicit links to various formulations of human rights adopted between 1945 and 1966.[44]

(Buenos Aires) and the International Development Research Centre (Ottawa) in 1976. Chichilnisky and Cole, "Human Rights and Basic Needs in a North-South Context," in Paula R. Newberg, ed., *The Politics of Human Rights* (New York: New York University Press, 1980), p. 141.

42. Henry Shue, *Basic Rights: Subsistence, Affluence, and U.S. Foreign Policy* (Princeton, NJ: Princeton University Press, 1980).

43. *Follow-Up of the World Employment Conference*, pp. 27–52.

44. See Héctor Gros Espiell, "The Right of Development as a Human Right," *Texas International Law Journal* 16 (1981): 189–205, reprinted in Richard P. Claude and Burns H. Weston, eds., *Human Rights in the World Community: Issues and Action*, 2nd ed. (Philadelphia: University of Pennsylvania Press, 1992), pp. 167–174; International Commission of Jurists, *Development, Human Rights of Law* (Oxford: Pergamon, 1981); Jack Donnelly, "The 'Right to Development': How Not to Link Human Rights and Development," in C. Welch, Jr. and R. Meltzer, eds., *Human Rights and Development in Africa* (Albany: State University of New York Press, 1984), pp. 261–284; Richard L. Siegel, "A Policy Approach to Human Rights Law: The Right to Development," in D. Cingranelli, ed., *Human Rights: Theory and Measurement* (New York: St. Martin's Press, 1988), pp. 72–88.

Yet such criticisms offered by certain Western scholars have not deterred the linkage of employment rights to the right to development in major international instruments and statements. This has been most consistently evident in positions developed under ILO and U.N. auspices. The Declaration on the Right to Development adopted by the U.N. General Assembly in December 1986, the most authoritative statement of the right to development thus far, links it to socioeconomic rights in general and to equal employment opportunity in particular.[45]

It cannot, however, be clearly demonstrated that employment and other socioeconomic rights have been assisted by the recent contentious debates on the right to development. The primary thrust of the Third World effort to promote a right to development has been to broaden the human rights agenda to include "third generation" issues ranging from disarmament to the creation of a new international economic order. References to greater responsibility of developing states to their own destitute and unemployed people are sometimes placed in such documents as a tradeoff for language asserting the need for greater responsibility of leading industrial countries for the welfare of Third World peoples. The right to development debate emerged from efforts to explore and promote the realization of economic, social, and cultural rights in the developing countries. Some important new directions for human rights and policy have emerged from this debate, including a stress on broader public participation in national decision-making regarding development. Yet efforts to connect the right to development explicitly to socioeconomic as well as to civil-political rights have yet to achieve a clear international consensus.

The 1976 ILO Declaration noted above also suggested that unemployment offends human dignity, a concept that has taken on new meaning in association with human rights scholarship concerning such values as self-respect, wealth, and skill.[46] Many studies have stressed the great importance of work to the psychological well-being of individuals. The central role played by work and its variations (labor,

45. See U.N. General Assembly, 41st Sess., Declaration on the Right to Development, adopted December 4, 1986. *Official Records*, Supplement No. 53 (A/41/53) (New York: United Nations, 1987), pp. 186–187.

46. See Christian Bay, "Self-Respect as a Human Right: Thoughts on the Dialectics of Wants and Needs in the Struggle for Human Community," *Human Rights Quarterly* 4, 1 (Winter 1982): 53–75; Jack Donnelly, "Human Rights and Human Dignity: An Analytic Critique of Non-Western Conceptions of Human Rights," *American Political Science Review* 76, 2 (June 1982): 303–16; McDougal et al., *Human Rights and World Public Order*, pp. 154–156.

callings, workmanship) in expressing ourselves as humans has been articulated by writers from Marx to Arendt.[47]

Other significant frontier efforts to bolster the legitimacy of the right to employment have been greatly influenced by John Rawls's *A Theory of Justice*, a work that emphasizes the value of self-respect and the provision of at least minimum standards while placing primary emphasis on the value of liberty.[48] While Shue and others find Rawls's perspective inadequate as a framework for a general entitlement to socioeconomic rights,[49] Nickel utilizes Rawls's core proposition to help bolster the right to employment by arguing:

The justification for a universal right to employment would lie, in this view, in the fact that because of class interests and various group prejudices any non-universal distribution of employment opportunities will be unfair to the disadvantaged classes and minorities. Hence the only fair distribution available is one that guarantees each person a job.[50]

Nickel also stresses the Rawlsian conception of the centrality of dignity and self-respect in his effort to promote a right to employment. An even broader Rawlsian case is made by Charles R. Beitz, who explicitly cites the Rawlsian social justice model and recalls the social justice arguments for socioeconomic rights proposed in 1945 by the Inter-American Judicial Committee.[51]

The development of frontier concepts and the reinterpretation of some older perspectives may have marginally broadened the base of support for a human right to employment. Employment has been a central issue in the discourse on global distributive justice and a New International Economic Order. The integration of employment with conceptions of basic needs and development represents a potentially important development.

The present section reviewed the development of new sources of the

47. Hannah Arendt, *The Human Condition* (Chicago: University of Chicago Press, 1958); For the development of labor, workmanship, and calling as conceptual criteria see Gregory E. Pence, "Toward a Theory of Work," *Philosophical Forum* 10 (1978–79): 306–320.

48. John Rawls, *A Theory of Justice* (Cambridge, MA: Harvard University Press, 1971).

49. Henry Shue emphasizes that a major part of his work on subsistence rights "is intended to be, among other things, a reply to the Rawlsian doctrine of the priority of liberty." Shue, *Basic Rights*, p. 92.

50. Nickel, "Is There a Human Right to Employment?" p. 161.

51. Charles R. Beitz, "Human Rights and Social Justice," in Peter G. Brown and Douglas MacLean, eds., *Human Rights and U.S. Foreign Policy: Principles and Applications* (Lexington, MA: Lexington Books, 1979), pp. 45–63. This Beitz view is challenged in Donnelly, "Human Rights as Natural Rights," p. 403.

right to employment by contemporary intellectuals, policy-makers, and diplomats. It was suggested that this right has been given greater breadth by subsuming into it such issues as employment security, basic needs, and equal opportunity, and that such efforts may have enhanced its legitimacy. Yet from the perspective of the early 1990s the future of the right to employment seems highly problematical due to ideological, geopolitical, and economic developments that have blunted efforts to establish this right more firmly at the national and international levels. The concept of a right to work has remained highly controversial and difficult to formulate.

The 1984 ILO Employment Policy Recommendations: A Case Study

In the quarter century since the adoption of the 1964 ILO Employment Policy Convention and Recommendation, many countries made formal commitments to full employment goals and instituted various unprecedented national programs designed to promote employment and develop human resources. Further, a growing international commitment to the concept of a right to work could be inferred from such steps as the ratification of the International Covenant on Economic, Social and Cultural Rights and the explicit references to that right in various U.N. General Assembly resolutions.[52]

These steps pointed toward a breakthrough in ILO acceptance of the right to work in a new convention or recommendation on employment policy scheduled for adoption in 1984. However, various political factors determined that such an instrument would include only a formalistic acceptance of the right to work. The pattern of steeply rising unemployment in developed and developing countries alike in the decade following the 1973–74 oil crisis sharply increased concern about the issue. Yet these developments also made the goals associated with full employment and the right to work seem more elusive than ever. Further, growing inflation, concerns about unstable export markets, and other economic concerns led many countries to target their macro- and microeconomic policies on other objectives. Several forces and trends undercutting international and national commitments to the right to work are discussed below.

52. For example, see U.N. resolutions No. 36/29 of November 13, 1981, and No. 37/49 of December 3, 1982. International Labour Conference, 69th Session, 1983, Report VI(1), *Employment Policy* (Geneva: ILO, 1982), pp. 9–10.

The Focus of Third World Support

While evidence could be assembled to demonstrate both growing support and loss of momentum for the right to work in the 1980s, debate in the ILO primarily reflected the limited nature of the gains made to that point. The search for new linkages connecting this right to basic needs and a New International Economic Order did bolster Third World support somewhat in the 1970s. Yet these themes faded in the 1980s, replaced by efforts to secure more immediate and practical concessions from the industrialized countries in such areas as debt relief and trade preferences. Third World support for a right to development and the New International Economic Order emphasized the shifting of responsibility for economic development from developing to industrialized states. One result was to reduce the possibility of any ILO convention or recommendation that would stress additional obligations of Third World governments to their own unemployed.

Disillusionment Regarding Keynesian Policies

Further, the governments of various Western industrialized states became demonstrably hostile to new international prescriptions of the right to work during the 1980s. This opposition derived from several sources. One was their declining confidence in the capability of Keynesian or other macroeconomic policies to return advanced economies to the favorable unemployment rates of the 1960s without contributing to unacceptably negative impacts on inflation and other critical national economic outcomes. In the 1940s and 1950s powerful elements in many Western states came to accept full employment as a feasible national objective and a paramount national priority. Support for the right to employment and full employment in Western industrialized countries grew out of favorable economic conditions, the perceived potency of Keynesian demand-management and other economic policies, and ideological attachments to full employment as a basic goal of the welfare state. These preconditions of full employment policies faded or were shattered in the wake of the oil shocks and stagflation of the 1970s. In the face of such forces, major international organizations (including the European Community, the International Monetary Fund, and the OECD) and the most influential Western governments increasingly supported deflationary economic policies, especially tighter monetary policies, that were virtually certain to increase rather than decrease unemployment in the short and medium term.

Such goals as stable currencies, control of inflation, and the repayment of international debt acquired vastly greater weight relative to full employment in an environment that appeared to force choices and trade-offs.[53] Further, no single economic medicine or known combination of prescriptions offered real hope to large numbers of developing and developed states affected by economic upheavals. Although a wide variety of economic policy packages were formulated and implemented in the early and mid-1980s, international pressures often mandated relatively tight monetary policies and the slowing of the rate of government expenditure increases. Periodic OECD and European Community calls for marginally more expansionary economic policies for the majority of their member states often met with limited national responses due to continuing concerns about inflation and pressures on national currencies. Even greater pressures to create austerity affected much of the developing world and Eastern Europe as structural adjustment became a condition for new loans and debt rescheduling for countries ranging from Poland to Brazil.

By the early 1980s an increasing majority of informed observers concluded that even a strong and widespread economic recovery would not recreate labor market conditions approaching full employment. Even many European trade union leaders increasingly shifted emphasis from the promotion of expansionary macroeconomic policies that could create new jobs to the protection of the jobs of those still employed.

Global Politics

From 1948 to 1966 the ebbs and flows of East-West and North-South conflicts did much to shape intergovernmental prescriptions of the right to employment. One of the worst of those ebbs came between 1979 and 1984, precisely the time that the ILO formulated and adopted updated policies on employment. The negative consequences of that political environment on the ILO consideration of what became the Employment Policy (Supplementary Provisions) Recommendation of 1984 is reviewed below in order to indicate aspects of continuity over a forty year period and to provide a baseline for review of potential changes in the subsequent era of perestroika and post-Cold War politics.

53. In contrast, Schmidt concludes that "there is no clear-cut relationship between unemployment on the one hand and economic growth, wage flexibility and inflation on the other." Manfred G. Schmidt, "The Politics of Unemployment: Rates of Unemployment and Labour Market Policy," *West European Politics* VII (July 1984): 8.

The political environment for the ILO deliberations included the causes and effects of the U.S. government's departure from that organization in 1977 and its return in 1980. This extraordinary action was part of a concerted effort on the part of the United States and some of its allies to pressure certain member states of various intergovernmental organizations to be less defiant of Western political interests. It was followed in the Reagan years by U.S. withdrawal from UNESCO and the withholding of dues owed to the United Nations and other organizations. These policies responded to the perceived politicization of such organizations by Third World and Communist-ruled states, particularly the positions taken by them on such issues as Israeli-Palestinian relations.

In retrospect the assertive position taken in the 1983–84 ILO debate by the Soviet Union and most of its close allies and clients was a poorly chosen strategy. States facing decline and imminent crisis proceeded on the basis of ideological reflex that still seemed appropriate to their leaders in the years before perestroika and New Thinking, and their principal Western adversaries were more than pleased to reply in kind.

Organizational and Bureaucratic Politics

The formulation between 1979 and 1984 of a new ILO policy instrument on employment policy revealed the balance of forces regarding the prescription of the right to work that existed just prior to the Gorbachev era. That this right would be a major issue in the debates and votes concerning a new ILO convention or recommendation on employment was assured by the attention given the concept by the 1979 Session of the International Labor Conference. Subsequently, the Soviet Union and its allies decided to make the prominent treatment of this concept in a new ILO convention a principal political objective. Other ILO participants, particularly certain Western governments, formulated contrasting objectives involving more limited or alternative formulations of the right to work. They also opposed altogether any new legally binding convention on employment, especially one that advocated a right to employment.

The ensuing deliberations took place within the unique tripartite structure of the ILO, involving voting participation by representatives of employers and workers as well as governments. With a global approach to membership, the organization developed by the 1960s a built-in Third World majority, at least when these countries were not sharply divided. However, the cross-cutting impacts of the employers' and workers' caucuses complicated the maintenance of government-based coalitions.

It is also pertinent that the ILO was created and has been maintained as an organization concentrating on social policy, with its primary constituents in national governments being Labor, Employment, and Social ministries. Even affiliated employers' organizations generally understand and often accept most ILO social priorities and usually avoid stating positions based wholly on cold economic calculations or laissez faire ideology. It is assumed by most observers that the International Labor Office, the ILO's secretariat, will actively promote actions by national governments that advance the interests of workers at the expense of some employers. In this sense the Office resembles a progressive International Labor Ministry.

The Office developed an initial draft of an Employment Policy instrument in response to the replies of member states to a questionnaire. One is impressed with the considerable leeway left to the Office at various stages of policy development.[54] Meetings with various Office officials and reviews of its published materials suggest to me that ILO adoption of the right to work concept was never an Office priority. This is consistent with the general Office preference for what it considers to be tangible and achievable objectives rather than what one prominent official referred to as "big statements."[55] The Office's important introductory report on law and practice emphasized that interest in the right to work in the ILO arena was late to emerge and that only a minority of member states recognized the right in their constitutions.[56] However, the Office also recognized that the degree of emphasis to be placed on this concept would be a political decision that it could influence but not control.

As to the appropriate meaning of the concept, both the Office and the ILO's Committee of Experts on the Application of Conventions and Recommendations consistently viewed it as excluding guaranteed employment. They considered it to involve such ingredients of international labor standards as active labor market policy, rejection of forced labor, non-discrimination, and protection against arbitrary termination of employment. This perspective was consistent with the incremental development of organizational ideology that included only a few areas of human rights as "fundamental human rights." The Office was reluctant to accept the positive obligation of governments to de-

54. See Robert W. Cox, "ILO: Limited Monarchy," in Cox and Harold K. Jacobsen, *Anatomy of Influence: Decision Making in International Organization* (New Haven, CT: Yale University Press, 1973), p. 112.
55. Interview conducted by this writer at the ILO, Geneva, October 19, 1983.
56. International Labour Conference, 69th Sess., *Employment Policy*, pp. 9–10.

velop policies and programs to maximize employment as the basis of a fundamental human right equivalent to non-discrimination, freedom of association, and the absence of forced labor. However, the right to work concept was viewed as useful for tying together seemingly separate ILO priorities and for increasing acceptance of government programs designed to promote full employment.

Although the ILO's provisional resolution of the right to work issue in 1983 was greatly influenced by the Office and by the views of government and employers' representatives, it was largely decided by the representatives of non-Communist trade unions. The immediate questions at issue included: (1) Would endorsement of the right to work be limited to a reference to the existence of the relevant article in the International Covenant on Economic, Social and Cultural Rights, or would the concept be endorsed independently in an ILO instrument? (2) Would the ILO support an interpretation of the concept different from that in the Covenant, particularly in regard to guaranteed employment? (3) Would reference to this right be restricted to the new instrument's preamble, or would it also appear in the main body of the text? (4) Would the concept be incorporated into a convention or in a less-binding recommendation?

The objectives of the U.S. government regarding such right to work issues reflected the deepening of the chasm between East and West in the wake of strained international developments and the highly ideological and often confrontational approach of the Reagan administration in its first term. Some of its views were echoed by the Thatcher administration as well as by certain other Western governments.

The strong Reagan administration counter-attack to the Soviet initiative on the right to work was intensified by the strong input of business-oriented and highly ideological Department of Commerce officials.[57] A position paper on employment policy prepared by Commerce for the U.S. delegation (USDEL) to the 1983 ILO Conference dealt with most of the issues introduced by the International Labor Office that had survived the initial member state questionnaire. That paper presented the right to work as a vehicle for Communist propaganda and as a Communist euphemism for denial of "such basic human rights as freedom to choose their jobs or career paths, to participate in the determination of their wages, or to emigrate."[58] The idea of

57. Before the withdrawal of the United States from the ILO in November 1979 U.S. government involvement with international labor issues was concentrated in the Department of Labor to a greater degree than subsequently.

58. "69th Session of the International Labor Conference, June 1–22, 1983," Position

a governmental guarantee of employment was challenged directly, the concept deemed "dangerous because the only way it can be implemented is by restricting imports and/or artificially depressing wages, thereby exporting unemployment to other nations."[59] As such, older human rights complaints are joined with some economic arguments that I had not encountered earlier in the right to work saga.

The major goals of the U.S. delegation regarding the right to work were set as follows:

USDEL [the U.S. delegation] may support reference to the 1966 International Covenant on Economic, Social and Cultural Rights (Article 6), but should propose that the "right to work" be elaborated in either: (a) its positive form (e.g., policies that maximize individual opportunities to find freely chosen and productive work); or (b) that it be qualified to express what it does not mean (e.g., that an individual is obliged to work at a specified job which he has not chosen and for wages which are determined without his consent). USDEL should support amendments to delegate this provision if the suggested changes noted above are rejected.[60]

In June 1983 a tripartite ILO Committee on Employment considered a draft document that included numerous issues that had become more salient in the years after the 1964 Employment Policy Convention and Recommendation.[61] These included the relationships of employment to policy developments in the areas of population, technology, regional development, international economic cooperation, and migration. The debate also provided opportunities to raise issues that many, especially Western representatives, considered to be more appropriate for other instruments or for other organizations, these topics including disarmament and multinational investment.

At the 1983 ILO Conference the Workers' Group tentatively supported (subject to review in 1984) a supplementary recommendation in preference to a convention and also endorsed major limitations on references to the right to work in that recommendation. As a result, the Communist-ruled states were largely isolated in their efforts to have the Committee endorse their conception of that right and expand upon the language in the International Covenant on Economic, Social and Cultural Rights. The Employment Committee endorsed the idea

---

Paper for the United States Delegation, Agenda Item 6, "Employment Policy," unpublished and undated, p. 1.

59. Ibid., p. 4.

60. Ibid., p. 6.

61. The deliberations of this committee are summarized in International Labour Conference, 70th Session, 1984, Report IV(1) *Employment Policy* (Geneva: ILO, 1983).

that "The promotion of full, productive and freely chosen employment provided for in the Employment Policy Convention and Recommendation, 1964, should be regarded as the means of achieving in
practice the realization of the right to work."[62] This formulation, endorsed years earlier by various ILO organs, seemed designed to credit
the previous work of the ILO without breaking new conceptual ground
or acceding to the political agenda of the Soviet Union and its supporters.

Some of the major choices made during the struggle over the International Covenant's article on the right to work were revisited in the
1983–84 ILO arena. A proposed mandate that the "full recognition by
member states of the right to work" be included in domestic legislation
was defeated handily despite Workers' Group support. Proposed Socialist state amendments relating the right to work to other social
values (e.g., human dignity, the development of the personality, and
social justice) were also rejected, often by crushing margins. Despite
the continued stress by Communist representatives on the concept of a
state guarantee of employment, this proposition had no chance of
acceptance.

The Soviet delegation had to take solace from the references to the
right to work included in an accompanying ILO resolution concerning employment. This less-binding action of the 1983 Conference
affirmed "the leading role that the ILO should play within the United
Nations system in the promotion of that right," and closely linked
the right to work theme to the ILO's evolving World Employment
Program.[63]

Despite efforts by the Soviet and like-minded delegations to reverse
the major decisions taken in 1983, the 1984 Conference incorporated
the right to work in the Employment Policy (Supplementary Provisions) Recommendation essentially along the lines decided the previous year. (The Recommendation appears in Appendix I of this volume.) Although it could be argued that the right was kept alive by the
1984 Recommendation's references to the International Covenant and
by the 1983 Resolution, it would be more accurate to view the process
as one of diminution of support for this right, both as a symbolic
objective and as an element of a strategy for promoting full employment. Major Third World governments and Western trade union rep-

62. Ibid., p. 54.
63. International Labor Conference, 69th Sess., 1983, "Resolution Concerning Employment," adopted June 21, 1983, *Record of Proceedings* (Geneva: International Labor
Office, 1983), pp. LXXXII–LXXXIV.

resentatives again turned down numerous proposals advanced by the Soviet Union and its allies to further develop a rights approach to employment.

Conclusions about the ILO and U.N. formulations of the right to work must be stated cautiously. Socioeconomic context, organizational processes, intellectual thought, and global political relations contributed to the outcomes in each case. As compared to the earlier United Nations considerations, the role of intellectual thought was somewhat smaller in the later ILO forum and the contribution of political considerations manifestly greater. The ILO proceedings were so highly politicized partly because ILO prescriptions often directly affect the allocation of staff time and other organizational resources. Further, tripartite politics is often more complex than policy-making that is more completely controlled by government representatives.

It remains to be seen whether the 1979–84 ILO process represents turning away from a human rights approach to the horrendous problems of unemployment and underemployment in the long-term. In the ILO debate it seemed evident that larger ideological and organizational considerations dominated. The strongly ideological Reagan and Thatcher administration representatives had persuaded a sufficient number of governmental and non-governmental representatives to perceive the right to work as an ideological issue of the renewed Cold War and to vote accordingly. In the wake of the U.S. withdrawal and return to the ILO, these Western governments marshaled increased political weight in such matters.

Conclusion

The processes through which the right to work or employment has been incorporated into significant international legal instruments and the factors that have determined the nature of those formulations were analyzed in this chapter. As these developments involved the history of ideas, socioeconomic trends, international politics, and organizational processes, the conclusions cannot be tidy ones. Major divisions persist among scholars, trade unionists, and officials of national governments and international organizations concerning the legitimacy and utility of a human right to work. Only a limited consensus has emerged concerning the philosophical and legal sources of such a right.

Despite the mostly negative positions taken by ILO delegates in 1984, the process of prescribing a right to work, formulating its meaning, and associating it with tangible international and domestic programs continues. The most influential historical experiences that advanced this right in the present century were the Great Depression and World War II. Additional support has come from the growing recognition of the seriousness of recent mass unemployment and underemployment in Europe and the Third World. As a result, the right to work has repeatedly been placed on the agenda of international organizations. Although the endorsement of this right in some form by such organizations has rarely been in doubt, the form of the endorsement and the definition of the right have invited debate and struggle. In the 1940s and 1950s there was little or no scholarly consensus and minimal official interest in providing a comprehensive justification for a right to work. However, broad agreement existed then concerning the desirability and feasibility of full employment even as proponents differed about the means to achieve that goal. The right to work seems to have thrived on a sense of the achievability of full employment, at least in industrialized countries, and to have faltered when full employment again appeared to be a distant or impossible dream after 1973.

It is not certain whether academic and political supporters of the right to work will seek to further legitimize this concept through future international instruments. Scholars from various regions and political orientations continue to reinforce as well as challenge efforts to associate the right to work with such perspectives as basic needs and the right to development. The goal of full employment has lost ground even as an element of Marxism-Leninism while it has gained from wide-ranging critiques of internationally supported austerity measures in Eastern Europe and the developing world.

Efforts to advance a positive definition of the right to work have been marked by the defeat of a guaranteed employment focus, except perhaps in relation to youth programs. However, the foundation of a meaningful right to work has been partially built on the elements of equal opportunity, free movement of labor, attention to job security, and commitments to active labor market policies.

A right to work must be built on a foundation of principles, goals, and rules. The principles include equal opportunity, free choice, and state and international responsibility. The stated goals relate to full employment and the achievement of a decent standard of living for all. The rules can be explicit, at least in regard to equality of treatment and limited aspects of employment security, and should also mandate that no state may consciously disregard responsibility to maintain high rates of productive employment as a principal policy objective.

The power of the idea of human rights elevates such principles, goals, and rules even in the absence of effective sanctions or compliance mechanisms. Indeed, it is not the weaknesses regarding sanctions or compliance that most clearly separates the international protection of the right to work from that for certain precious political and civil rights. Rather, it is the lack of consensus about the nature of state responsibilities and the appropriate tradeoffs with other socioeconomic objectives that makes the right to work exceptionally problematical even as a goal. This became increasingly clear when the international community sought to implement certain of its elements during the past forty years, a story told in the following chapters.

Chapter 5
The Limits of the International Response

The historical chapters of this book revealed the ingrained reluctance of the international community to accept such concepts as the right to work and full employment except during brief interludes of crisis and solidarity. This is consistent with my political analysis of the efforts to prescribe the right to work concept through the United Nations and ILO, processes that reflected pervasive cynicism as well as the subordination of such efforts to Cold War considerations.

In this chapter an effort is made to systematically review the international efforts of the past several decades to affect global, regional, national, and subnational policies and outcomes relating to employment generally and as a domain of human rights. Concepts from international regime and global policy analysis are introduced to facilitate the review. The principal vantage point of this chapter is the period from the oil crisis of 1973–74 to just prior to the collapse of the Marxist-Leninist regimes in Europe. More recent developments are discussed in the concluding chapter of this book.

As such, a major focus of this chapter is evaluation of efforts to influence policy. This requires the separating out of international factors in a policy area still dominated by national and subnational authority. Similar problems exist for such policy areas as, for example, education, human rights and the physical environment, although each of these policy areas differs regarding the legitimacy and level of development of international roles. Comparison of international roles might begin with such factors as the availability of international resources and legal authority. It is necessary to contrast internationally imposed or stimulated policies designed to have major impacts on outcomes with those policies that are essentially symbolic, serving mainly to give the observer only the impression that outcomes are meant to be significantly affected.

Another major problem is the meaning of the term international in the context of this chapter. In the issue area of employment distinctions among transnational, national, and intergovernmental actors are somewhat blurred. Transnational actors in this context include multinational enterprises, international trade unions, and other international non-governmental organizations. Transnationalism principally involves the movement of goods, money, people, information, and ideas across national boundaries without a high degree of direct participation or control by governmental or intergovernmental actors. Yet in areas of employment policy and employment rights transnational actors sometimes also assume authoritative roles. Tripartite representation of labor unions and employers' organizations in the International Labor Organization is the epitome of such roles. Yet the potential veto power over national and international employment policies exercised by vaguely defined transnational markets for government bonds, export goods, national currencies, and other commodities may exercise even greater authority than more tangible transnational actors. As such, the term international as used here includes certain transnational influences.

However, the focus of this chapter is on the intergovernmental processes and organizations that are directly created by national governments. As we saw earlier, the frequent efforts of intergovernmental organizations (IGOs) to prescribe goals, rights, and norms usually constitute very limited first steps in the direction of effective international action. Experience has taught us that effective performance by international organizations requires competent bureaucracy, independent will on the part of international civil servants and elected organizational leaders, widespread support from the leading national governments involved in the given issue area, meaningful legal authority, and a measure of autonomy in the control of financial resources. The mobilization of each of these elements in an intergovernmental organization is rare even when issues clearly challenge global human survival. They are scarce indeed when national interests of critically positioned states appear to conflict with global interests, when issues are stubbornly viewed as essentially domestic, or when policy is immobilized by conflicts among social, economic, environmental, and security values.

Nonetheless, it is evident that intergovernmental agencies are the principal vehicles for intergovernmental policy coordination and direct implementation. Global and regional policy regimes have advanced much further than many political realists imagined forty to fifty years ago even as they have thus far failed to match the hopes of contemporary globalists. As such, it is mainly the performance of these agencies that is judged here, together with the contributions of their leading member governments. In this chapter credit and blame is assigned to a wide variety of agencies as well as to other actors and factors influencing global and regional employment policy.

The employment policy effort described here has most often incorporated a strong ideological aspect. It may not seem fashionable to perceive basic ideological divisions in this age of breakdown of Marxist-Leninist power and the alleged end of history. Yet employment issues are at the nexus of so many ideologies and ideological issues, being central to positions taken by, for example, Social Catholicism and Reagan-Thatcher neoclassicism or radical conservatism. They are so intrinsically ideological because employment is heavily implicated in myriad social, economic, and political issues relating to status, wealth, alienation, liberty, responsibility, and lifestyle. It is a focal point of discussions of equality of opportunity, citizenship, poverty, economic development and competitiveness, social mobility, and social control. Further, employment is implicated in many choices concerning international trade, debt, foreign aid, and security for which the impacts on employment are scarcely predictable.

International Regimes

In recent years major collaborative efforts by students of international law, politics, economics, and organization have sought to identify the attributes of international regimes in issue areas ranging from nuclear weapons to oceans. These regimes, which constitute a major part of the external environments of national public policy in various issue areas, are of central interest to students of public policy and international relations. An effort is made here to identify the extent to which an international employment policy regime has taken shape and to assess its impacts on nation-states, especially those of Western Europe and North America. Potentially, an international regime offers a firm political, legal, and economic context for the development and implementation of policy in an issue area in which transnational and intergovernmental processes are important.

The editors of a 1982 special issue of *International Organization* claimed widespread acceptance for a definition of an international regime as "sets of implicit principles, norms, rules, and decision-making procedures around which actors' expectations converge in a given area of international relations."[1] This definition raises as many important questions concerning the core content of an international regime as it answers. Yet the sorting out of such terms is crucial to understanding much that has been done in the name of international organizations and national governments during the past forty years. Founding legal instruments of major international organizations and major international instruments in policy areas ranging from human rights to ocean pollution lean heavily to what Dworkin terms "principles, policies and other sorts of standards" as distinct from rules.[2] Principles state goals and declare them to be worthy ones, reinforcing the case for a particular choice without requiring that decision. In contrast, rules are specific prescriptions or proscriptions for action. If a formulation is accepted as a legal rule, it presumably must be obeyed and enforced without exception. However, as argued by Dworkin, a principle is followed only when it is not judged to be outweighed by one or more other principles or policies.[3]

Few students of regimes posit structural requisites. Oran R. Young legitimizes structural eclecticism by contending that "real-world regimes are typically unsystematic and ambiguous," varying with respect to extent, formality, direction and coherence, and not even requiring explicit organizational arrangements.[4]

However, structural analysis is unavoidable in thinking about regimes. Such analysis can be compatible with realist perspectives that emphasize the central role of the state in the international system. Robert Keohane stresses that international regimes are "the products of voluntary agreements among independent actors within the context of prior constraints."[5] Less attention is given to international agencies or organizations in the writings of Keohane and most of the other contributors to the *International Organization* special issue as compared with representative earlier writings on international regimes.[6] This

1. Stephen D. Krasner, "Structural Causes and Regime Consequences: Regimes as Intervening Variables," *International Organization* 36 (Spring 1982): 186.

2. Ronald M. Dworkin, "The Model of Rules," *University of Chicago Law Review* 35 (1967): 14–26. The authors of the *International Organization* special issue on regimes define principles as "beliefs of fact, causation and rectitude." Krasner, "Structural Causes and Regime Consequences," p. 186.

3. Dworkin, "Model of Rules," p. 26.

4. Oran R. Young, "International Regimes: Problems of Concept Formation," *World Politics* 32 (1980): 341.

5. Robert O. Keohane, "The Demand for International Regimes," *International Organization* 36 (Spring 1982): 330.

6. See David Leive, *International Regulatory Regimes*, 2 vols. (Lexington, MA: Lexington Books, 1976).

literature has shifted somewhat from identifying regimes with one or more international organizations to emphasizing the roles played by major national governments in those regimes.

Both leading national governments and international organizations tend to be major, if not dominant, actors in international regimes. The relevant international organizations may be non-governmental or intergovernmental, or a hybrid such as the tripartite (government, employers, workers) ILO. Various other transnational actors, including multinational enterprises, may be given, or allowed to retain, authoritative roles in a given regime.

Most developers of the regime concept are reluctant to insist on functional requisites other than those of formulating and implementing principles, norms, and rules appropriate to the interests of the relevant actors. However, John Gerard Ruggie and Ernst Haas offer some requisites and options on regime functions that can assist our search for an employment regime. In an early formulation of their thinking on this subject they required that a regime constitute "international arrangements for jointly managing a resource," these aimed at such purposes as "problem search and definition," "harmonization/ standardization of national responses," "defining property rights," and "collective elaborations of welfare choices."[7] Nicholas Onuf and V. Spike Peterson proposed a categorization of functions involving (a) monitoring/publicizing (tutelary regime); (b) codifying/mediating (regulatory regime); and (c) promulgating/enforcing (governmental regime).[8]

In sum, major efforts have been exerted to develop some consensus perspectives about international regimes, thereby allowing others to build on a stronger conceptual foundation. These efforts have not satisfied all close observers, as indicated by Susan Strange's wide-

7. John Gerard Ruggie and Ernst B. Haas, "Environment and Resource Interdependencies: Reorganizing for the Evolution of International Regimes," in *Report of the Commission on the Organization of the Government for the Conduct of Foreign Policy* (Washington, DC: U.S. Government Printing Office, June 1975), 1, Appendix B, pp. 222–223. Ruggie and Haas identify an international regime for social-economic planning.

8. Nicholas G. Onuf and V. Spike Peterson, "Human Rights from an International Regimes Perspective," *Journal of International Affairs* 38 (Winter 1984): 329–342. In fuller terms their functional categories are monitoring and publicizing behavior for consistency with principle, mediating contested claims and codifying classes of solutions, and promulgating and enforcing decrees. For perspectives on the requisites of an international environmental regime see R. Michael M'Gonigle and Mark W. Zacher, *Pollution, Politics, and International Law* (Berkeley: University of California Press, 1979) and Oran R. Young, *International Cooperation: Building Regimes for Natural Resources and the Environment* (Ithaca, NY: Cornell University Press, 1989).

ranging critique of certain conceptualizations of regimes as faddish, imprecise and value-biased.[9] However, it is now necessary to proceed with additional testing of the still-abstract concepts and to do more case and comparative studies of regimes. This book constitutes such an effort.

International Regimes and Global Policy Studies

The regime approach blends the legal and political aspects of policy-making, stresses the evolution of structures and functions in an issue area, and has led to enormous scholarly interest in patterns of hegemony and other leadership and transformation issues. While these and related aspects of regime analysis are of great interest and can be considered powerful analytical tools, Marvin Soroos and other students of global policy studies have found it necessary to provide a complementary approach that is, presumably, applicable to the kind of issue area that is central to this book.[10]

As presented by Soroos, the global policy approach differs from the regime approach in a variety of ways but primarily in its view of global policies as "the actual courses of actions adopted" to deal with relatively narrowly defined problems.[11] Whereas international regime analysis emerges largely from the fields of international law and organization, Soroos builds from U.S. public policy studies, offering in practice a strong emphasis on policy-making processes. Whereas Soroos claims to de-emphasize structure in favor of outputs, structural elements are introduced as "policy making and implementing arenas" and as governmental and non-governmental actors.[12]

A major difference between Soroos's global policy analysis and that of mainstream international regime literature is his more limited view of policy outputs. For him, most global policies can be viewed as regulations or programs. While these terms can be interpreted broadly, they would not easily stretch to include international efforts to respond to issues through such less tangible methods as harmonization, coordination, and social learning. Effective international contributions to policies that were only recently viewed as essentially domestic neces-

9. Susan Strange, "Cave! Hic Dragones: A Critique of Regime Analysis," *International Organization* 36 (Spring 1982): 479–496.

10. See Marvin S. Soroos, *Beyond Sovereignty: The Challenge of Global Policy* (Columbia: University of South Carolina Press, 1986); and Stuart Nagel, ed., *Symposium on Global Policy Studies*, special issue of *International Political Science Review* 11, 3 (July 1990).

11. Soroos, *Beyond Sovereignty*, p. 21.

12. Marvin S. Soroos, "A Theoretical Framework for Global Policy Studies," in Nagel, ed., *Symposium on Global Policy Studies*, pp. 314, 316.

sarily take many forms and utilize a wide range of approaches. Such contributions need not, for example, involve legislation or implementation of formal policy. The objective of making a difference or assuring that a regional or global interest is considered may well result from informal processes of communication that do not depend on international bureaucracies or threats of sanctions.

In this chapter elements of global policy studies are incorporated in order to augment the contribution to employment policy offered by the international regime approach. This contribution, most evident in regard to policy outputs, will be discussed here in ways that go beyond Soroos's focus on regulatory and programmatic responses.

Elements of an International Employment Policy Regime

Structural Dimensions

The existence or non-existence of a distinct international employment policy regime depends primarily on judgments concerning such a regime's autonomy from broader economic and social policy regimes. Conscious efforts to create a distinct employment regime through a specialized intergovernmental organization have centered primarily on ILO developments, and even in that context the broader rubrics of economic, social, or labor affairs apply. Virtually every other intergovernmental organization involved with employment policy deals with this subject together with an array of other economic and social issue-areas and as part of a broad mandate for economic or social stabilization and development.

The case for an international employment regime is based on evidence that is both structural and functional. In structural terms there is the reality of myriad substructures within an array of IGOs that have specialized responsibility for employment. These include the OECD Manpower and Social Affairs Committee and Directorate for Social Affairs, Manpower and Education; the European Community Standing Committee on Employment and Directorate-General for Employment, Social Affairs, and Education; and the ILO World Employment Programme, Employment and Development Department and Employment Policy Committee. These bureaucratic units and committees maintain various degrees of contact with each other and with various national Labor and Social ministries and non-governmental international and national organizations. Meetings of Social and Labor ministers are convened within the European Community, OECD, and Council of Europe, and provide especially important forums for moving the policies of those organizations and the respective member governments in new directions.

A second category of specialized structures has broader jurisdiction than can be encompassed under the labels of employment and labor policy but often takes significant action pertaining to employment. These prominently include the ILO Committee on the Application of Conventions and Recommendations; the recently restructured U.N. Committee on Economic, Social and Cultural Rights; the Commission and Court of Justice of the European Community; and the Council of Europe Court of Human Rights, Committee of Independent Experts, and Governmental Committee of the Social Charter. These organs review national government compliance with the prescribed standards of their respective organizations regarding employment and related human rights matters, these often involving various claims of violated rights and neglect of governmental duties.

Such a structural focus is made problematic by the even greater influence on employment policy often enjoyed by other bureaucratic and committee structures within some of these same organizations. Reasons for this include tendencies to subordinate employment to other economic policy priorities and to place the most influential organizational experts in structures with economic policy responsibilities broader than that of the specialized employment units.

Beyond such intra-organizational structural rivalries, the main agencies in the employment regime may be overwhelmed by the power and influence of international organizations with principal responsibilities that may only occasionally focus directly on employment issues. Considerable impacts on employment have been generated by the raw economic and political power of such monetary and development assistance organizations as the World Bank, the International Monetary Fund (IMF), regional banks, the Bank for International Settlements, such trade agencies as the General Agreement on Tariffs and Trade (GATT) and such broad policy forums as the G-7 economic and political summits. Although these organizations and forums vary greatly in their impacts on global and regional employment, they demonstrate that leverage over monetary, trade, and fiscal policies, as well as access to billions of dollars in funds for development and stabilization loans, can negate or overwhelm most social and microeconomic policy initiatives of the core organizations of the employment regime. The austerity measures often promoted through the conditionality requirements of the International Monetary Fund and the World Bank, as well as the coordinated fiscal and monetary stimulation or restraint periodically advanced at G-7 summits or in the leading organs of the European Community, often have major impacts on national and regional employment policies and outcomes. Increased unemployment may be the unfortunate byproduct, at least in the short term, of policies focused on financial stabilization or of judgments concerning preferred systems of political economy. The impacts of such policies may be far greater than those designed primarily to ameliorate unemployment, and thus must be considered in any analysis of global and regional employment regimes.

There are, of course, still other intergovernmental actors and forums with considerable periodic influence on employment outcomes. For example, NATO and its member states can do a great deal to accelerate the conversion of human resources toward or away from military roles. OPEC and its members have demonstrated both the ability to generate burdensome levels of stagflation in much of the world and to promote stable employment in oil-importing nations through restraint on prices.

The most limited geographic levels of the international employment regime include bilateral international structures as well as small regional organizations such as the Benelux Economic Union and the Nordic Council. Even these can affect member countries' employment policies in significant ways. At an intermediate level in size and geographic scope are the twenty-six-member (at the close of 1991) Council of Europe, the twenty-four-member OECD, and the twelve-member European Community. Agencies with intermediate geographic scope but less defined roles regarding employment include intergovernmental regional banks and trade groupings (e.g., the now defunct Council for Mutual Economic Assistance as well as the European Free Trade Association). This leaves as the major intergovernmental organizations that can hope to advance global policies relating to employment and related human rights issues the specialized ILO and UNESCO, the periodically interested United Nations, and the inevitably influential World Bank, IMF, and GATT.

However, the embryonic regime suggested here includes far more than intergovernmental organizations. Employment is a subject in which world leadership is diffused, at least as compared with such other economic realms as trade and finance. As such, it is difficult to limit the number of interested or potentially influential national governments or non-governmental organizations or to defer to a single hegemonic power. This international regime is unusually complex because national and international interest groups representing what the Western Europeans call the "social partners"—trade unions and

employers' associations—have been augmented by a plethora of representatives of farmers, women, and foreign migrant workers, among
others, and various subgroupings of all such interests.[13] The European
Community in particular has demonstrated that effective power and
resources can attract to an international arena an array of interest
group representatives comparable to those contending in the arenas of
power of leading industrialized countries.

As such, the employment policy regime has a Western European
core, reinforced by such factors as the relatively great authority of the
European Community and the traditional and continuing major roles
of many Western European states and interest groups in the staffing
and politics of such other important agencies as the ILO and OECD.[14]
The Western European core role is reflected by such other indicators as
their leadership in the ratification of ILO conventions, the location of
IGO headquarters, and the influence of Western European social,
economic, and political developments on the agendas of the various
organizations.

The OECD and ILO offer substantial opportunities for such non-EC
states as Sweden and the United States to become heavily involved in
the employment policy regime. The early history of the Manpower and
Social Affairs Committee of the OECD was dominated by the effort of
Gösta Rehn to use that forum to spread various active labor market
policy ideas originating in Sweden throughout the OECD member
states. The United States, though sometimes viewed as a pariah state in
the ILO setting due to such factors as its refusal to ratify most conventions and its withdrawal from that organization between November
1977 and February 1980, retains an avid interest in both of these
organizations. It has both shared its varied experiences and experiments with such employment policies as job creation for targeted
groups and new approaches to women's rights and learned from other
leading member states through such organizations.

Although until the 1990s most East European countries had limited
contact with the organizations of the employment regime centered in
Western Europe, this is beginning to change rapidly and markedly.
Even before the dramatic political changes of 1989–90, the Soviet
Union and various East-Central European countries had altered con-

---

13. See Barbara Barnouin, *The European Labour Movement and European Integration*
(London: Frances Pinter, 1986).

14. Robert W. Cox, "ILO: Limited Monarchy," in Cox and Harold K. Jacobson, eds.,
The Anatomy of Influence: Decision Making in International Organization (New Haven, CT:
Yale University Press, 1973), p. 130.

siderably some of their postures on basic issues relating to labor and employment in global forums.[15] By 1990 some post-Communist states were moving toward associate or full membership in major Western Europe-based organizations.

Many Third World countries affect and are affected by employment policy initiatives through their participation in such global organizations as the ILO, United Nations, GATT, IMF, and the World Bank. Given the ILO's leading role in the setting and supervision of employment standards on a global level, its activities have drawn the most involvement of Third World states in that sphere. However, agencies that control major funding for projects and economic stabilization can far outweigh the impacts of the ILO on employment outcomes in developing countries.

Of the organizations that have devoted major attention to employment there is a certain dichotomy between those that have stressed the connection between employment and human rights, particularly the United Nations and the Council of Europe, and those for which employment is primarily an element of economic and social policy, especially the European Community and the OECD.[16] The ILO is a special case, viewing employment essentially as social policy and not as a domain of fundamental human rights except in a few particular dimensions like forced labor and non-discrimination. The differences

15. Philip Alston and Bruno Simma, "Second Session of the UN Committee on Economic, Social and Cultural Rights," *American Journal of International Law* 82 (1988): 603–615. Although the formerly Communist-ruled states of Eastern Europe had little claim to a regional human rights regime, they can be viewed as having prescribed and implemented, within limits that included pervasive political discrimination, such employment policy principles as the right to work and full employment. See Blair A. Ruble, "Factory Unions and Workers' Rights," in Arcadius Kaham and Ruble, eds., *Industrial Labor in the USSR* (New York: Pergamon Press, 1979), pp. 59–79; Anna-Jutta Pietsch and Heinrich Vogel, "Displacement by Technological Progress in the USSR," in Jan Adam, ed., *Employment Policies in the Soviet Union and Eastern Europe* (New York: St. Martin's Press, 1982), pp. 145–165; and Mark Harrison, "Lessons of Soviet Planning of Full Employment," in David Lane, ed., *Labour and Employment in the USSR* (New York: New York University Press, 1986), pp. 69–82. For a strong dissenting view see Leonard Schapiro and Joseph Godson, eds., *The Soviet Worker: Illusions and Realities* (New York: St. Martin's Press, 1981), especially the essay by Fyodor Turovsky.

16. The European Community has moved slowly but perceptibly toward accepting the need to struggle against unemployment on social policy grounds. The OECD, in contrast, continues to subordinate social policy considerations despite jurisdictional expansion into such areas as social insurance and women's rights. On the increasing attention of the European Community to human rights principles see P. D. Dagtoglou, "Human Rights and European Community Law," *Tulane Law Review* 56 (1981): 294–311.

are reflected in the endorsement of the right to work prescription by
the United Nations and the Council of Europe, but not by the OECD
or the European Community. This difference in emphasis is also reflected in the type of national ministries that interact with the respective organizations and the relative size, quality, and status of economic
and social policy units within each international organization.

Much of what has been described thus far militates against the idea
of a single international employment regime. We have described different organizations, representing important variations in priorities,
membership, and territorial and functional jurisdictions, among other
considerations. Further, the degree of integration of these various
organizations has not been very great. The concerns of international
agencies have often focused on preserving or altering jurisdictional
boundaries. Member countries and such interest groups as employers
and trade unions have too often shopped around for the IGO forum
that promises to maximize their interests. However, it still seems to me
that a single international employment regime exists, at least in embryonic form.

The idea of a single regime is most obviously supported by the
existence of the prescription and implementation processes of the
nearly global ILO and United Nations. Although limited by global
political and cultural diversity, these organizations both provide forums and mechanisms that require national governments to report on
their employment policies. The ILO has also voiced some rather sharp
criticism of national performances in this policy area. The single
regime idea is also supported by the ability of leading centers of communication, research, and policy experimentation to share their conclusions with national governments and with international and subnational organizations in many parts of the world. To some degree this
results in propagation and, increasingly, acceptance of norms that
relate to governmental and employer responsibilities regarding employment. However, such acceptance of norms and principles has been
limited in all regions of the world, suggesting the need to analyze the
sources of the regime's weakness.

Intergovernmental efforts on behalf of workers date back at least to
the 1890s, when several international conferences on the subject were
held by governments and private professionals. An International Association for the Legal Protection of Workers was established in Basle
before the turn of the century, and the first international labor conventions were adopted by governments in 1905 and 1906.[17] The Treaty of

17. Nicolas X. Valticos, *International Labour Law* (Deventer, Netherlands: Kluwer
Publishing, 1979), p. 3.

Versailles concluding World War I provided for the establishment of the International Labor Organization, which soon became one of the most active international agencies prescribing and seeking to implement international social policy standards concerning employment and related issues.

The contemporary international employment regime is derived from these earlier developments as well as the profound impacts of the Great Depression, World War II, and such more recent global and regional developments as the progress of North American, European, and global economic interdependence and integration. These first two events promoted the ideal conditions of heightened national solidarity, involving increased support for economic and social policies that offered greater security to the entire populations of various industrialized countries. The progress of European integration resulted from and further stimulated a heightened sense of international interdependence. Further, the horrors of the Holocaust made possible for the first time a consensus in favor of prescribing numerous civil/political and socioeconomic "fundamental human rights" deserving international protection. Just as a human rights regime unfolded most evidently at the global (U.N., ILO) and Western European levels during the quarter century after World War II, a closely related employment regime developed at the same geographic levels, with major roles being played by some of the same international agencies.

Regime Principles and Goals

The principles adopted by the creators of the employment policy regime necessarily must be drawn from an even larger body of principles developed for economic and social policy. ILO employment policy standards promulgated in conventions and recommendations address the need to assert a high priority to employment in programs of national social and economic development, to develop some version of an "active labor market policy" in relation to human resources and the availability of alternative employment, and to advance such particular approaches to this field as training, vocational guidance, recruitment, and placement. When the ILO was called upon to suggest which parts of its "International Labor Code" related most closely to the right to work developed by the United Nations, its Committee of Experts on the Application of Conventions and Recommendations concluded that such a right involves "general measures to promote equality of opportunity and treatment in employment," "policies and measures pursued with a view to achieving full employment," and issues of forced labor that relate to "free choice of employment."[18] The International Labor Office has also supported the inclusion of "protection against arbitrary termination of employment" as a basic ingredient of the right to work.

The *right to work*, the most controversial and amorphous principle of the regime, has been most consistently expounded by the United Nations. The U.N. formulation of this right, which won limited ILO endorsement in 1983 and 1984, refers to "the right of everyone to the opportunity to gain his living by work which he freely chooses or accepts."[19] Statements proclaiming such a right have also appeared in legal instruments of the Council of Europe, the Organization of American States, and the Organization of African Unity.[20] It should be noted that several of these organizations explicitly rejected formulations that involved government-guaranteed employment or the availability of national governments as providers of jobs in the last resort. The principle of the right to work that has survived is a lowest common denominator that emphasizes non-discrimination and freedom of choice. It also substitutes for the goal of "full employment" in certain international instruments in which rights terminology is preferred to the language of economic growth and development.

The *full employment* goal represents the other umbrella concept of the international employment regime. It has been the preferred formulation of organizations that view themselves as promoting employment in an economic or socioeconomic policy context rather than one of human rights. The ILO's 1983–84 qualified endorsements of the right

18. Committee of Experts on the Application of Conventions and Recommendations, "The Concept of the Right to Work in International Law: Note Prepared by the International Labour Office," July 1982, unpublished, pp. 8–9.

19. Article 6(1) of the International Covenant on Economic, Social and Cultural Rights (see Appendix IV in this volume). See also Article 23 of the Universal Declaration of Human Rights (adopted December 10, 1948, G.A. Res. 217A [III], U.N. Doc. A/810, at 71 [1948]) and U.N. Resolutions No. 36/29 of November 13, 1981 and No. 37/49 of December 3, 1982 on youth unemployment. G.A. Res. No. 36/29, adopted November 13, 1981, *Resolutions and Decisions Adopted by the General Assembly During Its 36th Session* Supp. No. 51 (A/36/51) (New York: United Nations, 1982), p. 170 and G.A. Res. No. 37/49, adopted December 3, 1982, *Resolutions and Decisions Adopted by the General Assembly During Its 37th Session* Supp. No. 51 (A/37/51) (New York: United Nations, 1983), p. 183. The ILO endorsed the right to work in 1983 with the adoption by the International Labor Conference of a Resolution Concerning Employment Policy. A qualified endorsement came in 1984 when the International Labor Conference took final action on the Employment Policy (Supplementary Provisions) Recommendation, No. 169 (see Appendix I in this volume).

20. See the Council of Europe European Social Charter (adopted 1961) (see this volume, Appendix III) and the OAU African [Banjul] Charter on Human and Peoples' Rights (OAU Doc. CAB/LEG/67/3 Rev. 5, adopted June 27, 1981, entered into force February 28, 1987).

to work did not alter that organization's preference for the full employment principle, as expressed in instruments dating from its pivotal 1944 Philadelphia Conference.[21] Together with the 1964 and 1976 OECD Council recommendations on employment and manpower policies, the ILO Employment Policy Convention and Recommendation of 1964 (No. 122) and Employment Policy (Supplementary Provisions) Recommendation of 1984 represent some of the most comprehensive and authoritative IGO efforts to define and promote full employment in relation to economic growth, social equity, and price stability.[22]

The full employment principle has been a vehicle for the endorsement of a plethora of specific programs as well as a variety of social and economic policies and goals. The aims of the ILO and OECD instruments declaring the goal and principle of full employment include promoting (1) experimentation with an expansion of government-supported programs augmenting the quality and quantity and availability of the labor supply, including measures to improve job training, placement, and labor mobility; (2) new approaches to job creation where this is necessary to affect business cycles or to assist "targeted" regions or hard-to-place individuals and groups; and (3) efforts to coordinate government labor market and human resource development programs with measures in such closely related areas as education and regional development.

It proved necessary to constantly update prescriptions on full employment policy in response to evaluation research findings, economic conditions, and political responses to various proposals. Since 1973 this has meant ever greater efforts to link a wide variety of social, economic and other policies to full employment planning in order to ensure that employment would not be unduly harmed by policies emphasizing economic stabilization and other goals. Such efforts, which continue to this day in various international organizations, generate considerable

21. See the Declaration of Philadelphia, which was annexed to the ILO constitution, and ILO Recommendations Nos. 71, 72, and 73 of 1944. International Labour Conference, 26th Sess., *Record of Proceedings* (Montreal: ILO, 1944), pp. 621–623, 602–620. Note that the ILO concern with "measures taken or contemplated to combat unemployment" is expressed in such of its first labor standards as the Unemployment Recommendation (No. 1) and Convention (No. 2), both adopted in 1919. See also Jean Mayer, "The Concept of the Right to Work in International Standards and the Legislation of ILO Member States," *International Labour Review* 124 (1985): 225–242.

22. Resolution of the Council on Manpower Policy, May 21, 1964, and Recommendation of the Council on a General Employment and Manpower Policy, March 5, 1976 (see Appendix II in this volume). For a review of this effort from an OECD perspective see OECD, *A Medium Term Strategy for Employment and Manpower Policies* (Paris: OECD, 1978), pp. 43–58. While human resource or labor market are less sexist terms that incorporate many such policies, manpower policy was the term of choice through the 1970s.

controversy as attention shifts to the employment implications of a myriad of policies. These include the management of burdensome international debts, population control, migration, income maintenance, disarmament, technology, and foreign investment as well as more traditional concerns with fiscal, monetary, and incomes policies.[23] In this process the international organizations promoting employment have refined their advice on selective labor market policies while fitting those measures into the broader and more sophisticated policy packages that they seek to promote.

The European Community, founded with a commitment to full employment as one of several principal goals, presents opportunities for examining what can be accomplished when such a commitment is combined with significant legislative, judicial, and budgetary capacities as well as a finite territorial scope. The Community also emphasized *the free movement of labor and services* principle in their founding documents. This concept is given prominence in the drive for fuller economic integration expressed in the Single European Act approved in 1987 for full implementation in 1992. In the original six Community states, and the present twelve, free movement of labor is declared to mean borders open wide to job-seeking nationals of member states, even for long-term and permanent stays. Although this principle is qualified in the founding treaties by references to limitations justified on grounds of public policy, public security, or public health, and allows for exemptions regarding public service employment, the Community takes the principle of freedom of movement well beyond various international organizations with broader territorial scope that exclude the critical right of entry.[24]

23. These linkages were broadest in the ILO process of drafting the supplementary recommendation on employment policy approved in June 1984. See International Labour Conference, 70th Sess., 1984, Report IV(1), *Employment Policy* (Geneva: ILO, 1983).

24. Such a right of entry is also declared in instruments of the Nordic Council and Benelux Economic Union. See Title III of the Treaty of Rome establishing the European Economic Community (adopted March 25, 1957) in *Treaty Establishing the European Economic Community and Connected Documents* (Brussels: European Communities, 1961) pp. 57–65 and Commission of the European Communities, *Freedom of Movement for Workers Within the Community* (Brussels: European Communities, 1977. See also the Agreement between Denmark, Finland, Norway and Sweden concerning a Common Labour Market, signed May 22, 1954, in *Cooperation Agreements between the Nordic Countries*, second revised edition (Stockholm: Nordic Council and Nordic Council of Ministers, 1978), pp. 52–55. Social protection for migrant workers in the European Community is also reinforced by the 1989 Community Charter of the Fundamental Social Rights of Workers and the 1992 Protocol and Agreement on Social Policy. See Juliet Lodge, "Social Europe," *Journal of European Integration* 13, 2–3 (Winter–Spring 1990): 135–150;

Other organizations, especially the Council of Europe and ILO, have developed the principles of equal protection and equal opportunities for migrant foreign workers who were invited to establish or retain employment and/or residence (without right of entry or the right to stay).[25] As such, their contributions are viewed more accurately as reinforcing the principles of non-discrimination and equal (even compensatory) treatment for particular categories of residents who have special claims to international protection and exceptional needs for both legal protection and social services.[26] Among the most pathbreaking aspects of the prescription of equal protection for foreign workers has been that of political rights for alien workers, these including the right to vote in certain elections and freedom to engage in legal political activities without threat of deportation.[27]

The principles of *non-discrimination* and *equal opportunity* have been perhaps the most commonly invoked by the employment regime, and prescriptions against racial discrimination have special mechanisms for implementation in the U.N. and ILO contexts.[28] Yet it is probably in the area of equal treatment of women that the employment and human rights regimes of Western Europe and the industrialized West have had their greatest impacts. The principles of non-discrimination and equal treatment for women have expanded greatly since the initial

---

Council and Commission of the European Communities, *Treaty on European Union* (Luxembourg: European Communities, 1992), pp. 196–201.

25. According to Swart, "Up to the present time the Council of Europe's conventions have hardly mentioned such a right [of entry], though there are exceptions and a certain evolution can be traced." A. H. J. Swart, "The Legal Status of Aliens: Clauses in Council of Europe Instruments Relating to the Rights of Aliens," *Netherlands Yearbook of International Law* 11 (1980): 6. Among the areas of evolution of the right to entry is that promoting reunification of families.

26. See ILO Convention No. 143 (1975) and Recommendation No. 151 concerning migrant workers, in International Labour Conference, 60th Sess., 1975 *Record of Proceedings* (Geneva: ILO, 1976), pp. 908–919, 964–973; John Claydon, "International Protection of the Welfare of Migrant Workers," in Ronald St. John Macdonald, Douglas M. Johnston, and Gerald L. Morris, eds., *The International Law and Policy of Human Welfare* (Alphen aan den Rijn, Netherlands: Sijthoff and Nordhoff, 1978), pp. 347–372.

27. See A. C. Evans, "The Political Status of Aliens in International Law, Municipal Law and European Community Law," *International and Comparative Law Quarterly* 30 (January 1981): 20–41; Zig Layton-Henry, ed., *The Political Rights of Migrant Workers in Western Europe* (Newburg Park, CA: Sage Publications, 1990).

28. The U.N. International Convention on the Elimination of All Forms of Racial Discrimination (adopted December 21, 1965, entered into force January 4, 1989, 660 U.N.T.S. 195) called for the establishment of the U.N. Committee on the Elimination of Racial Discrimination. United Nations, 20th Sess., *Official Records of the General Assembly*, Supp. No. 14, pp. 47–52. In 1973 the ILO established special surveys with respect to its Discrimination (Employment and Occupation) Convention No. 111 (1958).

IGO emphasis on protection against allegedly unsafe or unhealthy working conditions (a focus now widely viewed as responsible for additional discrimination) and on largely symbolic affirmations of the justice of equal pay.[29] By 1976 this response was transformed into something potentially much more meaningful in the European Community as a result of court decisions and Council directives that called for national legislation and implementation designed to assure advanced concepts of equal pay for equal work as well as wide-ranging entitlements to equal or compensatory opportunity and treatment in other dimensions of employment and training. It is notable that such pioneering international efforts were based on treaty law that does not emphasize human rights, the primary concern of the Treaty of Rome's article on equal pay being to prevent distortion of competition among member states.[30] This is one of many examples of how the basic principles of the employment regime derive from a variety of sources, instruments, and concerns.

Methods, Process, and Policies: Social Learning

The relative lack of success of the embryonic international employment regime during the past decade stems from less than complete devotion of many major actors to its basic principles as well as from structural shortcomings. These interrelate with the methods and processes that any international regime must utilize to move from the prescription of principles to success in sponsoring, enacting, and implementing significant ideas and rules that solve major problems in a given issue area. In the case of the international employment regime, the available processes and resources vary greatly in their nature and adequacy.

Although many modes of operation have been developed by and with the international employment regime, three broad approaches stand out. The first is the promotion of social learning by the regime actors. A second is the development of programs that may involve financial and technical support for international, national and subnational agencies. Such resources are usually provided by member states and reallocated among those and other countries through intergov-

---

29. ILO Convention No. 100 (1951); Article 119 of the EEC Treaty of Rome (1957).

30. See EEC Council Directives, "On the Approximation of the Laws of the Member States Relating to the Application of the Principle of Equal Pay for Men and Women," February 10, 1975, Dir 75/117/EEC, OJ, L45, 1977; and "On the Implementation of the Principle of Equal Treatment for Men and Women as Regards Access to Employment, Vocational Training and Promotion, and Working Conditions," February 9, 1976, Dir 76/207/EEC, OJ, L39, 1976.

ernmental organizations. Third, the regime adapts its basic principles and prescribes rules through international legal instruments that may or may not be effectively implemented or supervised. These are similar to the basic methods employed by national political systems to resolve or ameliorate many domestic problems. However, a relative lack of formal authority or adequate resources makes utilizing them at the international level more complex and difficult. The use of each of these three types of methods and processes, as well as the policies that they promote, beginning with social learning, is traced below.

Hugh Heclo, Ernst Haas, Peter Haas and others have focused on the concepts of social learning and epistemic communities to pull together a wide range of efforts to learn from other countries' experiences in various issue areas.[31] Such processes now routinely proceed with the assistance of the staffs of international agencies, who often see their primary roles as facilitators of research and discussion. It is quite possible for an international regime to be successful solely through such activities. Regime actors are often judged on the quality of their policy initiatives as well as their ability to gain acceptance from member governments and other actors.

Social learning processes subsume the Ruggie-Haas categories of coordination of problem search and definition, the defining of property (and other) rights, and the collective elaboration of welfare choices. Participants include the staffs of the committed international organizations together with both political representatives and experts of the various national governments. In the international employment regime the social learning network also often includes representatives of employers' organizations, trade unions, women's groups, and a host of other non-governmental interests, as well as consultants from universities and research centers.[32] The system is designed largely to help national government agencies to be responsive to emerging issues, aware of evaluation research concerning ongoing programs, and privy to discussions about the pros and cons of possible new policy options.

31. See Hugh Heclo, *Modern Social Politics in Britain and Sweden: From Relief to Income Maintenance* (New Haven, CT: Yale University Press, 1974), p. 306; Ernst B. Haas, *When Knowledge Is Power: Three Models of Change in International Organizations* (Berkeley: University of California Press, 1990); and Peter M. Haas, ed., *Knowledge, Power, and International Policy Coordination*, special issue of *International Organization* 46 (Winter 1992). The current discussion of social learning utilizes the term "epistemic communities," focusing on networks of knowledge-based experts.

32. The various categories of actors are allowed widely varying degrees of contact and influence in the several organizational settings. Trade unions and employers' organizations are given the largest roles in the tripartite ILO, significant but lesser roles in the European Community, and are often held at arm's length by the OECD staff and national representatives.

Given the interdependence of societies, the similarity of many countries' employment problems to those of many others, and the numerous directions that policy can and does take in this field, social learning must proceed at the international as well as the national level.

Although not all relevant international communication takes place under the auspices of IGOs, and epistemic expert communities free of direct intergovernmental control often frame the range of political controversy surrounding an issue, there is a tendency to bring much of the process of policy evaluation into their domains. For example, in 1978 the Danish Labor Minister initiated an informal meeting on employment issues with several of his counterparts from OECD member states. Later an expanded "Copenhagen Group" was staffed by the OECD Secretariat. Although IGO staffs tend to formalize regime communications, less formal discussions are also maintained, these including regular bilateral telephone, mail, and fax contacts by counterparts in national ministries, irregular study visits by the entire range of governmental, academic, and interest group actors, social activities at IGO headquarters sites, and the system of labor and social attachés in various embassies.[33]

The OECD has been particularly successful in giving national government officials and experts a sense of "ownership" in new approaches to policy through their participation in "working parties," high-level meetings, and other formats. Similar activities are also organized under ILO and European Community auspices.

The regime also encourages dialogue among those who initially approach controversial proposals from different interests and/or ideological positions. The bridging task varies somewhat in each organizational setting, this in response to differences in membership, communications, norms, power relations, and organizational structure. However, great pressures for consensus exist in virtually every IGO, except in relation to certain efforts to bring symbolic political issues into such forums, with most participants recognizing that ideas cannot be imposed on key actors and that a watered-down, consensus-based document is normally superior to a stronger instrument that lacks the critical support of major powers.

International organization staffs and committees often take posi-

---

33. Other devices have included comprehensive on-site reviews of national labor market programs (undertaken by the OECD in the 1960s and early 1970s), systematic comparative reviews of national legislation and policies, seminars and conferences sponsored by various regime actors, and the mutual information system on employment policies in Europe (Misep) set up to collect and disseminate information through a network of national correspondents.

tions on major issues that begin as subjects for discussion. Advocacy by units within regime organizations often involves complex efforts to persuade powerful actors within the organization's network. International employment regime program proposals must be appropriately packaged and "sold" to other staff units, the major policy makers in the secretariat, the "social partners" and, most crucially, the government representatives of powerful member states.

With these various processes of social learning and organizational advocacy, major and minor policy thrusts of the international employment regime are set out, maintained, modified, or abandoned. The extent to which such initiatives are subsequently supported by the technical resources, financial incentives, or legislative authority of the regime's leading IGOs depends largely on such advocacy efforts within particular organizations.

The ideas that result from social learning and advocacy processes are the basis of all regime contributions to the solution of employment problems. As such, the ability of a regime to generate sound policies is the key to its success or failure.

Despite major disagreements among the principal intergovernmental organization staffs and member government representatives there has been consensus on certain basic issues within the employment regime. In part this results from factors of power and influence. It has consistently mattered more what the main line was in the OECD, G-7 summits, the European Community, World Bank and the IMF as compared with the ILO, United Nations, Council of Europe, and other organizations without comparable major economic power or expertise. As such, the main line on employment policy has most often been determined by the United States and leading OECD member governments in conjunction with the top officials of the IGOs in which these countries maintain decisive power.

The quality of analyses of current aspects of the employment situation and forecasts of near-term trends by IGO staff economists have improved steadily since 1970, though such major developments as the recession of 1980–82 and the effects of the subsequent international debt crisis were not fully anticipated. Refinement of economic measurements and predictions techniques, involving such matters as the harmonization of national governments' measurements of unemployment, has been an area of steady progress by regime research units. Additionally, ameliorative programs have been subjected to increasingly sophisticated evaluative studies designed in part to transcend objections or support based on ideology or supposition.

The analytic work of the intergovernmental components of the regime can be faulted for the failure of political analysis to match economic analysis. This regime too often avoids political judgments concerning feasibility and public support, preferring the apparent security of quantitative economics. Further, regime organizations and national governments are often willing to ignore the poor meshing of certain policy prescriptions with major social policy principles promoted by the regime, as occurs when austerity unmodified by social protection is advocated.

The thrust of the regime's economic analyses and proposals has been marked by major shifts that can be attributed to the various "schools" with which contributing social scientists, principally economists, have identified. In particular, the OECD has had distinct periods in which Keynesian, monetarist, and other thinking has dominated. However, some of the most interesting regime contributions have involved efforts to move beyond the teachings of any one economic school.

Gösta Rehn, the Swedish economist and OECD Manpower and Social Affairs (MSA) director between 1962 and 1973, long advocated far-reaching new conceptions of "active labor market policy." Beginning in 1964, Rehn persuaded the MSA Committee to endorse his proposals to supplement macroeconomic counter-cyclical policies with "selective labor market measures" that promised to counter inflation while minimizing unemployment levels. Based primarily on the sophisticated and costly Swedish labor market programs, the Rehn/MSA package involved public capital investments, employment subsidies, the promotion of geographic mobility of workers, and the flexible use of greatly increased resources for vocational training.[34] (These OECD instruments of 1964 and 1976 are reprinted in Appendix II of this volume.) Rehn's primary objectives were to get the OECD governments to adopt such major programs and to view such active labor market policies as means to address both inflation and unemployment. Major efforts were made to convince governments that by resorting to selective action they might be able to avoid stop-go macroeconomic policies. Yet even OECD officials acknowledged in 1978 that the counter-inflationary concept of an active labor market policy "met with considerable skepticism and in the end gained much less ground in actual policy-making than the original long-term development objectives of active manpower policy."[35]

Rehn could take some comfort from the knowledge that member government expenditures on the programs that he advocated grew by 500 to 1,000 percent during his decade as OECD manpower director.

34. On Swedish policies see Helen Ginsburg, *Full Employment and Public Policy: The United States and Sweden* (Lexington, MA: Lexington Books, 1983), pp. 127–160.

35. OECD, *Medium Term Strategy*, p. 52.

However, as he wrote in 1975, "Because the start usually was near zero, . . . this high rate of growth in relative terms should not lead to too optimistic conclusions about the adequacy of presently existing machinery for the implementation of manpower policy."[36]

Several lessons can be learned from the Rehn/MSA Committee efforts. First, a major economic prescription is not likely to go very far without strong support from leading research and policy-development staff units and committees as well as the highest ranking officials of such international organizations as OECD. Rehn failed to win over the OECD's dominant Economics and Statistics Department, and he received less than full support from that organization's Secretary-General or from the British and U.S. permanent delegations. Second, to maximize its impact the new policy guidance must be supported by major research efforts that broaden endorsements by major independent economists as well as experts in national governments. The fact that Rehn obtained partial results despite these weaknesses and failings was largely due to untiring personal efforts by a few people to sell the policies within and outside OECD, the established program of formal evaluation of national labor market programs by leading experts, and the applicability of his proposals to diverse national circumstances.

A more recent employment program flowing substantially from OECD contrasts sharply with the Rehn/MSA effort in terms of process. In the decade following 1973 the OECD searched for a policy line to meet its members' political and economic needs at a time of economic crisis and adjustment. The chosen policy rubric, "positive adjustment policies," was packaged and sold by its sponsors as the antithesis of "negative" policies designed to "prop up" weak industrial sectors, "impede" technological change, and "distort" trade flows.[37] This rhetorical battle had more to do with the requirements of internal regime debates than with scholarly analyses of differing viewpoints.

Various versions of the OECD positive adjustment package have emphasized structural change rather than counter-cyclical policies, sought greater consistency between macro- and microeconomic policies (discouraging microeconomic policies that create new "rigidities" and mitigating the effects on employment of "non-accommodating"

36. Gösta Rehn, "Recent Trends in Manpower Policy," *European Yearbook* 21 (1973): 86. The manuscript was completed in January 1975. Considerably greater sums for these programs were allocated by many OECD states in response to the 1974–75 recession.

37. OECD Council, Communique of June 15, 1978, "Policies for Adjustment: Some General Orientations," in OECD, *Positive Adjustment Policies: Managing Structural Change* (Paris: OECD, 1983), pp. 111–114.

macroeconomic policies), stressed "real wage flexibility," and relied mostly on market forces.[38] Few national government interventions other than those promoting competition and wage restraint and providing "information and guidance" were given unqualified support in the OECD's restatements of classical economic liberalism.

This OECD effort was well prepared by in-house research as well as such prestigious outside consultants as Paul McCracken and Hans Tietmeyer, who were widely viewed as co-sponsors.[39] It was developed with somewhat more unity among OECD committees and directorates than the earlier Rehn effort, though the Manpower and Social Affairs constituency sought opportunities to modify and moderate the prevailing line. In 1979 the MSA directorate accepted the challenge to discover employment policies that "promote, or *de minimus*, do not hinder the process of adjustment which is necessary for a dynamic and growing economy."[40] In this changing environment MSA even became the constructive critic of some selective labor market measures that it had advocated a decade earlier, these including public sector job creation and marginal subsidies to private employers. OECD's thrust shifted toward structural policies designed to facilitate wage reductions, limits on payroll taxes, "enterprise efficiency," and the shedding of unneeded workers.[41]

Though it would have been consistent with ideological trends in leading OECD member states for the OECD to hold onto the main lines of its positive adjustment policies throughout the 1980s, a partial mid-course correction was signaled in 1985 when a broad-based "high-level group of experts" was created to review labor market flexibility issues.

The pet phrase of the Dahrendorf Group Report was "Labor market flexibility is not a panacea for all social and economic ills."[42] While strongly influenced by the earlier McCracken line, the new report clearly strived for workable policies that could be supported by a broader range of interests in the OECD and within each member state. As noted in a 1990 publication by the MSA Committee, "The emphasis

38. See "Summary and Conclusions," in OECD, *Positive Adjustment Policies*, pp. 7–22.
39. Each headed study groups associated with the OECD's Economic Policy Committee. See Paul W. McCracken, *Towards Full Employment and Price Stability: Summary of a Report* (Paris: OECD, 1977) and OECD, *Positive Adjustment Policies*, pp. 5–6.
40. Manpower and Social Affairs Committee, *Manpower and Employment Measures for Positive Adjustment: Note by the Secretariat* (Paris: OECD, June 1979), p. 20.
41. OECD, *The Challenge of Unemployment: A Report to Labour Ministers* (Paris: OECD, 1982), p. 110; OECD, *Positive Adjustment Policies*.
42. OECD, *Labour Market Flexibility: Report by a High-Level Group of Experts to the Secretary-General* (Paris: OECD, 1986), p. 6.

in labor market policies on flexibility and adjustment policies did not meet with general approval. In fact, some observers regarded the focus as biased by employers' interests. . . . Many of the deregulations suggested a serious attack on achieved social standards."[43] The Dahrendorf Group endorsed a tripartite social compact approach to national policy-making, proposed that the OECD-wide unemployment rate be returned to the 1979 level of 5.5 percent, challenged some assumptions about the negative effects on employment and competitiveness stemming from employment protection and worktime reduction policies, and focused attention on residual poverty issues. The effect of such perspectives was evident in the subsequent work of the Manpower and Social Affairs Committee and Directorate and, to a lesser extent, in the OECD as a whole. While leading OECD voices continued to stress anti-inflationary macroeconomic policies and support for structural adjustment policies identified in the late 1970s and early 1980s, assaults on social protection were blunted somewhat. The theme of "the active society," promoted by MSA spokespersons in the late 1980s, gave a renewed thrust to certain microeconomic and social policies supported by worker representatives. It also redirected policy to the problems of societies needing to train old and new groups of workers for skilled employment and rapidly changing technology.[44]

Although the OECD certainly did not come full circle in its approaches to unemployment, with direct employment creation still warned against, one can note a renewed or increased emphasis on "active labor market policies" in some subsequent OECD publications and recommendations. A major OECD publication editorialized in 1989 that, "the underlying goal is to enhance the effective productivity of the population as a whole by drawing on previously unused talents, and harnessing them in a more effective and comprehensive division of labour."[45] Having succeeded in helping to undermine direct employment creation and having provided ammunition for opponents of most worktime reduction schemes, among other measures, the OECD seems to have returned to an approach that seeks to promote consensus on those active measures, sponsored by governments or enterprises, not deemed to create rigidities or inflexibility.

References to full employment in some OECD publications in the 1980s used that term to disparage national efforts to maintain jobs in enterprises that had "ceased to respond to technological requirements

43. OECD, *Labour Market Policies for the 1990s* (Paris: OECD, 1990), p. 17.

44. "The Path to Full Employment: Structural Adjustment for an Active Society," editorial in *OECD Employment Outlook*, July 1989, pp. 7–12.

45. Ibid., p. 9.

or consumer preferences."[46] Yet in response to the needs of certain targeted groups the OECD has responded to more traditional meanings of full employment.

In relation to at least two major problems the international regime has kept faith with the full employment and right to work principles even in the short-term context. These relate to youths in transition from school to work as well as the needs of depressed or underdeveloped regions, particularly in Western Europe. Both concerns have been articulated by a wide range of participants in the international regime, and the search for solutions in Europe has been supplemented by EC financial resources.

School-leavers, long classified as one of several hard-to-employ groups requiring special attention and program "targeting,"[47] emerged in the 1970s as a primary object of attention within the international employment regime. Statistical evidence of horrendous levels of youth unemployment in many OECD countries beginning in the 1970s, and the greater awareness of the social as well as economic costs and dangers, led major actors to seek new kinds of state interventions in this sphere.[48] Such regime institutions as the European Commission went so far as to endorse a "minimum employment guarantee," involving job creation as well as training, to young people unable to find or keep work.[49] Although the member states deflected the notion of a guarantee at the EC level, youth unemployment emerged throughout the OECD countries and globally as one of the foremost employment issues, and many countries responded in the 1980s with unprecedented spending on "youth initiatives" involving such programs as training guarantees, occupational guidance, vocational training, and work experience.[50] However, although international organizations sought to give order to this response it has been difficult to remedy what one British observer termed in 1983 a "confusion of schemes, subsidies and make-work programmes."[51]

A similar lack of coherence and adequacy marks various national

46. Ibid., p. 12.
47. Other targeted groups include women, the disabled, migrants, racial minorities, the long-term unemployed, and older workers.
48. Youth unemployment in twelve selected OECD countries averaged 17.3 percent in 1982. *OECD Employment Outlook*, September 1983, p. 26.
49. "Coping with the Shortage of Jobs in the 1980s: Communications from the Commission to the European Council," March 21, 1983, p. 6.
50. See OECD, *Challenge of Unemployment*, p. 110; OECD, *Youth Without Work: Three Countries Approach the Problem* (Paris: OECD, 1981).
51. Ian Hargreaves, "Frantic, Haphazard Efforts to Help the Young," *Financial Times* (London), January 17, 1983.

and international efforts at regional policy in Western Europe despite decades of interest in such programs.[52] The involvements of the OECD and EC, among other organizations, in youth and regional efforts suggest limits of the social learning process when overriding factors include the insufficiency of available funds and the political nature of efforts to redistribute resources to members and non-members of particular IGOs.

Yet such programs as youth and regional initiatives have enjoyed the benefit of widespread consensus, at least concerning goals, compared to most other employment issues. For example, constant debates relating to the appropriate roles of national governments, international organizations, and firms, often rooted in ideological conflict, have prevented the adoption of a coherent position on industrial policy at the OECD or European level, though significant elements of such policies have advanced.[53] While generally in accord with OECD views on positive adjustment policies, the European Commission has tended to be more supportive of governmental industrial policy interventions than the Paris-based organization, especially interventions coordinated at the European level.[54] The European Commission has also expressed greater support than the OECD secretariat for worktime adjustments favored by trade unions.

For various reasons the social learning processes of the employment regime have worked far less effectively at the global level, particularly in relation to Third World and East European unemployment and underemployment, than within the domains of Western Europe and the OECD. To a considerable extent the global regime has not even broken through the stage of problem definition. For example, despite emphasis on the severity and worsening state of the unemployment and underemployment issues in much of the developing world by ILO and various non-governmental advocates, IMF and World Bank publications and spokespersons have too often demonstrably played down Third World unemployment as a reality and as a concern. A more concerned, unofficial perspective is reflected in an Overseas Development Council estimate that Third World unemployment and under-

52. See G. J. Croxford et al., "The Reform of the European Regional Development Fund: A Preliminary Assessment," *Journal of Common Market Studies* 26 (September 1987): 25–38.

53. See Paul G. Taylor, *The Limits of European Integration* (New York: Columbia University Press, 1983), pp. 213–227; and Jeffrey Harrop, *The Political Economy of Integration in the European Community* (Hampshire, Eng.: Edward Elgar, 1989), pp. 92–104.

54. See Étienne Davignon, "The End of the Road for Europe, or a New Beginning?" in Ralf Dahrendorf, ed., *Europe's Economy in Crisis* (New York: Holmes and Meier, 1982), pp. 119–138.

employment combined stood at 40–50 percent in 1987, adding that, "In the next two decades, at least 600 million new jobs—more than the total number of jobs in all the industrial market economies—will have to be created just to accommodate new entrants into the labor force who are already alive today."[55] In contrast, various experts have noted the fact that IMF and World Bank publications have often played down the incidence of Third World unemployment.[56] Richard E. Feinberg has argued that "In essence, . . . the Fund adheres to the trickle-down approach whereby aggregate growth in GNP is thought to lead to full employment and rising real incomes."[57] The World Bank did not place employment on a par with other basic needs deserving of its promotion during the Robert McNamara and A. W. Clausen eras, and is widely considered to have lessened its interest in alleviating poverty in the 1980s.[58]

The International Labor Office worked throughout the 1980s to make the world more conscious of the negative effects on employment of structural adjustment and related policies, gaining some support for this difficult endeavor from such agencies as the United Nations Department of International Economic and Social Affairs and the OECD Development Center. ILO staff economists have continued to challenge World Bank and other more sanguine perceptions of labor markets, stepped up their research output, and emphasized the failure of the international finance and monetary system to prevent hardship in many developed countries.[59]

55. John W. Sewell and Stuart K. Tucker, eds., *Growth, Exports and Jobs in a Changing World* (New Brunswick, NJ: Transaction Books, 1988), p. 17.

56. For example, in the IMF's *World Economic Outlook* (1987) unemployment is only very briefly discussed in relation to Western Europe and the United States and not at all for the Third World. The contention that the World Bank downplays Third World unemployment to an unacceptable extent was made in a controversial article by Guy Standing of the International Labor Office. Standing, "Underemployment and the Recomposition of Labor Reserves," in Bertram Gross and Alfred Pfaller, eds., *Unemployment: A Global Challenge*, vol. 492 of the Annals of the American Academy of Political and Social Science (Newbury Park, CA: Sage, 1987), pp. 80–87.

57. Richard E. Feinberg, "The International Monetary Fund and Basic Needs: The Impact of Standby Arrangements," in Margaret E. Crahan, ed., *Human Rights and Basic Needs in the Americas* (Washington, DC: Georgetown University Press, 1982), pp. 214–235.

58. T. Addison and L. Demery, "Alleviating Poverty Under Structural Adjustment," *Finance and Development* 24, 4 (1987): 41–43; *New York Times*, July 16, 1990, p. A3.

59. See comments by Gerry Rodgers in Bernard Salome, ed., *Fighting Urban Unemployment in Developing Countries* (Paris: OECD, 1989), p. 97; See also International Labour Organization, *World Recession and Global Interdependence* (Geneva: ILO, 1987), pp. 133–139.

Further, major ILO spokespersons have decried the abandonment of full employment and right to work as goals and objectives.[60] While recognizing that the employment problems of the Third World extend beyond unemployment and involve "the prevalence and growth of precarious, casual, and often exploited forms of labour," they have insisted that attention be given to urban unemployment.[61] Regularly scheduled forums to advance the principal objectives relating to employment have been advanced through "high-level conferences" on employment and structural adjustment. These conferences have apparently exacerbated North-South tensions within the ILO.

As such, the component organizations and forums of the international employment regime vary considerably in both processes and substantive outcomes of social learning regarding employment. Many of the inconsistencies and inadequacies of the regime are rooted in jurisdictional rivalries, ideological differences, and limited interest on the part of organizational staff, top leadership, and member state representatives. Yet it is likely that no aspect of regime functioning has greater potential than social learning. Communication and research have pointed toward more effective solutions and helped to avoid wasteful and counter-productive detours. Social learning processes have significantly increased the body of knowledge about the range of policy options available to national governments and intergovernmental organizations and have validated and promoted some effective approaches. Myriad policies and programs have been promoted across national lines, including measures to advance equal opportunity and vocational training as well as those closely identified with structural adjustment.

Nonetheless, it is evident that the research and other social learning processes have been of significantly less value outside the OECD countries than for those developed market economies. For the developing world the research agenda remains centered on basic work on concepts and data. Frances Stewart of the Institute of Commonwealth Studies presented a broad overview of this research in 1989, concluding that on a global level "employment has largely been ignored in the formation of structural adjustment programmes, and has had only a minor role in research."[62] Stewart added that, for developing countries, "past employment research has shown that it was not effective in policy

---

60. International Labour Conference, 75th Sess. 1988, *Human Rights: A Common Responsibility, Report of the Director-General*, Part I (Geneva: ILO, 1988), pp. 35, 42.

61. Ibid., p. 40.

62. Frances Stewart, "Summary of Discussions and Suggestions for Future Research", in Salome, ed., *Fighting Urban Unemployment in Developing Countries*, p. 28.

terms, partly because of weaknesses in the concepts, assumptions and models, and also because the policy conclusions were rarely accepted by decision makers."[63] I agree with Stewart's assessment but contrast this experience sharply with the far more effective experience of research and social learning by and for industrial market economies.

Other Policy Responses

While elements of the global and international policy response to unemployment have been alluded to above, an effort is made here to present a fuller exposition of the diverse outputs of intergovernmental organizations as well as aspects of transgovernmental cooperation by national political leaders and experts. The responses include proclaimed intentions of national leaders to coordinate macroeconomic and structural policies; studies and borrowing of successful approaches to particular labor market programs that have such aims as improved labor mobility and adaptation; the substantial investments of the European Community in vocational training, regional policies, and the adjustment of workers to changing competititve impacts; and the modest investment of the ILO in studies and technical assistance to promote employment and the meeting of that organization's labor standards. Also involved are project, structural adjustment, and liquidity loans to national governments from such agencies as the World Bank and IMF, which often offer direct support for employment-generating programs but also frequently force retrenchment in national government spending, public sector employment, and subsidized private employment.

It is probably not possible to confidently assess even the overall direction (positive or negative) of the sum of such global and regional policy efforts to affect employment. At any given time varying conclusions can be drawn about actual short-term international impacts on employment and projected long-term results. Further, impacts are often subject to disputes concerning substitution effects and other modifying factors.

Legislating and Supervising Employment Policies

Legislation and supervision of labor and employment standards are major means to reinforce the international employment regime. More binding and non-binding employment-related prescriptions exist than could possibly be discussed or even mentioned in this study. It seems

63. Ibid.

best to start with the following generalizations concerning the relationship of such standards to the basic principles of the regime.

First, some subjects are deemed more appropriate for international rule-making than others. The many reasons for prescribing binding rules include the desirability of protecting states and firms from the advantages obtained from competitors' exploitation of workers. The various regime actors also want to affirm certain human rights principles on behalf of individuals and groups and to meet the appropriate international responsibility for the regulating of such transnational phenomena as ocean shipping and the treatment of migrant workers. Less acceptable as binding prescriptions are attempts to mandate the scope and direction of overall national employment policies. The difficulties here begin with doubts about the appropriateness of rule-making in the face of the desire of national governments to have maximum scope to choose and change their own policy emphases. They also may involve, at the broadest level, major philosophical differences over such concepts as guaranteed employment and state intervention in the private sector.

Second, accepting a subject or principle for international standard-setting does not ensure that a sound and appropriate legal instrument will be formulated or implemented. Both prescription and implementation of rules are highly political processes that test the political powers and judgments of each significant actor. The outcomes often reflect current power relations among employers, trade unions, and various coalitions of member states. The resulting instrument may or may not go beyond the lowest common denominator of member states' law, thought, or practice. One often finds winners and losers in the processes of prescribing and implementing instruments in the employment regime. These processes will also determine whether enough states will ratify a convention to allow it to go into effect legally and have a maximum impact on subsequent national law and practice.

Critical decisions have to be made in relation to the necessary degree of flexibility to be left to states in fulfilling regime objectives. The flexibility issue has been particularly important in efforts to prescribe national full employment policies and programs. The best-known such instrument, the ILO Employment Policy Convention (No. 122, 1964) has been termed by the ILO itself a "promotional" instrument that is binding on ratifying states only in limited ways. As stated by the ILO's Committee of Experts on the Application of Conventions and Recommendations:

As regards the way in which the commitment to the goal of full, productive and freely-chosen employment is carried out, the Convention is a very flexible instrument, leaving member states free to decide both the measures to be adopted and the type of machinery to be instituted for the formulation and implementation of those measures.[64]

Issues of whether or not to endorse new solutions to long-standing issues come up regularly. Should equal protection for women require affirmative action and equal pay for comparable work?[65] Should the prohibition of forced labor apply to military conscription, criminal convictions, or emergencies?[66] Although all important international legal instruments involve important policy choices, the failure to achieve consensus on basic principles may undercut the broader purpose of the endeavor.

At the center of the standard-setting and implementing efforts of the international employment regime are the ILO and European Community. Both of these organizations combine broad powers to enact and implement binding rules with a major emphasis on employment issues. However, the legislative and judicial powers of the Community organs have attributes that are not matched by any other international organization. The Community's founding treaties provide for regulations that create rights and obligations directly applicable to member states and individuals throughout the Community, directives that call upon member states to legislate in conformity with common standards or to carry out treaty obligations, and decisions that may authoritatively implement regulatory powers. Further, the European Court of Justice may develop authoritative case law. As stated by A. G. Toth, "Community law, as a whole, constitutes a new, independent [autonomous], supranational, self-contained, uniform and unitary legal order of a sui generis type, with a limited field of operation."[67] As suggested by Paul Taylor, such a summary may well overstate the federal or supranational pretensions of the Community.[68] However, few dispute the fact that Community law varies in major ways from traditional international law in areas central to the employment regime.

64. International Labour Conference, 57th Sess., *Report of the Committee of Experts on the Application of Conventions and Recommendations*, Vol. B, *General Survey on the Reports Relating to the Employment Policy Convention and Recommendations, 1964* (Geneva: ILO, 1972), p. 3. The OECD Council has taken a similar approach regarding its 1964 Resolution on Manpower Policy as a Means for the Promotion of Economic Growth and its 1976 Recommendation on a General Employment and Manpower Policy.

65. See Ronnie Steinberg Ratner, *Equal Employment Policy for Women* (Philadelphia: Temple University Press, 1980).

66. See David Ziskind, "Forced Labor in the Law of Nations," *Comparative Labor Law* 3 (1980): 253–283.

67. See A. G. Toth, *Legal Protection of Individuals in the European Communities* 1 (Amsterdam: North-Holland, 1979), p. 8.

68. Taylor, *Limits of European Integration*, p. 294.

In contrast to the frequent use of such law-making devices by the EC, the OECD makes sparing use of the binding decision clause in its founding convention.[69] It prescribes mainly through declarations, resolutions, and recommendations, which are officially non-binding even though at least some of the most important of these may be recognized as customary international law and have had significant impacts on the resolution of disputes concerning such issues as the appropriate compensation of employees laid off because of abrupt plant closures.[70]

The primary sponsors of traditional conventions as instruments of binding law for the employment regime are the ILO and the Council of Europe. The former organization has adopted conventions and recommendations that pertain to each major principle of the employment regime. In contrast, the contributions of the Council of Europe to the regime have been concentrated in the areas of equal protection and freedom of movement for such groups as migrant workers and refugees.

Legal obligations in the area of employment are also generated by major international charters and covenants designed to provide overall frameworks for the enjoyment of economic and social as well as political/civil rights. The most notable of these documents include the U.N. International Covenant on Economic, Social and Cultural Rights (adopted 1966) and the Council of Europe European Social Charter (adopted 1961). Such instruments are particularly important for early and sometimes original formulations of the basic principles of the employment regime. However, broad formulations tend to be particularly difficult to interpret and apply.

Other than the choices of flexibility and principle made in the process of formulating and adopting such international instruments, the major determinants of practical impact are the processes and degrees of commitment involved in implementation and supervision. The employment regime has devised a wide variety of systems for reporting and review and has demonstrated considerably different degrees of commitment from organization to organization and, within a particular agency, from instrument to instrument. The implementation efforts that clearly stand out for their ability to get the attention of the member states and broader community of states are those employed by

69. Article 5 of the Convention on the Organization for Economic Cooperation and Development, adopted December 14, 1960.

70. This is affirmed in relation to the Declaration of June 21, 1976 by Governments of OECD Member Countries on International Investment and Multinational Enterprises, which incorporated "Guidelines for Multinational Enterprises," in Norbert Horn, "International Rules for Multinational Enterprises: The ICC, OECD, and the ILO Initiatives," *American University Law Review* 30 (1980): 936–939.

the ILO regarding conventions and by the European Community respecting its several forms of legislation.

The ILO has developed processes for supervision of its conventions and recommendations that are models for other international organizations. These processes involve regular reporting obligations by national governments, opportunities for comments by non-government organizations, annual and special periodic reviews of evidence by a committee of experts, and special committees for particular conventions or subject areas. This effort proceeds in an atmosphere of substantial commitment by the reviewing committees, as evidenced by the difficulty experienced periodically in gaining Conference approval of the annual reports as well as the repeated efforts by various groups of member states to moderate or prevent particular criticisms found in these reports. Demonstrating the paramount importance of the commitment of staff, committee members, and others to the principles of the regime is the fact that major parts of the ILO process have been adopted without comparable results thus far by such organizations as the Council of Europe and United Nations.[71] Fortunately, hopeful developments in U.N. enforcement of economic and social rights emerged in the late 1980s and early 1990s. These are discussed in the following chapter.

Even in the case of the ILO, however, major variations can be observed in terms of which standards are chosen for emphasis and, to a lesser degree, which member states are subjected to greater or lesser scrutiny. The conventions deemed to have greatest priority have been the "basic human rights" conventions, these officially designated as those concerned with freedom of association, forced labor, and discrimination.[72] A major effort was made between 1980 and 1983 to secure an increased emphasis on the Employment Policy Convention

71. It is necessary to distinguish the Council of Europe's weaker enforcement of the European Social Charter and the employment-oriented conventions from its impressive system for implementing the mostly political and civil rights in the European Convention for the Protection of Human Rights and Fundamental Freedoms (adopted 1950). Swart concludes that the Council of Europe "is able to do little more than keep an eye on the effectuation of conventions and agreements at a fairly superficial level." A. H. J. Swart, "Legal Status of Aliens," p. 49. See also David Harris, *The European Social Charter* (Charlottesville: University of Virginia Press, 1984); *European Social Charter: Origin, Operation and Results* (Strasbourg: Council of Europe, 1991); and the reports of the ILO's Committee of Experts on the Application of Conventions and Recommendations to the U.N. concerning various articles of the International Covenant on Economic, Social and Cultural Rights (transmitted annually by the U.N. Secretary-General to the U.N. Economic and Social Council).

72. International Labour Organization, "Final Report of the Working Party on International Labour Standards," special issue of *Official Bulletin* 57 (1979), Series A, p. 14.

(No. 122, 1964), in order to challenge the alleged abandonment of the full employment principle by Chile, Britain, and other (mostly Western) governments. Increasingly critical statements by the Committee of Experts on the Application of Conventions and Recommendations culminated in the 1983 finding regarding Britain that "it is not apparent that employment considerations as defined by the [1964 Employment Policy] Convention are the subject of an active policy on the part of the Government."[73]

However, the process by which the ILO has supervised the Employment Policy Convention in recent years reflects the limits of its ability to influence member states in this area even as it periodically exhibits boldness in taking a few states to task. The Committee of Experts indicated in 1983 that "it finds the supervision of Convention No. 122 to be very difficult" due to such factors as the need to supplement government reports with independent information and the lack of appropriate expertise on the committee.[74]

In summing up the experience of the ILO with Convention No. 122, it should be stressed that the organization's efforts to make member states feel accountable to its supervising bodies were partly successful. As a result the ILO can be said to have at least slowed the trend toward the discounting of the full employment principle. Yet it has lacked sufficient expertise, legitimacy, and will to point the states under review to a policy orientation much more specific than having an "active labor market policy."

Perhaps the greatest failure of the international employment regime has been the unwillingness or inability of the European Community to use its impressive legal authority more effectively to promote full employment. The EC has made important contributions to the equal protection and freedom of movement concepts and has marginally enhanced legal protections against collective dismissals. Yet its legislation has operated only on the periphery of the broader policy issues that determine a commitment to full employment. Indeed, Community organs have sometimes exacerbated short-term unemployment by ordering closures of industrial plants (e.g., by implementing mandatory production quotas) and by challenging certain national subsidies viewed as implicit subsidies of exports.

73. International Labour Conference, 69th Sess., 1983, *Report of the Committee of Experts on the Application of Conventions and Recommendations* (Geneva: ILO, 1983), Report III (Part 4A), p. 254. In 1983 the Committee of Experts reviewed the application of Convention No. 122 in 51 countries and commented on the full employment policies of 18 states, these including 12 OECD member states.

74. Ibid., p. 18. The committee, made up largely of judges and law professors, is not well chosen for the evaluation of social and economic policies.

To the credit of the EC Commission, it devoted increasing attention in the 1980s to the development and promotion of official measures aimed at the unemployment crisis. However, this effort was slow to begin and has been racked by delays and failures to secure the needed consensus. As a result it has produced mostly non-binding resolutions and recommendations on issues of central importance and various binding acts concerning narrower issues. Binding measures continue to be selected in areas, including part-time and temporary work and social security, in which the focus of the proposed legislation is the elimination of discrimination against certain categories of workers. The promotion of opportunities for young workers, the reorganization of working time, and harmonization of national vocational training policies have been handled mainly through proposed and adopted recommendations and resolutions. Even such non-binding instruments have often been excruciatingly difficult for the Commission and its allies to promote in the Council.

The result is that the ILO and European Community, both with politically and legally impressive supervisory mechanisms, have few major binding full employment measures to implement that reach to the heart of the full employment principle. This contrasts sharply with the present situation regarding equal treatment and discrimination on such grounds as gender, race, and political views. Since 1976, the will and capabilities of the EC Commission and Court of Justice have been demonstrated repeatedly regarding the implementation of directives and treaty provisions pertaining to equality for men and women in pay, training, hiring, promotion, and social security.[75] The ILO also has demonstrated a high level of determination in its activities relating to racial and political discrimination. Indeed the ILO's supervisory procedures have won renewed respect in many parts of the world due to its activities in such areas as discrimination and freedom of association. Unfortunately, its efforts to implement the Employment Policy Convention have frustrated almost everyone involved in the process.

The form of global policy instruments is addressed by Soroos when he asserts that "Most global policies are set forth in treaties or resolutions, which are adopted either in the regular meetings of the central organs of the United Nations, in the affiliated specialized agencies, or in ad hoc conferences convened to focus world attention on a particu-

75. The Court combines the role of interpreter of both constitutional (treaty) law and particular legislation. Both have been used in these and related policy areas. See Elizabeth Meehan, "Sex Equality Policies in the European Community," *Journal of European Integration* 13, 2–3 (Winter–Spring 1990): 185–196.

lar problem of widespread concern."[76] This assertion raises issues about whether all global policy areas are amenable to conference policy-making that results in major public declarations and legal obligations.

Various resolutions, conventions, recommendations, and other official instruments have played roles in global and international employment policy. These have included affirmations of the right to work, agreements that national governments have obligations to promote full employment, and recommendations concerning the kinds of measures useful to achieve or to approach full employment.[77] Such instruments often affirm the principles and goals of employment policy while giving vague and skeletal presentations of endorsed policies. They rarely compare in directness or comprehensiveness with leading instruments dealing with such major global policy issues as, for example, nuclear proliferation or ozone depletion.[78] Battles have raged over symbolic and ideological language and over linkages of employment policy with some policy areas of marginal relevance to employment. Rarely have even the most positive participants and observers felt that the cause of full employment has been advanced significantly by such intergovernmental instruments standing alone.

There has been little praise for the overall results of global and international efforts to ameliorate high unemployment and violations of internationally accepted norms relating to employment policies and practices. Kurt Rothchild argues, "Apart from relatively inconsequential summit and other declarations, there have been no significant international agreements on—or commitments to—employment objectives."[79] Bertram Gross asserts that "the United Nations has deserted

---

76. Soroos, *Beyond Sovereignty*, p. 20.

77. Statements of national obligations are combined with recommendations of national policies in Resolution of the [OECD] Council on Manpower Policy as a Means for the Promotion of Economic Growth, May 21, 1964 [CF C/M(64)10 (Final) Item 84, Doc. No. C(64) 48 (Final)] in OECD, *Acts of the Organization* 4 (Paris: OECD, 1964), pp. 185–195 and Recommendation of the [OECD] Council on a General Employment and Manpower Policy, March 5, 1976 [CF C/M(76)4 (Final) Item 46(a), (b) and (c), Doc. No. C(76) 37] in OECD, *Acts of the Organization*, vol. 16 (Paris: OECD, 1976), pp. 31–35; see also ILO Convention No. 122 and Recommendation No. 122 (concerning Employment Policy), both adopted July 9, 1964, and Employment Policy (Supplementary Provisions) Recommendation, No. 169, adopted June 26, 1984 (Appendix I in this volume).

78. See Richard Elliot Benedick, *Ozone Diplomacy: New Directions in Safeguarding the Planet* (Cambridge, MA: Harvard University Press, 1991).

79. Kurt W. Rothchild, "The Neglect of Employment in the International Economic Order," in Gross and Pfaller, eds., *Unemployment*, p. 50.

its earlier commitments to full employment,"[80] reflecting the attitude of most of its member states. He contends that Eastern Europe follows the example of the OECD in "dodging the subject" and that developing nations "touch on it cautiously."[81] Yet some very real differences in emphasis exist among such organizations and geographic spheres.

Programs and Financial Subsidies

The intergovernmental organizations of the employment regime are generally denied substantial resources for major distributive programs, though there are a few significant exceptions. Intergovernmental programs may be operated directly by the international organizations or funneled through non-governmental organizations or national and subnational governments. Such European Community programs as its Social and Regional Funds certainly are much more than token or symbolic, though they were dwarfed until recently by the EC's Common Agriculture Fund as well as by the available resources of most member countries. Allocations to the Regional and Social Funds reached 7 billion European Currency Units (ECUs), more than U.S. $8 billion, by 1988 and were projected to increase rapidly even before new Community agreements accelerated that growth in the 1990s.[82]

Through the 1980s the Community struggled to agree on adequate financing, the targeting of efforts to such groups as youth, women, foreign workers, and needy regions, the assertion of "European control" over critical aspects of projects, and the integration of the several structural funds. However, by the late 1980s these funds were a key to future Community influence in industrial and labor market policy and a potentially critical factor in the integration of poorer countries and regions into the growing Community. They were also a key bargaining chip in negotiations concerning Community geographic and functional expansion.

The ILO's World Employment Programme is impressively broad in its geographical scope but can be viewed as token when measured against the needs of the many client states for technical assistance and the means to carry out the ILO's advice and achieve its standards. The ILO has been given significant, though clearly inadequate, funding for programs that are intended to reinforce its educational and standard-setting efforts and to stimulate much more responsive national efforts on behalf of employment. While their programs are sufficient to dem-

80. Bertram Gross in Gross and Pfaller, eds., *Unemployment*, p. 182.
81. Ibid., p. 184.
82. *The Economist*, February 27, 1988, p. 42.

onstrate the potential value of technical assistance and program seeding, they also reflect the huge gap between the organization's missions and its resources in the employment field. The ILO's programs generally follow the pattern of the United Nations agencies insofar as they direct their resources primarily to developing countries. Through such vehicles as the World Employment Programme the ILO provides assistance for national employment and development planning, public works, and human resource development. Unfortunately, even with supplementary contributions from Western governments and the U.N. Development Program, the meager available resources are dwarfed by the range of needed services and the number of countries requesting assistance.

The World Employment Programme accounted in 1987 for approximately 36 percent of the organization's technical cooperation activities, these mainly in the fields of public works, labor market and employment planning, information systems, appropriate technology, rural development, and refugees.[83] With an ILO annual budget of only U.S.$350 million for 1990–91, and little more than U.S. $100 million available to the ILO from all sources for technical cooperation, it is not difficult to accept the conclusions of Walter Galenson and others about the limited impacts of such a program as operated in more than one hundred countries.[84] ILO programs have been limited by the lack of priority for employment in the development strategies of many ministries of development as well as major donor countries.

Explaining the Weak Global Response

The inadequate global response to unemployment is attributable to such factors as the constitutional and organizational limits of intergovernmental institutions, the application of ideology and schools of economic analysis within those organizations, and conflicting organizational missions. The limited response is due primarily to the secondary place of employment policy on international agendas when placed against other economic and human rights concerns. While such other labor issues as free trade union association have been given a more prominent place on the global agendas—as in the Polish and Chilean cases—unemployment per se has not reached the level of a problem demanding urgent or expensive global or regional action. Various countries, Sweden most prominently, have raised it to the top of their

83. International Labour Conference, 75th Sess., 1988. *Report of the Director-General: Activities of the ILO, 1987* (Geneva: ILO, 1988), p. 22.
84. *ILO Information* 15, 2 (May 1987): 1; 17, 2 (May 1989): 2.

national political agendas. But this has not been matched at the global level because of a continuing inclination to view it as a separate national issue for each country, the tendency of elected governments to seek all the credit even for symbolic and ameliorating policies, and the greater perceived political risks associated with inflation and other economic problems. Moreover, unemployment is often believed to be a problem that is even more difficult to ameliorate at the global or regional level than at the national level, particularly when demographic trends, debt obligations, or collapsing national economies render the contributions of global policy structures largely irrelevant and ineffective.

Organizational Factors

Factors involving the nature of particular intergovernmental organizations and the milieu in which they function include not only variations regarding language and customs but also geographic representation, whether constitutional power is based on financial contributions, and the roles of national and transnational interest groups.

The financial and legal authority of the European Community is itself a by-product of the geographic and political affinity of its member states. While employment was not a primary function of the three original Community organizations, it became obvious by 1974 that Community structures needed to respond effectively to serious unemployment problems of member states and to the rapid changes in the region's labor markets. The Community needed grassroots support more than did other intergovernmental organizations, partly because it often placed various economic sectors and large groups of workers at risk in the course of its efforts to develop treaty powers and to create a genuine common market. Further, powers given to the Community by its member governments to achieve other fundamental goals could periodically be redirected to increasing employment, as in the 1970s, when Community organs moved ahead of most member governments on equal employment opportunity for women. Nonetheless, geographic cohesion has not overcome the tendency for national and Community leaders to stress other economic, political, or social values or to protect national primacy regarding employment policies.

By contrast, the ILO has maintained a consistent rhetorical, legislative, and programmatic emphasis on the employment-related aims of organized labor and many national Labor and Social ministries. Unfortunately for organized labor and its allies, such ILO orientations were usually not supported by sufficient agency muscle. The ILO has led the way in developing procedures for supervision of its conventions. Yet the enormous political and socioeconomic diversity of its membership has meant that it must move slowly in advancing labor standards, lacking substantial financial incentives or instruments of legal or political coercion.

Conflicting organizational missions complicate intergovernmental efforts to deal with unemployment. These conflicts exist within such organizations as the OECD and European Community as well as between such organizations as the IMF and World Bank. The Bank emphasized employment less than other basic human needs during the McNamara and Clausen eras.[85] It also increasingly aligned itself with the IMF's practice of establishing difficult conditions for major loans, some of which explicitly require reducing employment in public sector enterprises and in the civil service.[86] Several studies indicate that governments affected by the kinds of structural adjustment policies promoted by the Bank and the Fund during the 1980s "find themselves dealing with the unemployment effects of their adjustment policies."[87]

Although the Fund and Bank have developed many overlapping functions and missions since the early 1970s and have established close collaboration in dealing with their borrowers, the Fund in particular has promoted a high degree of austerity through its loan conditionality agreements. Although the Fund professes concern for economic growth,[88] the conservative macroeconomic and structural reform measures that it has demanded of many member countries have had some harsh short- and medium-term impacts on their employment rates.[89]

Ideological Differences

The impact of ideology on employment policy has been great at the global level. Both East European and Western representatives singled out employment as a subject for potentially advantageous discussion as early as the sharp debates in the United Nations on the Universal Declaration on Human Rights and as recently as the ILO's efforts to develop an employment policy in 1983–84. During the various debates, delegates spoke across East-West lines in terms that often must have been incomprehensible to each other, while placing greater emphasis on winning debating points than on advancing global policy on employment and human rights.

The Cold War was not the only source of ideological friction affect-

85. Addison and Demery, "Alleviating Poverty," pp. 41–43.

86. *New York Times*, March 25, 1986, p. 32.

87. Addison and Demery, "Alleviating Poverty," p. 42.

88. M. de Vries, *Balance of Payments Adjustments, 1945 to 1986: The IMF Experience* (Washington, DC: International Monetary Fund, 1987).

89. *New York Times*, April 14, 1985, p. E2.

ing global and international employment policy. Within the Western alliance, social democratic and social market orientations often confronted more conservative and radical ones when major decisions were made affecting employment policy.[90] The shift to the right by most of the Western powers in the 1980s was apparent at the annual summits and had an impact on the employment-related policies of the OECD, European Community, World Bank, IMF, and other global institutions. The OECD shift to the positive adjustment approach was anticipated by internal divisions within that organization and, especially, the bureaucratic and policy dominance of its Economics and Statistics Department. Increasingly, but not invariably, the ideological shifts noted here tilted macroeconomic policy consensus from a stimulative to a restrictive direction, unless the stimulative measures were coordinated and the overall risk of inflation was considered to be acceptable, using conservative standards of analysis.

Conclusions

Unemployment is not a problem that can be readily addressed by global policies such as international legal instruments that embody regulations. Moreover, resources available for global programs do not approach the huge needs of the many nations losing ground due to growing labor forces and declining employment opportunities. There is no single obvious fix, quick or slow, in this post-Keynesian era. Furthermore, the outside world has no special interest in the unemployment problems of most individual countries. This situation can be attributed to the greater political salience of such related issues as inflation and balance of payments stability, the perceived inability of the unemployed to threaten the political order in most cases, the availability of such ameliorating programs as unemployment insurance, and the positive political effects of various symbolic programs that offer the appearance of government concern.

Employment is an issue that is dealt with much less adequately globally than regionally. This tendency can be explained by the greater impact of ideological divisions and by the paucity of financial resources dedicated to employment creation at the global level. Furthermore, conflicting missions in important intergovernmental organizations often aggravate global efforts.

An international regime approach reinforces global policy analysis

---

90. See Robert D. Putnam and Nicholas Bayne, *Hanging Together: Cooperation and Conflict in the Seven-Power Summits*, rev. ed. (Cambridge, MA: Harvard University Press, 1987).

insofar as it stresses the development of regime structures and capabilities as bridges between recognizing problems and making policy choices. In the case of employment, significant regime developments included the emergence of a United Nations commitment to socioeconomic human rights and the European Community's decision to stress subsidies to national employment development programs. Moreover, a regime perspective highlights the weaknesses of the contributions of those global institutions that give priority to reduced unemployment.

The tendency for employment policy to fall through the cracks of both economic and human rights policy must be overcome. Higher priorities have been asserted in both areas by national and intergovernmental organs, the most obvious of these being inflation and gross violations of the right to life.

International efforts to affect employment have failed to equal those in behalf of such other affirmed socioeconomic human rights as food, social insurance, and some areas of health care, but compare more favorably in meaningfulness and effectiveness with programs in such other proclaimed entitlement areas as education and shelter. Systematic research should be done to confirm these comparisons and to examine the underlying causes. It is apparent that the global society gives much greater attention to deprivations that are more visible and conscience-pricking (e.g., lack of food and imprisonment for political offenses) than to mass unemployment and underemployment.

Chapter 6
New Directions in the Nineties

Almost every leading commentator on current international developments assumes that recent momentous changes at the international and national levels will produce profound but often unpredictable outcomes. Certain changes from the mid-1980s to the early 1990s are, in many ways, "sea-changes."[1] They include developments that are global in impact and previously almost unimaginable in scale and scope. Taken together they drastically alter the balance of ideas as well as more conventional elements of power that shape such fields as employment and human rights. Such developments include the collapse of Marxism-Leninism as an ideological weapon and the consequent loss of will and motive to contest dominant Western perspectives concerning many employment and human rights issues. As a result, debates in these subject areas increasingly reflect other alignments, including struggles between North and South and within the widened Western sphere.

The global and regional changes that will determine how we think and act regarding employment in the final years of this millennium are, like the forces discussed in earlier chapters, a mixture of the political, economic, social, cultural, and military. In many cases the connections between these forces and aspects of employment are indirect and less than obvious. Yet they provide, individually and collectively, an international context for policies that greatly determine our welfare and well-being now and in the foreseeable future.

This book has chronicled the impact of a definable Soviet bloc on the international politics of employment and human rights. This bloc, consisting primarily of the nation-states associated with the Warsaw

---

1. See Nicholas X. Rizopoulos, ed., *Sea-Changes: American Foreign Policy in a World Transformed* (New York: Council on Foreign Relations, 1990).

Treaty Organization and the Council for Mutual Economic Assistance, utilized internationally, and benefited domestically, from proclaimed constitutional guarantees of employment. Each of these states built into their economies and legal systems a variety of policies that kept overt unemployment to a minimum—including onerous requirements before certain kinds of dismissals could proceed and incentives that led enterprising managers to maximize persons on payrolls by under-employing and featherbedding.

The members of this bloc, perceiving that the provision of employment and job security constituted an area of major ideological and political advantage over many capitalist systems, took advantage of various opportunities to use this perceived favorable dimension of their domestic policies at international forums. Although such efforts were usually politically clumsy, they constituted for bloc spokespersons an issue that seemed to confirm Marxist-Leninist ideology and sometimes caused visible squirming in the ranks of Western adversaries.

Subsequently, there began the era of East European political transformation, privatization, uneven transition toward market economies, and negotiations for debt relief and Western economic assistance. This period also brought wide-ranging East-West cooperation in the very intergovernmental organization forums that had provided significant battlegrounds in the recent history of the right to employment. The politics of ideas and systems shifted drastically as Soviet, successor state, and East-Central European leadership increasingly competed for Western favor and support.

Yet this shift in the rhetorical struggle and the blurring of East-West social and economic systems constitutes only one part of the sea-change regarding Eastern Europe. Another is the advent or threat of horrific levels of unemployment in the aftermath of the collapse of Communist rule. This has perhaps been most dramatic thus far in the territory of the former German Democratic Republic, which registered a jobless rate of 14.6 percent in mid-1992, for which the term "employment catastrophe" is being used.[2] Even this high level of unemployment, credited with leading to massive suicides and political disaffection, may have less long-term impact than the ongoing economic free-fall of the early 1990s in most post-Soviet republics.[3]

---

2. *Week in Germany* (New York, German Information Center), September 11, 1992, p. 4; *The Economist*, April 6, 1991, p. 67.

3. Projections of near-term Soviet unemployment reaching as high as 12 percent are made in the authoritative *A Study of the Soviet Economy* (Paris: International Monetary Fund, World Bank, OECD, and European Bank for Reconstruction and Development, 1991), 2: 149.

Various repercussions of the East-Central European experience can be expected to reinforce regional and global consciousness of the powerful negative impacts of mass unemployment. Together with recent political developments in France, the United States, and elsewhere they also can be expected to challenge assumptions made in the 1980s concerning the lack of substantial impact of unemployment on the political vulnerability of particular government administrations and on national political systems. It was one thing to have "unacceptable" levels of unemployment in stable democracies facing, at worst, slight declines in overall GDP. Evidence is building to demonstrate that the impact on political stability is much greater in regimes facing sharply rising expectations, few established political leaders or parties, and rapidly changing constitutional orders. Political trends in the united Germany of 1991–92 and in several East-Central European countries indicate that this backlash is already affecting the direction of politics in and out of the former Soviet bloc, increasing support for radical rightist, ultra nationalist, xenophobic, and even Communist elements.[4]

A second geographic area experiencing sea-change affecting employment and related human rights policies is the European Community. The essence of the consensus favoring the Single European Act of 1987 and its plan for the completion of the internal European market was a neoliberal one. The Cecchini Report, sponsored by the European Commission, promised that "a new competitive environment" fostered by the elimination of remaining national and market barriers was to result in "major reductions in chronic European unemployment after a short-term adjustment period."[5] The completed internal market would add 1.8 million jobs Community-wide, reducing the overall unemployment rate by some 1.5 percentage points.[6]

However, the Single European Act set off tremors in European labor circles as well as among other advocates of social causes. Fears centered on potential efforts by less affluent Community member states to compete for new investment through such measures as reduced social security obligations for firms, less social protection in such areas as working conditions, health, and safety, and the encouragement of lower wages and weaker trade unions. The expected short-term surge

---

4. Alan Riding, "Europe's Growing Debate Over Whom to Let Inside," *New York Times*, December 1, 1991, p. 2E.

5. Paolo Cecchini with Michel Catinat and Alexis Jaequemin, *The European Challenge: 1992—The Benefits of a Single Market* (Aldershot, Eng.: Gower Publishing House, 1988), p. xvii.

6.Ibid., p. 97.

in mergers, acquisitions, and joint ventures, posing threats of marked increases in plant closings and large-scale redundancies, also threatened to generate greater labor market instability.[7]

The leap of faith and action into a Europe in which barriers to free movement across national barriers were to be markedly reduced for goods, services, workers, and money was part of a search for a larger consensus about the future of Europe involving such issues as monetary and fiscal policy, the restructuring of national and Community political power, and defense cooperation. It also prompted renewed efforts to meet the social challenges posed by the new economic order.

One of the major considerations for the future direction of the Community on employment and related issues is the pressure to admit new member states. In several cases this is a matter of when rather than whether particular states will be included. New members will presumably come first from European Free Trade Association (EFTA) members, and may come later from states of the former Soviet bloc, Turkey, and other applicants. The consequences of such expansion will be enormous and will take various forms. The problems of relative industrial backwardness and societies in transition to free markets characterize the former Communist East, with Germany's Eastern laender offering an early trial run for the expansion of the geographic scope of subsidies, regional policy, and other methods of adjustment and equalization. The remainder of Scandinavia, Austria and Switzerland offer fewer problems together with prospects of increased interest in the Community in some of their approaches to active labor market programs. Throughout most of 1991 the EC and the seven EFTA states struggled to shape a new provisional economic and political relationship, which bore fruit in a treaty signed in October of that year.[8] The implications of that agreement are discussed below.

One of the major problems of further Community expansion is the prospect of diversion of structural fund, investment bank, and other financial resources away from weaker regions of present member states to accommodate new states. Unless total resources available for redistribution and social programs are increased well beyond present levels, income inequality and regional disparities within and among the

7. See Charles V. Ciccone and Gail McCallion, "EC-92: The Potential Consequence for European and U.S. Labor Markets," in *European Community: Issues Raised by 1992 Integration,* report prepared for the Committee on Foreign Affairs, U.S. House of Representatives, by Congressional Research Service, June 1989, p. 55.

8. "EC and EFTA," *The Economist,* May 18, 1991, pp. 53–54; "Lest a Fortress Arise," *The Economist,* October 26, 1991, pp. 81–82.

present member states will be difficult to reduce when the internal market advances.[9] This prospect led to new agreements on augmentation and reallocation of Community budget obligations at the December 1991 Maastricht Summit that were signed by the participants in February 1992.

Perhaps the potential sea-change with the least predictable result is the prospective North American common market initiated by the establishment of the Canada-U.S. Free Trade Agreement that entered into force in 1989. The authorization of "fast track" treatment of U.S.-Mexican-Canadian free trade negotiations in 1991 by the U.S. Congress led to the signing of the North American Free Trade Agreement in 1992. Similar "fast track" treatment was promised in 1991 in regard to GATT's Uruguay Round. These decisions were stimulated by North American fears about Europe's proposed completion of its common market by the end of 1992 as well as Japanese and other East Asian competition. A vision of an enlarged European Community viewed as capable of creating major new barriers to external trade spurred free trade developments.

Many U.S. labor and environmental spokespersons, together with their allies in the Clinton Administration, the Ross Perot camp, Congress, and elsewhere, perceive the expansion of free trade to Mexico as threatening the wholesale exportation of U.S. jobs as well as the creation of major environmental risks.[10] Although the employment outcomes of the North American developments cannot yet be predicted confidently, certain warning signals are apparent. The European Community demonstrated how countries with unequal levels of industrialization and technology can succeed in moving toward a free trade area. This, however, required substantial transfers of resources to backward countries and regions, other political and financial payoffs, and the stimulation of increased efforts to train and retrain workers in the various participating countries. Although the U.S. government has responded rhetorically to such concerns on this side of the Rio Grande, there is ample reason to doubt that the U.S. federal government has the commitment or financial ability to match existing European programs. In any event, no foreseeable North American free trade community is likely to have political or financial strengths comparable to that of the European Community, and therefore will face greater risks of collapse in the face of major and prolonged losses of jobs and

9. Giuseppe Mele, "EEC Regional Policy and the Reform of the Structural Funds," *Journal of Regional Policy* 10, 4 (October–December 1990): 700.
    10. *New York Times*, May 8, 1991, p. C2.

national income in any of its three parts. Economic and political strains in Canada in 1992–93 illustrate those risks.

The forces of change noted above distort the reader's vision insofar as they stress trends in the OECD and post-Communist lands rather than in the developing countries that house most of the world's population. No single recent event, or combination of developments, has substantially shifted attention to the social and economic problems of the Third World, and it is unlikely that any soon will. For many of these countries the many ominous economic developments of the 1980s forecast continuing socioeconomic difficulties in the 1990s, especially the sharp fall in aggregate net financial transfers to developing countries from 1982 onwards.[11] Most intergovernmental and national lending, granting, and technical assistance organizations continue to downplay the significance of unemployment in most developing countries— even after receiving massive criticism of painful Third World experiences with structural adjustment and debt repayment demands imposed in the 1980s. Unfortunately, labor force growth in many regions of Asia, Africa, and Latin America will continue to outstrip the ability of most countries on those continents to create jobs. Although the anticipated slowing of labor force increases in various developing countries can be expected to improve prospects on the unemployment front in the coming decade, an average of some 35 million new members are expected to join the labor force in developing countries annually for the remainder of the 1990s.[12]

East-Central Europe and the former Soviet republics remind us that political and economic stability count as much as labor force trends in predicting unemployment and underemployment. The trends of the first years of the 1990s point to some possible improvement in overall political stability and democratization in Africa and Latin America, combined with growing risks of instability in parts of the Arab world, China and India. China, the world's most populous country, is at this writing continuing repression of human rights even as it continues with highly beneficial economic reforms and rapid growth in foreign

11. Independent Commission of the South on Development Issues, *The Challenge to the South: A Report of the South Commission* (New York: Oxford University Press, 1990), p. 59. It is recognized here that the term Third World, used here as a synonym for the developing countries that have not yet achieved the status of "newly industrialized countries," has always carried a questionable connotation of Eurocentrism and has lost even more meaning with the end of the Communist regimes in Europe that largely constituted the Second World.

12. United Nations, *Global Outlook 2000: An Economic, Social, and Environmental Perspective* (New York: United Nations, 1990), p. 214.

investment, production, and exports. Its highly profitable trade relations with the United States are increasingly at risk due to both human rights abuses and bilateral trade imbalances. The pro-democracy movement that set the stage for Tiananmen derived in part from patterns of labor force growth and mobility that shattered China's full employment commitments even as Communist political discipline wavered.[13]

India's 850 million people face the combined effects of high levels of political corruption and violence, much of the latter driven by nationalistic and religious separatism and chauvinism. Yet it is the underlying weaknesses of an economy that until recently won much credit for stability and moderate growth that will have the greatest effect on the employment situation. In 1992 India was struggling to avoid default on its foreign loans. One journalist notes that this is accompanied by "a spiral of 17 percent inflation, a strangling bureaucracy, poverty, illiteracy, overpopulation and huge environmental problems."[14] *The Economist* recently viewed India as a country in which development has gone tragically wrong, one that "has achieved less than virtually any comparable third-world country."[15] While solid progress on unemployment and underemployment remain out of reach, it is clear that competition for jobs by workers at all levels of educational attainment continues to be a volatile element of India's political situation.

Several trends in the international political economy deriving from the fall of Communism in East-Central Europe and the former Soviet Union have had major impacts on national and regional employment patterns. These include the accelerating tendencies to reduce arms budgets and dismantle certain weapons, the pressures to make Western economic assistance available to the former Warsaw Pact countries, the economic costs of violence in the former Yugoslavia and elsewhere, and the increasing threats of large-scale Westward migration. Each of these trends are probably in their early stages, assuming that the continuing radical transformation of the economies of the former Soviet republics proceeds. Such interrelated developments will offer opportunities as well as problems of short- to medium-term adjustment for East and West alike. Outcomes depend on the ability of the new regimes to adapt their economies and labor forces without shatter-

13. Jeanne L. Wilson, "Labor Policy in China: Reform and Retrogression," *Problems of Communism* 39 (September–October 1990): 44–65.

14. Bernard Weinraub, "Party in India Chooses Rao for Premier," *New York Times*, June 21, 1991, p. A3.

15. "A Survey of India," *The Economist*, May 4, 1991, p. 9.

ing domestic political support. For leading Western powers, new demands for bilateral and multilateral grants and credits create extraordinarily difficult decisions relating to quantity, form, and timing in the context of other large foreign economic obligations and, in several cases, exceptionally large national budget deficits.

A highly influential area of international political economy affecting labor markets is the trade arena. An era of evolving trade liberalization, begun with Bretton Woods nearly fifty years ago, has become one of emerging regional trading groups, renewed national and regional protectionism, and increasingly aggressive competition for high-value markets. Fears of being fully or partially shut out by regional trading blocs mount in much of the world even as hope is focused on the professed liberal goals of the Uruguay Round. Key trade issues of the early 1990s include agricultural subsidies and trade in services. In the minds of many experts the politics of trade and foreign investment are the principal politics of profits and employment. No one can deny its relevance. "Fair trade" is a rallying cry of those who fail to see equity or optimum employment outcomes from competing against and in protected markets.

Closely connected with trade developments in their current and future impacts on employment are issues of foreign direct investment and international debt. The 1990s began with a strong rush of transnational corporate investment in the Europe of 1992 and beyond, with increased emphasis by these firms on establishing privileged access to the Community's internal trade. This, however, is threatened by the contention in some European circles that certain foreign-owned assets should not be given such equal access—especially in the automobile industry. Robert Reich declared a death knell for the very idea of nationally based multinationals—positing "the coming irrelevance of corporate nationality."[16] The already existing realities of international political economy include the ignoring of home country national interests by many multinationals. They also include a conflicting intensification of national government efforts to exert influence, and in some cases direction, over multinationals in various industries and issue-areas. Japan may be one of the leaders in this continued nationalist concentration of effort, but it is not alone. U.S. and European industrial policy may be less obvious than Japan's but these countries are also increasingly proactive in such policy areas as competition/antitrust, subsidization, and the encouragement of meaningful efforts to meet

16. Robert Reich, *The Work of Nations: Preparing Ourselves for 21st Century Capitalism* (New York: Alfred Knopf, 1991), p. 136.

the challenges of cutting edge technology. In the present decade the increasingly subtle neomercantilist, authoritarian corporatism practiced in much of East Asia probably exerts more influence than the fading efforts to shape increasingly hyperliberal states in the United States and Britain.[17] As to the situation of ordinary workers, they face the increasing ability of firms and industries to dictate terms of employment. Although valuable research and managerial talent is benefiting from a seller's market for their labor, the bargaining power of various strata of workers below those levels is declining in an era of global production-sharing, markedly weakened trade unions, and "lean and mean" workforces.[18]

Although some progress has been made since the mid-1980s to reduce the overhanging impact of massive global debt, especially that in Latin America and East-Central Europe, on the world economy, the combined impacts of debts engendered by national budget imbalances and trade deficits continue to constrain economic growth. The impacts of debt are felt by lenders and borrowers alike, as leading Western countries lose potential markets in states forced to curtail imports. The impacts of this debt on employment are also felt through real interest rates that are much higher than normal at comparable stages of previous economic cycles. The world is being significantly affected by the growing budget deficits as well as trade imbalances experienced by the United States and many European countries. Kevin Phillips recently compared the U.S. situation with that of the Gilded Age of the 1920s.[19] The consequences for world employment from the excesses of that period were, of course, truly grave.

In most Western economies the ordinary worker is functioning in a global environment that is both forcing increasing migration of workers and engendering sharply increased resentment against this phenomena. This environment also typically includes the levelling off or contraction of indigenous labor force growth, an obvious enlargement of clandestine sectors of many national economies, and the ability of many industries to produce more goods and services with fewer workers. Although each of these trends significantly affects both interna-

17. The term hyperliberal is used in Robert W. Cox, *Production, Power, and World Order: Social Forces in the Making of History* (New York: Columbia University Press, 1987), pp. 286–289.

18. Reich, *Work of Nations*, pp. 122–125; James A. Caparoso, "Labor in the Global Political Economy," in Caparoso, ed., *A Changing International Division of Labor* (Boulder, CO: Lynne Reinner, 1987), p. 195.

19. Kevin Phillips, *The Politics of Rich and Poor* (New York: Random House, 1990), p. 65.

tional and national responses to employment, the negative and positive effects vary considerably from country to country. At present, factors presumably favorable to employment prospects include the slowing of the growth in the labor force in many developing countries, the creation of regional free trade areas, and the flexibility inherent in the expansion of clandestine economic sectors. The more obvious negative factors include, at least in the short run, the need to readjust from peak levels of military production in the United States and Russia, the poorer prospects for further major trade liberalization across regional lines, and the inability of large numbers of production workers to secure their jobs in the face of the increasingly flexible global division of labor.

The continuing power of internationally generated monetary discipline should be noted. Countries contemplating major efforts to stimulate employment and their economies as a whole through looser monetary and fiscal policies are faced with withdrawals of banked funds from abroad and competitive pressures to devalue national currencies. Efforts to maintain considerable stability in many European currency values accentuated this macroeconomic discipline until the European monetary system began to shatter in the fall of 1992. Such a linkage of currencies was crucial to the virtual collapse in 1992 of Sweden's ability to use its model labor market policy to hold unemployment well below most European Community states. Recession had compounded a loss of Swedish competitiveness in international trade, and rather dramatic fiscal and monetary measures became necessary by September 1992. By late 1992 Sweden's open unemployment was rising rapidly toward Western European norms.

In sum, the global political economy has experienced extraordinary turbulence in its structure and processes that has been described by James N. Rosenau and others as unprecedented.[20] All of the major seachanges involve enormous implications for workers on all continents. Some of these implications are great opportunities, as in the case of poorer countries set to benefit from some aspects of freer internal markets as well as liberalized foreign trade and direct foreign investment. Many others are mixtures of long-term opportunities and shorter-term dangers, risks that are faced most directly by elements in the labor force that are least educated or adaptable, inadequately trained, and in need of social protection.

20. James N. Rosenau, *Turbulence in World Politics: A Theory of Change and Continuity* (Princeton, NJ: Princeton University Press, 1990).

Emphases in Recent Writings About Full Employment and the Right to Employment

The major forces and sea-changes noted in this book are closely associated with a continuing evolution (and some recycling) of ideas about employment. The combined impacts of events and ideas have shaped public policy and thoughts about employment, related rights, and governmental obligations. An effort will be made here to review recent relevant academic and official writings about employment, and related issues intended for various national, regional, and global audiences.

Our task includes the separating of the wheat from the chaff in various writings about employment. One criterion for doing this is the inherent quality of particular proposals and analyses. Another is their expected and actual impact on policy. We have already noted the influence of a wide variety of intellectual contributions to the international consideration of employment issues, some written by and for national governments or international organizations, others primarily for academic or general audiences. Some presentations, including those of Beveridge and Keynes, had substantial impact at the national and international levels within a few years of publication.[21] Others, including early contributions of Hayek and Milton Friedman, had major impacts only decades after the ideas were first presented.

On the subject of employment a disproportionate share of articles, books, chapters, and pamphlets continue to have a utopian character, apparently lacking the potential to gain substantial political or intellectual support. Some of it constitutes a literature of protest or an isolated call to arms against technological, bureaucratic, corporate, or "imperialist" targets or realities.

The ideological orientation of recent writings on employment continues to lean toward the neoclassical. There are good reasons to expect continued dominance of neoclassical liberal views. The collapse of the Soviet bloc in East-Central Europe has left those countries in search of Western advice about transition to market economies. Many, though not all, providing that advice reflect neoclassical tendencies.[22]

---

21. For recent scholarship on the diffusion of Keynesian and other economic ideas see Mary O. Furner and Barry Supple, eds., *The State and Economic Knowledge: The American and British Experience* (Cambridge: Cambridge University Press, 1990), and Peter A. Hall, ed., *The Political Power of Economic Ideas: Keynesianism Across Nations* (Princeton, NJ: Princeton University Press, 1989).

22. Galbraith argued that the flow of advice reaching those countries in 1990 was marked by "its casual acceptance of—even commitment to—human deprivation, to unemployment, and disastrously reduced living standards." John Kenneth Galbratih, "The Rush to Capitalism," *New York Review of Books*, October 25, 1990, p. 51.

The transition of these economies as well as many developing states provide great opportunities for economists and others who can help guide the way to privatization and unsubsidized production, prices, and employment. At least in the short term, this seems to have given neoclassical economics a new lease on life despite the strained aftermaths of the Thatcher and Reagan eras. Yet criticism of its tenets has also been mounting both in the East and in the West.

Post-Soviet and East-Central European economic, social, and political transitions involve major economic and political risks that neoclassical approaches may well fail to adequately anticipate. This has already begun to bring more balanced advice from diverse directions. For example, the highly influential 1991 analysis of the Soviet economy prepared by the leading economic IGOs endorsed "exceptional programs" to deal with employment in the transition period, including diverse ameliorative programs developed in Western Europe and North America.[23] Although these proposals prominently feature neoclassical suggestions concerning self-employment, qualified support is also given to public works, a broadened approach to retraining, and a "carefully formulated" system of income support for the unemployed.

Despite a widespread inclination in East-Central Europe and in the West to reject the full employment traditions of former Communist-ruled countries, it has proved impossible to do that in every case. The continuing legacy of the constitutionally guaranteed right to employment in such countries is demonstrated even in the strongly neoclassical writing of János Kornai, a leading Hungarian economist. Kornai concedes that "one of the greatest achievements of the socially planned economies in Hungary and many other socialist countries was full employment."[24] Yet he adds that this was achieved before 1990 not by incorporating the right to work in their constitutions but by specific strategies of economic growth designed to sop up the labor supply. Kornai consciously echoes Hayek's title, *The Road to Serfdom*, in his review of what he conceives to be the reverse kind of voyage. In effect, only the idea of full employment as a long-range goal and area of government responsibility remain in his formulation, the objective being "the establishment of a lasting, long-run relationship between the labor market and job rights."[25] Yet few Eastern European writers dismiss the relevance of labor market stability as completely as do certain Western neoclassical theorists.

Soviet government officials and politicians and their Russian suc-

23. IMF et al., *Study of the Soviet Economy*, 2: 164–165.
24. János Kornai, *The Road to a Free Economy* (New York: W. W. Norton, 1990), p. 199.
25. Ibid., p. 198.

cessors felt the need to soothe fears of mass unemployment. One agency called in 1990 for a "new conception of social protection for the population during the changeover to market relations."[26] A draft position paper from the USSR State Committee on Labor and Social Questions was designed to elicit broad public discussions on social protection under market conditions.[27] Notably, this transitional Soviet conceptualization retained the idea that every able-bodied person should be guaranteed the right to work, this incorporating "the freedom to earn money and, consequently, the opportunity to improve his circumstances and raise his standard of living without any restrictions."[28] This was presented as part of an effort to contrast proposed state policy with the "shock therapy" suggested by others. Yet even with an approach that minimized the dangers of massive unemployment, the spokesman for the draft, Vladimir Shcherbakov, acknowledged the need to devise "new approaches to a definition of the 'right to work.' "[29] Unemployment would not be legitimized, and the unemployed would not be left to "the mercy of fate." There would be state assistance for training and "a system of legislatively codified social guarantees representing the minimal obligations of the owner and giving him the right to use the employee's labor." Experts from international organizations and various Soviet scholars reportedly participated in the development of this document, which constitutes a potentially important step toward a market-oriented, post-Soviet conception of full employment policies. It does not, of course, answer all the questions asked by workers and others in a country and era in which the pace and extent of the transition were still being actively contested.

Growing unemployment encouraged political forces termed conservative to challenge the more radical Yeltsin administration from their base in the Russian parliament in 1992–93. The president was forced to grant major concessions to those forces, slowing economic reforms, until his significant victory in several referenda in April 1993.

Current neoclassical prescriptions for Central and Eastern Europe and for much of the developing world often rely on the willingness of these societies to accept delayed gratification. Such conceptions must contend with the reality that delayed gratification was also basic to Communist and various previous Third World economic strategies and

26. Report on press conference of Vladimir Shcherbakov, chairman of the State Committee on Labor and Social Questions, *Izvestia,* August 7, 1990, p. 2, translated in *Current Digest of the Soviet Press,* XLII, 32 (September 12, 1990): 1.

27. Ibid.

28. Ibid.

29. *Izvestia,* August 8, 1990, in *Current Digest of the Soviet Press* XLII, 32 (September 12, 1990): 2.

that there is now insufficient public patience in many cases. The challenge for the West is to encourage social, economic, and political strategies that factor in an understanding of the many decades of frustration endured by the majority of the citizens whose economies are now to be restructured. Although such understanding is not altogether lacking in such works as *A Study of the Soviet Economy*, it needs to be more tangible and responsive. It must include the encouragement of social protection for pensioners, others on fixed income or dependent, and the unemployed.

Many countries in Asia, Africa, and Latin America have had even longer experience with the politics and economics of structural adjustment than have the post-Communist regimes. No overview of thought in such diverse countries can do justice to the existing range of views. Reports published in the *New York Times* in mid-1991 claimed to have detected a coalescing of elite opinion in a large number of developing countries on behalf of liberal economic reforms and fundamental structural adjustment.[30] That newspaper indicated that it was able to confirm World Bank optimism about the broadening of the base of countries with leaderships prepared to abandon protectionist foreign investment policies, to deregulate and privatize industry and finance, and to reduce subsidies and price controls. Related to this alleged consensus was a further weakening of commitments to employment security, especially as reflected in a resolve to reduce public payrolls and to allow companies greater flexibility regarding layoffs. The *Times* series indicated a growing sense that protectionist business as usual was increasingly seen as foreclosed by international carrots and sticks. As in Eastern Europe, the perceived collapse of sectors of various national economies also made new outlooks and policies inevitable.[31]

Although these positive orientations toward neoclassical policies are seen as increasingly influential, the post Cold War climate has not eliminated contrary orientations in the developing world. One set of at least partially contrary viewpoints results from the strong industrial policy orientations of leading East Asian countries, including South Korea and Japan.[32] In the Japanese case the idea of employment security, at least in the larger firms, helps underlie strategies for redeployment of the labor force and the replacement of fading industrial sectors by more advanced ones.

30. Sylvia Nasar, "Third World Embracing Reforms to Encourage Economic Growth," *New York Times,* July 8, 1991, p. A1.

31. *World Development Report 1991* (Oxford: Oxford University Press for the International Bank for Reconstruction and Development, 1991).

32. See William McCord, *The Dawn of the Pacific Century* (New Brunswick, NJ: Transaction Books, 1991).

The South Commission, formed in 1987, represents an effort on the part of intellectuals and officials from various developing countries to respond to neoclassical pressures from the West. It follows a path set by the United Nations Conference on Trade and Development (UNCTAD), the Brandt Commission, and other official and unofficial groups created for research and advocacy. This commission's work, spearheaded by former Tanzanian President Julius Nyerere, then Prime Minister Mahathir Mohamad of Malaysia, and Manmohan Singh of India, offers a further cooling off of the New International Economic Order rhetoric. Instead it emphasizes economic cooperation among Third World states and the need to focus on developing human resources in the South. The report is notable in the context of the present book for its insistence that social questions are as important as economic dimensions in the development process, its call for development strategies that emphasize employment policy, and its protest against the increased levels of unemployment resulting from externally forced fiscal retrenchment.[33] It strongly emphasizes technology-related education and training—thereby rejecting the idea that the problems of employment and development need be approached in fundamentally different ways in the North and South.

Although recent Third World perspectives on employment and related human rights issues have received some overdue attention, writing on these subjects continues to emphasize the context of particular Western countries and regions. Such publications reflect the enormous socioeconomic and political changes noted above but also involve an ongoing reassessment of public policies carried out by the leading Western countries. To what extent is there a residue of opinion in support of full employment policies and the right to employment at this juncture? On the whole not very much emphasis is being placed on either concept, and strong right to employment advocates continue to be rather isolated in various forums. Even many negative assessments of Reagan-Bush-Thatcher policies have tended to stress outcomes other than disquieting overall employment levels, targeting instead such issues as growing income and asset inequality as well as unfairness in tax systems.

A 1989 report that rallies support for full employment from Socialist and Social Democratic perspectives itself confirms the collapse of broader support for this concept in Western Europe. The report of the Commission on Employment Issues in Europe, formed in 1986 and known as the Kreisky Commission,[34] combines some worthy updating

33. Independent Commission of the South, *Challenge to the South*, pp. 13, 15, 68.
34. Named for its President, former Austrian Federal Chancellor Bruno Kreisky. See

of thinking about economic stimulation and active labor market policy with the rallying of political forces that had been forced on the defensive throughout the 1980s. It presumes that, in Western Europe, fighting unemployment then had relatively little political support and that a kind of depoliticization of the issue had taken place. It also argues that few European politicians or governments remained wedded to the principle of full employment and that "a new orthodoxy" encouraged governments to concentrate on improved functioning of markets.[35] From their somewhat narrow ideological base, which they view as gaining increased support in the wake of the absence of progress against unemployment in the 1980s, the Commission's authors frame a new call for full employment and the right to employment. Yet even they limit their conception of full employment to the restoration of the 5 percent unemployment level of the late 1970s, this to be achieved in a half decade. Further, the right to work is now phrased as labor market and not job security, a personal right to employment opportunity but not necessarily a right to be maintained in the same job. This conception is based on Scandinavian models of rights to training and increased employment opportunity for all.[36]

Perhaps the most notable theme in the Kreisky Report is the full recognition that the best answers to mass unemployment need be developed through highly developed international coordination and harmonization, most particularly efforts to stimulate economic expansion. The report consciously builds on the European Commission's conceptions of social protection and job creation through the completion of the Community's internal market. It agrees with John Kenneth Galbraith's rejection of "the pursuit of full employment in one country,"[37] recognizing the power of other major economies to frustrate national macroeconomic policies in the absence of appropriate coordination.

A major barometer of official opinion about those rights and state duties is the ongoing flow of papal encyclicals on this subject. The one

Commission on Employment Problems in Europe, *A Programme for Full Employment in the 1990s* (New York: Pergamon Press, 1989). This Commission included John Kenneth Galbraith, former French Socialist Prime Ministers Raymond Barre and Michel Rocard, and such notable players in this chronicle as Guy Standing of the ILO and Gösta Rehn (former OECD official). Principal credit for the writing of the report is given to Ewald Walterskirchen of the Austrian Institute for Economic Research and Clas-Erik Odhner of the Swedish Trade Union Confederation.

35. Ibid., pp. xxii, 107.

36. Ibid., p. 146.

37. John Kenneth Galbraith, "Fat Years and Lean," *New York Times Book Review*, August 19, 1990, p. 11. For Phillips's views see *Politics of Rich and Poor*.

hundredth anniversary of Pope Leo XIII's *Rerum Novarum* was observed in 1991, providing an opportunity for Pope John Paul II to
provide a current perspective on the Catholic social thought advanced
by that work. It has been argued here that papal perspectives on labor
issues have often been underestimated as influences on social policy in
many Catholic and other countries. With the current trends toward
democratization in Central Europe, Catholic social thought has some
new opportunities to help shape public and elite opinion. This weight,
most evident in the close relationship of the church with Poland's
Solidarity Movement, can be exercised through the expanding role of
official church bodies and organizations as well as through Christian
Democratic and other party and trade union organizations.[38]

Centesimus Annus (The 100th Year) is limited in terms of new ground
because the Polish pope had expounded on *Rerum Novarum* a decade
earlier. The newer concerns include a stronger criticism of the treatment of much of the Third World by leading capitalist powers as well as
its focus on the needs of transitional East-Central Europe. On the
whole the guidance offered is consistent with previous recent interpretations of Catholic social thought, with no evident curtailment of
earlier themes about the materialism, consumerism, and bureaucrati-
zation of capitalist states and societies. In one memorable passage the
pope refers to a risk "that a radical capitalistic ideology could spread
which refuses even to consider such problems as global exploitation
and human alienation."[39]

The concept of a right to employment is advanced further in the
latest encyclical only in its insistence that the church's engagement with
social questions must focus on work as an essential part of its task of
preaching the Gospel. As in the 1981 *Laborem Exercens* (On Human
Work), John Paul II seeks to be more explicit than his predecessors on
this subject. The explicitness is, however, both positive and negative.
On the positive side the 1991 statement embraces various aspects of
what might be termed "active labor market policy," insisting that the
state has a duty to create economic conditions that ensure job opportunities, especially in time of crisis.[40] On the other hand the several
references to a right to work are undercut by his argument that "the
state could not directly ensure the right to work for all its citizens unless
it controlled every aspect of economic life and restricted the free initia-

---

38. See *New York Times*, May 14, 1990, p. A7.

39. Pope John Paul II, *Centesimus Annus*, May 2, 1991, in *Origins: CNS Documentary
Service* 21, 1 (May 16, 1991): 17.

40. This directly follows such an emphasis in "Economic Justice for All: Catholic
Social Teaching and the U.S. Economy," put forward by the National Conference of
Catholic Bishops in November 1986.

tive of individuals."[41] The net result is a church position that can be utilized by Catholic-oriented and other politicians holding a wide range of positions on state obligations to workers.

If the dominant character of official and quasi-official writing on employment and workers' rights was defensive between 1987 and 1991, writings by academicians in that period moved the debate both back to themes worked over decades before and forward to ideas stimulated by a new internationalism. Motivated by evidence of decline in the quality of employment in such regions as East-Central Europe and the United States, Norway's Jon Elster challenges continuing emphasis on the proportion of the population that is working for pay. He contends that in a capitalist economy "full employment can only be achieved at the expense of creating a second-rate work force that is paid lower wages than private-sector workers performing the same tasks."[42] In the United States both Kevin Phillips and Robert Reich agree that the increase in the number of American jobs in the 1980s constituted something other than a net achievement given the growth in low-paying service employment.[43] They both raise the question of job quality in ways that force the recognition that guaranteed minimum- and low-wage employment accomplishes little for the individual and even less for the country. Reich, a liberal Democrat who became the Clinton Administration's Secretary of Labor in 1993, reciprocates Phillips's ideological iconoclasm when he directs attention away from the redistribution of benefits, including work, and stresses instead enhanced skills and capacities for the population as a whole. Reich argued in 1991 that "unemployment is now less of a problem" and that the "the more important issue over the longer term is the quality of jobs, not the number."[44]

The decline of ideologically based support for full employment was remarked on by Robert W. Cox in his 1987 *tour d'horizon* of the global political economy. This neo-Marxist and neo-Gramscian writer with former ties to the ILO notes, "It is remarkable, in the light of scholarly stress on the 'legitimacy' function of the welfare states, how little opposition there has been to the tendency to sacrifice employment in the fight against inflation and how little of that has been clearly grounded in alternative ideology."[45] Cox provides a penetrating analysis of why

41. Ibid., p. 19.
42. John Elster, "Is There (or Should There Be) a Right to Work?" in Amy Guttmann, ed., *Democracy and the Welfare State* (Princeton, NJ: Princeton University Press, 1988), p. 74.
43. Phillips, *Politics of Rich and Poor*, p. 169; Reich, *Work of Nations*, esp. chapters 14, 17.
44. Reich, *Work of Nations*, p. 203.
45. Cox, *Production, Power, and World Order*, p. 445.

this lack of full employment policies occurred, stressing the roles of international non-governmental organizations (e.g., the Trilateral Commission) and intergovernmental organizations in preparing the demise of the conception of the state as the ensurer of high employment levels. He points to the OECD's McCracken Committee Report of 1977 as a negative turning point and stresses the role of the IMF in supervising a global order that set limits on national efforts to reduce unemployment in the short term. Cox emphasizes the role of what he terms "the international financial network" as "the principal external constraint" on such national policies as increased state expenditures in support of welfare state and full employment objectives.[46]

The recent academic debate on the future of employment continues the discussion, begun in 1946, concerning governmental responsibility for full employment and the possibility of a right to employment. Some new wrinkles have been added, but the student of these issues will note frequent allusions to ideas and arguments offered decades and even centuries ago.

By and large the issue of a right to employment in academic discourse has long been less an interest of economists and more one of other social scientists as well as philosophers, historians, and legal scholars. Yet few who are not economists or political economists are fully comfortable writing in practical terms about the economic requisites of full employment. As a result many discussions of the crucial concepts of this book remain amorphous or contain unconvincing prescriptions.

The calls of late-twentieth century scholars for a right to work differ in important respects from those rooted in the desperation of nineteenth century French workers or of Americans and others caught up in the Great Depression of the 1930s. Even the very high Western unemployment rates of the early to mid-1980s and 1990–93 failed to generate well-articulated demands that reflected the anguish of the long-term unemployed and others receiving diminished real social benefits. A large part of the recent Western academic discussion had an air of unreality and lacked an element of serious intent to transform public policy at the national or international level. Instead of established economic theorists debating the feasibility of a universal right to employment in the nineties, the discussion is characterized by philosophical argument that fails to achieve great urgency.[47]

46. Ibid., p. 305. Major themes of Cox's argument are supported in Caporaso, ed., *Changing International Division of Labor.*
47. Richard J. Arneson, "Is Work Special? Justice and the Distribution of Employ-

The current discussion sometimes retreats from proclaimed universal rights, shifting back to arguments for the right to employment as a dimension of national citizenship. Such an approach, mapped out by American political theorist Judith Shklar in 1991, can be viewed as setting back the clock by returning to the line of thought about citizen (and not human) rights developed by William Beveridge and T. H. Marshall, among others.[48] Shklar discovers some impressive centuries-old American roots for the right to work and argues for the essentiality of employment as a dimension of full American citizenship. However, even as a right of citizenship it is advocated as a presumption that should guide U.S. policy rather than a constitutional or legal right, a right because it is viewed as implicit in American citizenship. This "right to earn," as Shklar wisely phrases it, is "a right not to be deprived of one's standing as a citizen."[49] In her view the minimal political obligation of the state must include the creation of paying jobs that are geographically close to the unemployed and that offer them a legally set minimum wage and the chance for advancement. Such a view may well advance the present excessively limited American conception of citizenship. Yet it is not framed to project such a conception of citizenship into the international discussion of the scope of human rights.

Of course, even in the 1940s and 1950s philosophical and legal arguments for and against a right to employment were far more common than economic ones. Such themes as self-esteem, basic human needs, and distributive justice continue to be related to employment rights in the writings of Richard Arneson, British political scientist Raymond Plant, and others.[50] Such contemporary views are characteristically offered in direct reply to neoclassical opponents who have collectively succeeded in inhibiting the advancement of redistributive conceptions of rights. The political barriers to advancing a right to employment are emphasized both in the highly supportive book published in 1989 by Philip Harvey and in a strongly negative contribution

---

ment," *American Political Science Review* 84, 4 (December 1990): 1127–1147; Elster, "Is There (Or Should There Be) a Right to Work?" pp. 53–78.

48. Judith N. Shklar, *American Citizenship: The Quest for Inclusion* (Cambridge, MA: Harvard University Press, 1991). Notably, Charles Lockhart proposed in 1989 to base his proposals for additional U.S. socioeconomic rights on a conception of "producers' rights" in contrast with human or citizens' rights. Lockhart, *Gaining Ground: Tailoring Social Programs to American Values* (Berkeley: University of California Press, 1989), p. 34.

49. Shklar, *American Citizenship*, pp. 99–100.

50. See Raymond Plant, "Welfare and the Value of Liberty," *Government and Opposition* 20, 1 (1985): 297–314, and Plant, with Harry Lesser and Peter Taylor-Gooby, *Political Philosophy and Social Welfare* (London: Routledge and Kegan Paul, 1980).

by Jon Elster. Harvey argues that in the United States "groups opposed to the idea exercise substantial political power and benefit from a well-articulated ideology supporting their position."[51] He adds that even their more interventionist counterparts are less inclined than before to promote measures that extend beyond macroeconomic manipulation. The Democratic Party's belated and exceptionally limited responses to the 1991–92 U.S. recession supports this judgment. Elster emphasizes that no Western democratic country has chosen to create a legal right to employment in the wake of growing doubts about its economic and legal feasibility.[52] England's Michael Rustin asserted in 1983 that, with no British political party currently advocating a program to restore full employment and the right to work, there is "little prospect of these being restored."[53] Given the subsequent non-socialist trends in Labor Party positions there is little reason to believe that Rustin would have a different judgment a decade later.

Yet support for the right to employment persists, often consciously or unconsciously echoing prior arguments. Elster acknowledged in 1988 that, "in the past ten or fifteen years, in particular, the proposal to create a legal right to work has been put forward and discussed in most Western countries."[54] One can still find a presentation of "a practical program to secure the right to employment," a term used by Harvey that could well have been taken directly from seventeenth century English tracts.[55] Harvey's proposal builds on the same foundation that Gösta Rehn stood on twenty years earlier—that such countries as Sweden and Japan already represented virtual full employment states and that the best lessons from such systems could be transferred flexibly and with cultural sensitivity to other strong economies. Michael Rustin's proposal centering on labor boards with overall responsibility for subsidies to employers and a mandate to create jobs has even closer links than Harvey's to the three hundred year tradition of English practical and utopian proposals.[56]

The idea of a right to employment is defined by Harvey as "the obligation of society to ensure adequate employment opportunities for all job-seekers."[57] Rustin calls for a similar "universal access to work at a

---

51. Philip Harvey, *Securing the Right to Employment* (Princeton, NJ: Princeton University Press, 1989), p. 113.
52. Elster, "Is There (or Should There Be) a Right to Work?" pp. 53–54.
53. Michael Rustin, "A Statutory Right to Work," *New Left Review* 137 (January–February 1983): 51–52.
54. Elster, "Is There (or Should There Be) a Right to Work," p. 53.
55. Harvey, *Securing the Right to Employment*, p. 5.
56. Rustin, "Statutory Right to Work," pp. 60–63.
57. Harvey, *Securing the Right to Employment*, p. 97.

fair income."[58] Arneson, concerned with devising a right that meets his standards of equality, self-esteem, and dignity, proposes a moderately high standard for the quality of state-guaranteed employment offered as a matter of right.[59] Less evident in the current proposals is the idea of an enforceable individual legal right to obtain a job. The consensus clearly supports a qualified state obligation to promote full employment rather than an individual legal right to a job.

Summing up this review of recent comments relating to employment issues, it is evident that advocates of both full employment obligations of government and the right to employment are on the defensive but are still active in the arenas of academic and public debate. This debate is marked by cyclical tendencies that peaked in the early to mid-1980s in the direction of downplaying concern for even mass unemployment. In that political climate advocates for social protection generally, and the right to employment and full employment obligations of governments in particular, often conceded in advance that their support was too thin to successfully advance such ideas at the national or international level in the short run. Some of this reluctance also derived from perceived structural changes relating to technology and the globalization of the corporation. It was argued that such forces were now too powerful to accommodate full employment obligations. As more people agreed with Dahrendorf that fewer workers would be able to produce the needed goods, public optimism tended to focus on the employment creation potential of political and economic integration and liberalized trade as well as more flexible labor markets more than on state obligations to the unemployed.

Nonetheless, it is evident that voices favoring public responsibility for the unemployed, many feeling a need to provide decent jobs as a human right, would not be stilled. Part of this relates to the opportunity provided by the passage of time for neoclassical or radical conservative approaches to political economy to alienate many left behind. Those appalled by associated income inequality, imposed austerity, and unfair tax practices again grew stronger.

At this writing, in June 1993, it is too early to read definitively the inconsistent and rapidly changing ideological trends in countries having or soon to have national elections. Neglect of mass unemployment ultimately brings very real demands for policies more consistent with societal needs for national solidarity and economic security. In several important countries pressures are building for new and recycled em-

---

58. Rustin, "Statutory Right to Work," p. 57.
59. Arneson, "Is Work Special?" pp. 1144–1145.

ployment measures that are consistent with prevailing national budget constraints.

While many of the serious discussions of employment, the welfare state, and socioeconomic rights discussed above incorporate awareness of the impacts of international forces, few systematically addressed the roles of international organizations and regimes. Exceptions to this include the South Commission's emphases on structural adjustment and conditionality policies of the IMF and the World Bank and the Kreisky Commission's effort to integrate its proposals with developments in the European Community. In the following section I will suggest further trends and prospects for affecting employment through international agencies and regimes.

International Regimes and Employment: The Current Phase

The dramatic changes in global and regional politics in the late 1980s and early 1990s markedly transformed many of the specialized international regimes that had been partially shaped by Cold War politics. While this has been most evident in areas of international security and finance, such other issue areas as employment and human rights have also been greatly affected by the ending of the Cold War and related realignments in international relations.

The transformation of international regimes has involved both the universalization of membership in international organizations and the intensification of regional integration. Universalization was greatly facilitated by the ending of the Cold War, which made possible the admission of some divided and new states as well as Communist and post-Communist regimes to such organizations as the United Nations, the IMF, and the World Bank. This process had already been underway by 1989, but new impetus came as economic aid for East Central Europe, the Soviet Union, and its successors became an important interest of the Western leaders. Economic interdependence was viewed as bolstering domestic political prospects for new regimes as well as regional peace. In this new climate neutral Western states also felt freer to make or explore new organizational ties.

Universalization of critical economic regimes has augmented the power of leading intergovernmental organizations as, for example, their stabilization and development loans flowed to a wider range of countries. Also, in the current climate new forms of cooperation have emerged between global and regional agencies, as exemplified by the association of two global (IMF, World Bank) and three Western regional organizations (OECD, the European Community, and the European Bank for Reconstruction and Development) in recent official efforts to promote the adaptation of the economies of Russia and East-Central Europe.

Such globalization already has had positive impacts on employment, providing new sources of funding, research, and advice in support of such aspects of active labor market policy as training, public works, and placement services. The pre-existing reliance on the ILO for global assistance for such programs is now being supplemented by more involvement by the OECD, IMF, and World Bank staffs in such regions as South Asia and Eastern Europe.[60] On the whole, Western economic organizations and political leaders have demonstrated somewhat greater concern for "the harsh by-products of reform" in East-Central Europe than in most of the rest of the world, presumably because of enhanced awareness of the political consequences of unmitigated economic shock treatments.[61]

In the short run this globalization will advance approaches to structural adjustment favored by the staffs of several of these organizations as well as by the consensus of leading Western governments. An example of this is the accelerated liberalization of markets and government regulatory and tax practices in India in 1991 in anticipation of IMF loan conditionality. However, these organizations and their principal donor countries should anticipate that full globalization may well eventually lead to new constraints on conditionality as the recipients of unwelcome pressures are encouraged to coalesce and resist various measures that increase unemployment and political disaffection.[62] Such inclinations to resist build in part on recognition that the highly successful East Asian models for growth featured strong national government intervention. They are also stimulated by consciousness that even the present level of $30 billion annually in combined IMF/World Bank/UN Development Program financing does not match the continuing reverse flow of funds from the South to the North resulting from the debt crisis built up a decade earlier. Pressures from within these organizations to markedly increase international liquidity were building in 1993.

60. On World Bank support for India's vocational training see International Labor Conference, 76th Sess., 1989, *Record of Proceedings* (Geneva: ILO, 1990), p. 8/10.

61. See the U.S. Secretary of State's appeal for assistance by the ILO and other organizations to ameliorate such "harsh by-products" in International Labour Conference, 77th Sess., 1990, *Record of Proceedings* (Geneva: ILO, 1991), p. 11/7.

62. See "Brazil Wins Skirmish with IMF," *New York Times*, July 25, 1991, p. C2. Such developments are placed in context in Thomas J. Biersteker, "Reducing the Role of the State in the Economy: A Conceptual Exploration of IMF and World Bank Prescriptions," *International Studies Quarterly* 34, 4 (December 1990): 477–492.

In an array of available forums, including UNCTAD, the ILO, and the United Nations itself, Third World spokespersons of various ideological persuasions have continued to challenge conditionality agreements and their implications. The ILO Director-General noted in 1990 that the International Labor Office "continued to present an alternative approach to adjustment policy in which equity and participation considerations figure prominently."[63] Yet no breakthrough in power has been achieved by developing countries working through friendly forums. The International Labor Office has apparently had to restrain its inclinations to challenge structural adjustment, and instead often facilitates it. This has been balanced in part by increased attention to the negative employment and poverty impacts of forced restructuring in U.N. organs, including the General Assembly, the Economic and Social Council (ECOSOC), the Commission on Human Rights, and the Commission's Sub-Commission on Prevention of Discrimination and Protection of Minorities. These activities have opened up channels through which human rights standards and implementing agencies are increasingly being turned to in order to challenge the raw political and economic power of the sometimes callous champions of restructuring.[64] Human rights implementation devices such as special rapporteurs and official reports have been introduced into the politics of economic restructuring to express the preferred approach of the United Nations to implementing socioeconomic rights in the context of enforced austerity. However, the ability of such U.N. organs to alter the policies of the leading lending agencies through such pressures does not seem great.

The central question for international global policy and regimes regarding employment is the potential for fundamental transformation in the wake of momentous political and economic developments. The international employment regime described in Chapter 5 reflected limited organizational development as well as a consensus that employment was still essentially and primarily a domestic issue. It also involved reluctance to utilize global or regional agencies to promulgate or implement authoritative international rules or policy mandates except in such limited areas as social security and where certain human rights principles were implicated. Questions remain as to how such

---

63. International Labour Conference, 77th Sess., 1990, *Report of the Director-General, Part II: Activities of the ILO, 1989* (Geneva: ILO, 1990), p. 8.

64. See Reed Brody, Penny Parker, and David Weissbrodt, "Major Developments in 1990 at the UN Commission on Human Rights," *Human Rights Quarterly* 12 (1990): 559–588; and Brody et al., "The 42nd Session of the Sub-Commission on Prevention of Discrimination and Protection of Minorities," *Human Rights Quarterly* 13, 2 (May 1991): 260–290.

factors as widening European Community policy and geographic scope will affect these tendencies, how the universalization of the principal financial organizations will affect employment at a global level, and what new roles such long-committed organizations as the ILO and the OECD will take on in the near and medium terms.

The international employment regime is still marked by ambivalence and compromise regarding the setting and enforcement of standards that touch directly on the right to employment as well as state duties to promote full employment. Although leadership in the enforcement of labor standards, including those connected to human rights, remains in the ILO, only dim echoes remain of the previous efforts of its Committee of Experts on the Application of Conventions and Recommendations to sharply criticize various national regimes for neglect of mass unemployment. My review of the 1989 and 1990 reports of the ILO's Expert Committee found a rather benign approach to the responsibility of most states for employment, with moderate criticism of selected Western European states (including Ireland, Italy, and France) standing as exceptions to this pattern. The Committee has been inclined to accept imposed structural adjustment as a sufficient excuse for Third World failures to deal with unemployment and give the East-Central European countries a substantial grace period. Such leniency was even extended to the absence of meaningful estimates of national unemployment and underemployment by many governments, an approach that seems unduly generous in some cases and a clear retreat from the Committee's posture less than a decade earlier.

A typical example of recent standard-setting regarding unemployment was the ILO's drafting of a Convention Concerning Employment Promotion and Protection Against Unemployment, adopted in 1988. It broke very little new ground regarding a right to employment or active labor market policy and focused on unemployment insurance. One workers' representative noted that the "essential standards—at least as regards the industrialized countries—do not even surpass those levels which had clearly become standard practice at the end of the 1920s" in leading Western European countries, referring here primarily to unemployment insurance.[65] New options to allow any ratifying state to suspend standards temporarily were accepted. Among the few gains since the previous ILO effort to deal with employment was the fact that a binding convention was adopted, a course that was not taken in 1984,

---

65. Mr. Adamy of the German Federal Republic, in International Labour Conference, 75th Sess., 1988, *Record of Proceedings* (Geneva: ILO, 1989), p. 35/24.

and the decision to stress the need to find "suitable" employment when denying insurance benefits.

The weakening of the ILO supervisory role is being partially balanced by a determined effort to enhance the processes and roles of the relatively new U.N. committee responsible for implementing the International Covenant on Economic, Social, and Cultural Rights. While the committee, under the leadership of Philip Alston and others, has not yet attempted to seek remediation of deficient national efforts, it has made substantial progress in just a few years to improve state reporting on Covenant provisions and to elaborate the meaning of that covenant constructively and authoritatively. Although a strong admirer of the committee indicated in 1991 that "no one would dispute that economic, social, and cultural rights remain de facto second class rights," he added that it is increasingly becoming a body in which people can vest hope for change.[66]

Perhaps an avenue for further breakthroughs in the implementation of economic and social rights will be the 1993 World Conference on Human Rights to be held in Vienna. Some of its ninety sponsors in the United Nations view further development of implementation, at national, regional, and global levels, to be a ripe diplomatic issue. However, at this writing the prospects for a constructive effort to set a new agenda for human rights are not promising.[67]

The current politics of international standard-setting and enforcement also reflects changing political and economic trends. The absence of various Communist spokespersons left the lines of contention in the ILO operating primarily along worker-employee as well as North-South lines. The major change in East-Central European rhetoric was epitomized by then Polish Prime Minister Mazowiecki's comment to the 1990 International Labor Conference: "Full employment—at the

66. Scott Leckie, "An Overview and Appraisal of the Fifth Session of the UN Committee on Economic, Social, and Cultural Rights," *Human Rights Quarterly* 13 (1991): 568–569. See also Cindy A. Cohn and Matthew Lenton, "The Gold Ring: The Fourth Session of the Committee on Economic, Social and Cultural Rights," *HRI Reporter* 14.1 (Summer–Autumn 1991): 89–91; Henry J. Steiner, *Diverse Partners: Non-Governmental Organizations in the Human Rights Movement* (Cambridge, MA: Harvard Law School Human Rights Program and Human Rights Internet, 1991); Philip Alston, "Out of the Abyss: The Challenges Confronting the New U.N. Committee on Economic, Social and Cultural Rights," *Human Rights Quarterly* 9 (1987): 322–381; and "A Turning Point: Two Views on the 2nd Session," *Human Rights Internet Reporter* 12, 3 (Spring/Summer 1988): 63–66.

67. Penny Parker and David Weissbrodt, "Major Developments at the UN Commission on Human Rights in 1991," *Human Rights Quarterly* 13, 4 (November 1991): 609; Pauline Comeau, "General Assembly Is Called Upon to Salvage the 1993 World Conference on Human Rights," *Human Rights Tribune*, 1, 3 (Fall 1992): 22–23.

price of waste and economic stagnation—is no longer the ideal situation for us. Unemployment is not ideal either, but it is a necessity that we have to learn to live with, just as the other market economies."[68] The Soviet government's representative endorsed both the 1988 ILO convention and the unorthodox and conservative-oriented conciliation process that shaped the final product. A few years later a delegate to the International Labor Conference referred to that organization's "first post-Cold War programme and budget."[69] Clearly the East-West dimension of the international politics of employment was being rapidly and profoundly transformed in various intergovernmental forums.

While a political struggle between workers' and employers' organizations was played out in the watering down of the 1988 ILO employment convention, it is the North-South division that has become distinctly more salient in an array of organizations shaping global approaches to employment and human rights issues. Although no single Third World position can be distinguished, frequently stated views include reluctance to codify additional labor standards or to be judged on public policy outcomes that are viewed as decisively influenced by external forces. Additionally, a broadened southern coalition has sought to use ILO and U.N. forums that can potentially be dominated by Third World spokespersons to challenge the dominance of structural adjustment advocates in the leading economic and financial organizations. Various Third World governments have also resisted making ILO technical assistance to particular member states contingent on that organization's assessment of previous compliance with certain ILO standards.

Having traced some specific changes in intergovernmental agency activities involving employment, we need to explore the potential for fundamental changes in the international order affecting unemployment, underemployment, and the conditions of workers. One reason to do so is the emerging evidence that international cooperation in a variety of issue areas is being fundamentally transformed in the 1990s in the wake of monumental global and regional changes. Sometimes with clear U.S. government leadership, as in the 1990–91 Gulf War, and other times as a result of broad coalitions mobilized by other states, the potential for breakthroughs in various global policy issues seems greater than before. From the August 1991 attempted Soviet coup to the postwar attempts to control Iraq's nuclear efforts, from attempts to

68. International Labour Conference, 77th Sess., 1990, *Record of Proceedings* (Geneva: ILO, 1991), p. 12/3.
69. International Labour Conference, 78th Sess., 1991, *Report II: Draft Programme and Budget 1992–93 and Other Financial Questions* (Geneva: ILO, 1991), p. 2.

dismantle South African apartheid to the environmental politics of ozone and rain forests, the willingness of the international community to respect national sovereignty seems to have lessened. This provides some hope for constructive international involvement with such issue areas as employment that have been viewed as essentially national responsibilities for so long.

The arena for which promising international policy responses are most possible is the European Community and its potential areas of expansion and influence. Other possible sources of augmented regional and global involvements affecting employment include the G-7 governments' efforts to improve international coordination of monetary and fiscal policies, old and new intergovernmental lending agencies with expanded financial resources, and the evolution of Britain and the United States away from radical conservative (or hyperliberal) policies. Further, there is a possibility that the employment problems of the Third World will gain greater saliency as they become increasingly linked with such issues as trade and environmental protection. None of these factors assures a major transformation of the politics of employment even in Europe, much less globally. Yet together they offer hope of greater than incremental change through such mechanisms as regional redistribution of funds, promotion of social learning in new contexts, and new rule-making.

The lack of substantial growth in financial resources experienced by most major IGOs in recent years will certainly limit the opportunities for transformation. And in several cases available additional funds are being competed for by governments as never before. In the principal new sphere of large-scale funding, the flow of Western monies to Russia and East-Central Europe, fiscal and monetary policy conditions have not always been met by receiving countries, delivery on commitments has been slow,[70] intergovernmental coordination has been frustrated, and the role of employment promotion and safety net issues have not been as prominent as might have been hoped.[71]

Many of the paradoxes noted in this book are rooted in European Community ideas and experiences. One central idea associated with the completion of the internal market is a liberal commitment to the efficiency of markets freed from barriers impeding the production and movement of goods, services, capital, and labor.[72] One of the central initial promises of the Single European Act of 1987 was very substan-

70. *New York Times*, May 5, 1990, p. A5.
71. Guy Standing and Gyorgy Sziracki, "Introduction: Labour Market Issues in Eastern Europe's Transition," *International Labour Review* 130, 2 (1991): 137–144.
72. See Cecchini, *European Challenges*.

tial job creation, specifically 1.8 million additional jobs and the reduction of the EC-wide unemployment rate by some 1.5 percentage points.[73] Yet another principal goal of the post-1985 transformation of the Community was to markedly increase the international trade competitiveness of its member states. As is evident in the large scale corporate reductions in force on both sides of the Atlantic in the early 1990s, competitiveness is not necessarily viewed as compatible with employment security—especially in the short run. It will be interesting to see how Europe will play out the built-in tensions between the social market pressures for employment and income security on the one hand and the increasingly difficult competitive pressures from North America, East Asia, and elsewhere on the other.

To a far greater extent than ever before the European Community of the 1990s is in a position to lead international efforts to minimize unemployment and promote active labor market policies. This results primarily from the nature of the negotiations associated with the Single European Act of 1987 that will double the Community's structural fund resources to about 14 billion ECU by 1993. It also involves the important role of the Community in aiding and guiding post-Communist East-Central Europe as well as the new opportunities for social legislation in the new era of completion of the internal market. Social learning has at least temporarily shifted from the boundaries of the Community and OECD to a broader external sphere of influence, and the intensity of Community and OECD cooperation with each other and with other intergovernmental agencies has grown markedly.

The year 1991 turned out to be one of the most significant for the European Community members and aspiring members. In December eyes were on Maastricht, Netherlands, where the twelve member states worked to negotiate a new Community order that would go beyond the Single European Act in a wide array of policy areas and also transform Community decision-making. Strikingly, this Community Summit functioned simultaneously with the first efforts to restructure relations among the emerging post-Soviet republics at the Brest Summit, and followed by only a few months the apparently successful negotiation of a new European Economic Area (EEA) that would take the EFTA states far beyond EC associate status. Although the structure, powers, and decision-making processes of the future European order were not settled by these summits and agreements, the outlines of a new European order seemed generally clearer in their aftermath.

The treaty creating the EEA potentially extends European Community social policy, together with many other areas of Community policy

73. Ibid., p. 97.

later expanded at Maastricht, to the EFTA nations.[74] If allowed to become operative it will inaugurate free movement of workers among the nineteen associated states (with Switzerland granted five extra years to comply). Most observers view the treaty as a transitional step toward amalgamating the twelve with all or most of the EFTA states, and are impressed by the extent that the EFTA states agreed to be governed by EC rules without receiving major interim power in Community decision-making.[75]

At the opening of the December 1991 Maastricht Summit it was not clear whether the Community would poise itself for further major political transformation that would allow it to go well beyond the 1987 Single European act. At the Summit the situation in such areas as monetary union and defense cooperation clearly advanced but the social policy issues relating to employment were partial victims of the compromises and creative diplomacy forced largely by British intransigence. Before Maastricht the Community had put itself further into the forefront on employment and related social issues through such means as the implementation of the Single European Act's commitment to double its structural fund resources and its assumption of a leading role in the coordination of aid and guidance to East-Central Europe. Additionally, many plans were being floated to redistribute power on social issues, still viewed primarily as employee-management matters.

At the close of Maastricht the monetary union appeared to have been given critical impetus, with agreement on the goals of a European central bank and a common European currency before the end of the 1990s. This process was tied to criteria on interim member state economic performance aimed at promoting low common levels of inflation and fiscal discipline. In the context of the ongoing widespread recession such measures did not bode well for further efforts to stimulate European economies. However, long-term prospects for a more competitive Community seemed to have advanced. It is much less clear whether democratization was advanced at Maastricht, with the European Parliament gaining only incrementally even as national parliaments were to be asked to cede very important policy turf. Maastricht again confirmed the point that "at the core, the Community has always been a mechanism for governments to bargain."[76]

Building on the catch-word "cohesion," the principle that poorer

74. "EC, EFTA Create a Larger Common Market," *Eurecom* 3, 10 (November 1991): 1.

75. "Into the Unknown," *The Economist*, July 13, 1991, p. 58; "Lest a Fortress Arise," p. 81.

76. Wayne Sandholtz and John Zysman, "1992: Recasting the European Bargain," *World Politics* XL, 1 (October 1989): 115.

countries should pay less into the EC's budget was placed in a legally binding protocol and a cohesion fund was to be set up by 1994 to help pay for environmental and transport projects.[77] Additionally, qualified majority voting was agreed to in new treaty chapters applying to sociocultural issues ranging from consumer protection to education. Maastricht built on the redistributive approach of the Single European Act compromise, which had already committed, in its most generous case, EC structural fund aid to Greece equal to 5 percent of that country's GNP by 1993.[78]

On an array of issues at the core of the present study politics at Maastricht was strained but the outcomes seemed moderately hopeful. At stake was the viability of potential new Community legislation in an array of social policy areas linked to a social market approach to political economy.[79] This policy has been embodied as a set of principles and standards in the EC Charter on Basic Social Rights (henceforth Social Charter), signed by eleven heads of government in December 1989, and was subsequently developed into a forty-seven-point Social Action Programme and a set of proposed European Commission directives.[80] This process has already demonstrated an ability to achieve effective advances through further standardization of the practices and approaches to labor issues of the most corporatist and socially protective member states. Yet its scope and strength have always been limited by the bargaining power of Community employer groups, the British government, and other less enthusiastic forces. Both the Action Programme and the provision at Maastricht for a separate Agreement on Social Policy are little more than statements of intent. However, it is now clear that if the Maastricht initiative for a Treaty on European Union can be ratified in a coherent version, the Social Europe initiatives in such areas as the labor market, freedom of movement, social protection, equal treatment of men and women,[81] and health and

77. Protocol on Economic and Social Cohesion in European Communities, *Treaty on European Union* (Luxembourg: European Communities, 1992), pp. 202–203; *The Economist*, December 14, 1991, p. 52.

78. Sandholtz and Zysman, "1992," p. 121.

79. See "Sozialpartnerschaft," *The Economist*, November 16, 1991, p. 74.

80. For a chronology of Community actions see Juliet Lodge, "Forward," in *Social Europe*, special issue of *Journal of European Integration* 13, 2–3 (Winter–Spring 1990): 131–133. For an authoritative Community viewpoint see Patrick Venturini, *1992: The European Social Dimension* (Brussels: European Communities, 1989).

81. Gender equality rules, perhaps the Community's area of greatest social policy leadership in the 1970s, had become less innovative by the late 1980s and were viewed by some observers as more subject to patriarchical national and Commission attitudes. Elizabeth Meehan, "Sex Equality Policies in the European Community," *Journal of European Integration* 13, 2–3 (Winter–Spring 1990): 194–195.

safety in the workplace can advance, at least in each member state other than Britain. Regarding employment policy per se, the Commission summarized the situation in 1988 as follows:

Although this remains the responsibility of Member States and is still therefore outside the scope of the Community, a start has been made on concerting national policies. There have been exchanges of information and experiences and resolutions have been adopted, dealing in particular with flexibility of retirement age, fighting long-term unemployment, the contribution of local employment-creation initiatives to the struggle against unemployment, and an action programme for increased employment.[82]

In 1989 Paul Teague and John Grahl suggested that the contemporary Community debate included the issue of "whether the Community should adopt interventionist legislation and policies to regulate the European labour market."[83] After Maastricht such an interventionist approach remains possible, but had not been explicitly endorsed. The principle of subsidiarity, involving deference to national solutions to commonly perceived problems, was affirmed at Maastricht while explicit reference to a federal European future was negotiated out of the final language. The eleven-nation Agreement on Social Policy signed at Maastricht affirmed in its Article I the objectives of "the promotion of employment, improved living, and working conditions, proper social protection, dialogue between management and labour, [and] the development of human resources with a view to lasting high employment and the combating of exclusion."[84] Maastricht was primarily the voice of the governments that will continue to dominate the Community through Council meetings and subsequent summits. Even more hopeful are the European Parliament's and Commission's commitments in the period leading up to Maastricht to emphasize labor legislation relating to such major issues as paid leave for training, children's work, gender equality, and the rights of refugees and guest workers.[85] In 1988 various Nordic spokespersons contrasted their own positive record on employment policies with that of the Community.[86]

82. "The Social Policy of the European Community: Looking Ahead to 1992," *European File* 13, 88 (August–September 1988): 4.
83. Paul Teague and John Grahl, "European Community Labour Market Policy: Present Scope and Future Direction," *Journal of European Integration* 13, 1 (Winter 1989): 1.
84. Agreement on Social Policy in European Communities, *Treaty on European Union*, p. 197.
85. "Up the Workers," *The Economist,* June 29, 1991, p. 64.
86. Cited in a review by Toivo Miljan of J. Jamar and H. Wallace, eds., "More Than Just Good Friends?" in *Journal of European Integration* 13, 2–3 (Winter–Spring 1990): 234.

Perhaps this perception can be altered before the end of the century in the wake of the initiatives of Francois Mitterand, Jacques Delors, Helmut Kohl and others from the mid-1980s to the aftermath of Maastricht.

Many of the developments relating to Maastricht are subject to further delay and compromise at this writing as a result of the close defeat of the Maastricht proposals in a 1992 Danish referendum (reversed in 1993), the severe monetary crisis in the fall of 1992, and continuing strong British opposition. Such developments can be welcomed if they result in subsequent adjustments that promote broader participation in European decision-making, raise new social concerns to the fore, and prevent present and future monetary integration and discipline from strangling national efforts to stimulate recessionary economies. The key requirements of European monetary union outlined at Maastricht appear to be on a collision course with existing monetary and fiscal policies in most Community states as well as in various countries seeking early admission to the EC.

Whereas the European Community is in the process of major transformations that will affect aspects of policy ranging from employment training to treatment of foreign workers, the OECD has changed much less quickly or fundamentally. Some OECD leaders would like the organization to become a vehicle for effective policy collaboration for a broader range of countries that would include the former Soviet republics and bloc as well as what it terms the "dynamic Asian economies" of East and Southeast Asia. It already serves to link Japan and Australasia with its expanding European area of attention. Yet at this point its influence in new geographical areas will be largely through data- and policy-monitoring as well as consultation.[87]

The OECD sees a likely growth in its involvement with "multilateral surveillance" as well as with legally binding international agreements.[88] The former will involve the strengthening of its "structural surveillance programme," relating to the basic elements of liberal structural adjustment, as well as somewhat increased attention to national programs needed to expand and upgrade labor forces. While a new round of OECD policy statements regarding the labor market emerged in 1990,[89] these fell short of being legally binding agreements and failed to advance its policy advice much beyond that in the 1964 and 1976

87. OECD, *The Annual Report of the OECD* (Paris: OECD, 1991), pp. 7–8.
88. Ibid., p. 9.
89. In the spring of 1990 the Manpower and Social Affairs Committee as well as the OECD Council approved the policy statement, "Challenges and Opportunities in the 1990s," and a Secretariat report entitled "New Framework for Labour Market Policies."

OECD Council instruments. Those documents added a new focus on broadened labor force participation and the upgrading of human resources, using the rubric of the "Active Society." Economic liberalization continued to hold a firmer and less conflicted hegemony in the OECD than in the Community in the early 1990s despite the OECD Secretary General's 1991 statement that "it would be a shame if the OECD was characterized at the end of the century as an economic success and a social failure."[90] It has been rarer for social market or social democratic approaches to employment to be effectively promoted in the OECD context as compared with the Community. OECD publications continued to support the reduction of industrial subsidies and social security taxes rather than their harmonization and to emphasize the pitfalls of interventionist industrial policies. The Organization's emphasis on labor participation and upgrading has in recent years been juxtaposed with statements that appear to devalue the need for regular, long-term, and full-time employment.

A recent returning visitor to OECD headquarters would find some significant changes made in the past decade. The Organization is much more likely than before to be working in formal cooperation with one or more of a half dozen regional and global economic and social policy IGOs, including the IMF, World Bank, European Community, Conference on Security and Cooperation in Europe, and ILO. Further, its leadership, like that of other major economic IGOs, takes credit for a somewhat greater staff capability in social science analysis outside of economics. This has facilitated improved and expanded research and monitoring of such topics as migration of workers and families as well as the relationship between technology and economic growth.

Yet the same visitor would also note that the work of the dominant Economic Policy Committee and Directorate continued to emphasize values and goals other than full employment even as the 1990–93 recession dragged on. The increasingly perceptive work of the Manpower and Social Affairs Committee on negative employment trends failed to be strongly reflected in the Secretary-General's Annual Report in 1990, which tended to stress the Economic Policy Committee's emphasis on control of inflation as the key to continued economic expansion. The OECD seemed quite slow to alert its member states to the risk of serious recession that began in 1990 and intensified in 1992 and 1993 in much of Europe, though the Manpower and Social Affairs Directorate and Committee did sound alarms about both the growing

90. *New York Times,* June 9, 1991, p. F7.

political crisis in Europe concerning worker migration and a sharp rise in unemployment in most of the members states in 1991.[91]

Conclusion

The central questions of this book revolve around the meaningfulness of regional and global influences on national employment policy and the potential for considering employment as an internationally recognized human right. Has employment been considered a distinct policy area meriting a global or regional policy response? Did an employment policy regime emerge, and to what extent did it overlap with international human rights regimes?

The 1985–92 period was one of great opportunity for those seeking to advance an employment regime as well as global and regional policy. It was a time of such momentous global and regional developments as the ending of the Cold War and the decisions of the European Community to move further toward political and economic union. Unemployment was increasingly perceived as a global policy issue, and not merely a problem of developed market economies. In many developing countries debt obligations, lending agency conditionality, and impacts of structural adjustment exacerbated national and regional employment trends while necessary actions were taken to promote market liberalization. Third World unemployment grew in the second half of the 1980s in the midst of what most of the First World experienced as a major economic expansion. Even in many favored developed countries the boom of the 1980s ended with unemployment at a higher level than at the end of the previous cyclical expansion.[92] And the recession of 1990–93 brought unemployment levels to politically dangerous levels in such countries as Britain, France, Spain, Germany, and Italy.

Despite these and other forces for transformation the global and regional employment regimes remained limited in structural development, resources, powers, and functions, and failed to more fully develop identities separate from those of extant economic and human rights regimes. Employment remained a recognized regional policy issue of considerable urgency only in some parts of Europe. It developed further as a human rights issue only in a few international forums oriented to socioeconomic rights. For the most powerful global IGOs and Western governments employment was not so much a distinct

---

91. OECD, *Employment Outlook: July 1991* (Paris: OECD, 1991), p. 5.
92. Ibid., pp. 37, 40.

global policy issue as a socioeconomic concern secondary to such regime-defining concepts as development and economic growth.

The structure of a global regime concerned with employment advanced with the emergence of an assertive United Nations Committee on Economic, Social, and Cultural Rights. Yet this step forward only seemed to balance out a loss of momentum for ILO supervision of standards in areas ranging from active labor market policy to social insurance. The OECD, a critical actor in the embryonic employment regime of the 1970s, spread its geographic reach but failed to intensify its activities in the most affluent countries on behalf of full employment policies. No highly influential rights-oriented or policy-based international rules or standards were produced in the most recent period. Notably, no broad-based rebirth occurred for the most positive concepts underlying national and international commitment to protect against mass unemployment, these being full employment goals and the right to employment or paid work. The most powerfully phrased endorsement of the full employment concept, the 1989 Kreisky Commission Program, resulted from the work of an independent Social Democratic and labor-oriented body, and not from a mainstream intergovernmental organization or conference. Contemporaneously, ideological support for these concepts declined greatly in the emergent independent republics of the former Soviet Union as well as in the politically liberated East-Central European states. Intellectual support for the core concepts continued to be expressed in academic circles, but this did not generate a groundswell at any national or international level for a new effort to prevent mass unemployment.

The failure to advance an employment regime was strikingly reflected in economic data for the 1980s. Goals of an employment regime based on international social learning and technical assistance, combined with significant financial redistribution and standard-setting in parts of Europe, were largely unmet. The OECD reported in a recent summary of the issue area that, "by historical, post-war standards, the 1980s were a decade of particularly high unemployment."[93] For the OECD countries as a whole, the average unemployment rate for 1980–89 was 7.3 percent, compared to a figure of 5 percent or less for the period from 1960–79. The share of unemployment that was long-term also grew markedly, and no overall progress could be reported for the facilitation of geographic mobility of employees within their own country.[94] Such a positive trend as the improved ratio of female to male

93. Ibid., p. 37.
94. Ibid., p. 53.

earnings also leveled off in the 1980s.[95] Finally, the dramatic differences in standardized unemployment rates among the leading market economies remained largely untouched by efforts to influence the outcomes in such laggard countries as Spain and Ireland. The gaps between, for example, Northern and Southern Europe and between North America and Southern Europe grew markedly from the 1970s to the 1980s.[96] The comparative unemployment situation of women and youth improved somewhat, but that of foreign workers deteriorated.

Perhaps even clearer evidence of the limited impact of an employment regime was the failure to influence greater harmonization of national policies in such areas as active labor market policies. For example, the following percentages of GDP expended on public labor market programs shown in Table 1 were reported for major OECD countries in 1985 and 1990. Overall, national expenditures showed no major trend to increase or decrease. Unemployment insurance declined markedly in relative terms in the large majority of OECD countries, even in countries without proportional declines in unemployment. Official concerns communicated through the OECD and other forums about the loss of labor market flexibility from overly generous unemployment programs may have been influential. Growing national budget deficits and more conservative national leadership also contributed. Although no OECD-wide trend appeared for spending on active labor market measures, there was an interesting tendency for European Community member states to partially catch up to the Nordic states. On the whole the Nordic states leveled off, with Sweden—the global leader—showing a significant drop. In the Community the states that rose closest to the Nordic level for active measures were Italy, Germany, Ireland, and Spain. With Belgium and the Netherlands already spending over one percent of GDP on active measures in 1985, the overall trend was one of considerable EFTA-EC convergence. Countries left out of the trend to more substantial active public programs included the United States, an earlier pioneer in this domain, as well as Australia, Austria, Canada, Greece, Japan, Great Britain, Luxembourg, Portugal, Switzerland, and Turkey. This produced a strong dichotomy between the European and non-European membership, with several exceptions evident in the European group. A further regime impact was to reinforce the inclination of political leaders not to engage in major public direct job creation programs. In 1989–90 only

95. Ibid., p. 55.
96. Ibid., p. 40; OECD, *Employment Outlook: July 1990* (Paris OECD: 1990), p. 36.

TABLE 1. Public Expenditure on Labor Market Programs as a percentage of GDP, Active Measures and Income Maintenance*

| | Australia | | Austria | | Belgium | |
	1985–86	1990–91	1985	1990	1985	1989
Active measures	0.39	0.25	0.28	0.30	1.23	1.12
Income maint.	1.31	1.07	0.96	0.97	3.43	2.80
Total	1.70	1.32	1.24	1.27	4.66	3.92

| | Canada | | Denmark | | Finland | |
	1985	1989–90	1986	1989	1985	1990
Active measures	0.63	0.51	1.06	1.35	0.91	0.94
Income maint.	1.87	1.57	3.90	4.49	1.34	1.11
Total	2.50	2.08	4.97	5.83	2.25	2.05

| | France | | Germany | | Great Britain | |
	1985	1989	1985	1990	1985–86	1990–91
Active measures	0.67	0.73	0.81	1.02	0.72	0.59
Income maint.	2.41	1.92	1.41	1.16	2.06	0.90
Total	3.07	2.65	2.23	2.18	2.79	1.49

| | Greece | | Ireland | | Italy | |
	1985	1989	1985	1989	1985	1988
Active measures	0.21	0.42	0.45	0.80	0.45	0.80
Income maint.	0.43	0.46	1.04	0.72	1.04	0.72
Total	0.64	0.88	1.49	1.52	1.49	1.52

| | Japan | | Netherlands | | Spain | |
	1987–88	1990–91	1985	1989	1985	1989
Active measures	0.16	0.13	1.09	1.04	0.34	0.80
Income maint.	0.40	0.32	3.24	2.30	2.89	2.41
Total	0.56	0.45	4.33	3.34	3.23	3.21

| | Sweden | | Switzerland | | United States | |
	1985–86	1990–91	1985	1990	1985–86	1990–91
Active measures	2.11	1.58	0.17	0.17	0.30	0.25
Income maint.	0.87	0.67	0.28	0.14	0.61	0.60
Total	2.97	2.25	0.46	0.30	0.90	0.85

*Active measures (line 1) include public employment services and administration, labor market training, youth measures, subsidized employment, and measures for the disabled. Income maintenance (line 2) includes unemployment compensation and early retirement for labor market reasons. Totals (line 3) reflect variations due to rounding.
Source: OECD, *Employment Outlook: July 1991* (Paris: OECD, 1991), pp. 237–250.

Belgium and Finland, among the 23 reporting OECD states, spent more than 0.25 percent of their GDP for this purpose.

A somewhat greater degree of convergence could be observed in the sphere of legal job security for those already employed. To a limited but important extent access to the courts for job protection grew in the United States while it declined somewhat in much of Western Europe. "Fire at will" was weakened at the federal, and especially at the state, level in the United States, as various public policy and other criteria were successfully raised in order to restrain American employers. Western European employees lost some of their administrative protection but remained substantially better protected than their American counterparts against both mass and individual termination.

The impact of the employment regime was limited in part by the absence of any one intergovernmental organization with a commitment to deal with unemployment and job growth from an integrated perspective that combined policy and rights. Full employment policy clearly requires far more than the strategies identified as active labor market policy. It must integrate the following strategies and approaches.

Human Rights and Ethics. A full employment strategy should incorporate a rights-based approach. Such an approach facilitates and builds on a spirit of national socioeconomic solidarity as well as on ethical concerns for social justice. Although the extension of such an approach from rights of citizens to human rights can be difficult to put into effect, the case for socioeconomic justice and at least minimal entitlements for all can be justified philosophically and morally. The rights that need to be assured in principle include equal employment opportunity, free association, and security against arbitrary and sudden termination of employment. These should be combined with a reinforced duty of all states to use all available policy instruments to prevent high levels of unemployment.

Many of the lessons of the history of advocacy of a right to employment are clearly negative, and have provided historical evidence of pitfalls and unanswered questions. Implementing such a right is not feasible without full integration of the establishment of such a right with a broad panoply of effective employment-oriented social and economic policies. If such a right is to exist it must be based on the duties of each state and a more effective international regime for implementation of full employment. This regime should effectively utilize the best of international social learning about employment-related policies and seek to elevate socioeconomic rights to the level that political and civil rights are held in the leading constitutional democracies. Without an effective rights dimension full employment has been repeatedly sacrificed to concerns and interests relating to inflation and trade competitiveness that may or may not have been valid. The right that must be championed must be more than an entitlement to mere subsistence or income maintenance. Rather, it should be recognized that the opportunity to receive pay for work is understood by a very large part of every society as an indication of full citizenship and even full humanity.

Many of the critical remaining questions about socioeconomic rights are presently being answered by organs of the ILO and United Nations as well as by scholars.[97] Obligations of states must be effective immediately and must grow with their resources and capabilities. States must not be permitted to trade mass unemployment or its exacerbation for other political or economic interests. Intergovernmental organs and forums can define responsibilities of national governments as well as their own obligations. Potential workers or the long-term unemployed may never be able to win lawsuits to gain particular jobs or the right to any employment, but they should have recourse to complain to international organizations when states ignore the interests of workers. National, regional, and global agencies should be held fully accountable on a frequent and timely basis regarding their efforts to promote full employment and to avoid mass unemployment. Rapporteurs and on-site visiting delegations must reinforce existing reporting and hearing processes, adapting methods already employed to guard against such violations as genocide and disappearances.

This is an era in which "down-sizing" and "lean-and-mean" corporate strategies are emphasized throughout much of the world, and job security and corporate responsibility for employee welfare lie far down the list of priorities. Pressures for international competitiveness and the opportunities provided by technological breakthroughs allow and encourage such "flexibility," and recent recessions have provided an environment enabling firms in and out of financial difficulties to reduce workforces drastically or to move large-scale operations to countries with cheaper and less protected labor without engendering substantial public criticism. Weakened labor unions are less and less able to contend with these pressures and actions, instead concentrating on such issues as required procedures associated with redundancies as well as the protection of pension and other assets owed to employees.

Another major manifestation of the ethical and moral gap is the relative lack of concern for Third World unemployment and under-

97. For an impassioned recent plea for "the human rights of the disadvantaged" see Clarence J. Dias, "Realizing the Human Rights of the Disadvantaged," *ICJ Review* 45 (December 1990): 37–45.

employment by many governments of those countries as well as the greater part of the international community. It is as if this issue is moot in the absence of fully acceptable national data and massive civil unrest. Economic development and structural adjustment strategies are evaluated and advocated without appropriate concern for predictable transitional or long-term mass unemployment.

At the root of full employment policy should be concern for individual victims of mass unemployment as well as for the potential social and political risks in affected societies. Without a sense of solidarity for all members of a society, no strategies involving policy or rights will be fully effective. Some of the core ethical and moral dilemmas about welfare rights from prior decades and centuries have been partly overcome. We no longer blame the victims of mass unemployment as much as we once did, recognizing now that personal motivation cannot overcome all adversity. Policy incentives and disincentives can motivate many unemployed workers to find and accept less desired work in some circumstances, and intentional overstaffing and most job creation schemes do not offer a sound long-term strategy for firms or government units. Yet the root of all full employment policy must be concern for the workers who are already victims or are vulnerable to economic cycles, technological change, and negative trade impacts. Workers need a trump card in the form of national and international commitments to full employment that have legislative, regulative, and financial teeth and meaningful methods for monitoring and implementation.

Macroeconomic Policy. Employment is necessarily only one of the concerns that national and supranational agencies must consider when steering national economies with fiscal, monetary, and other economic policies. Productivity, competitiveness, and price and wage stability are clearly also vital to the short- and long-term welfare of national and regional economies. The central issue is one of priorities and the weight that full employment plays in macroeconomic policies that dominate national economic policy. The critical British and American Employment Acts of the 1940s recognized the centrality of macroeconomic policy for full employment, and were initiated with confidence that Keynesian macroeconomic policies would successfully avoid mass unemployment. No rights-based or policy-based full employment strategy can succeed without a solid basis in macroeconomic policy dedicated to avoiding large-scale unemployment. Such fiscal and monetary policies of the various major states must be coordinated, with full employment as a major goal of such efforts. Coordination must not be allowed to choke off necessary stimulation of faltering or recessionary national or global economies.

Much of the failure to deal effectively with unemployment since the 1960s results from the frequent ineptness of national macroeconomic policies as well as intergovernmental efforts to seek financial stability together with growth. The priorities of most finance ministries and central banks and their counterparts in the OECD and IMF are quite different than those of many Labor and Social ministries and such of their counterparts as the ILO. The dominance of agencies controlling fiscal and monetary policy in national, regional and global economic policymaking is evident in the present study. Labor and Social ministries and the ILO are relegated to the promotion of microeconomic and social policies that cannot compete in total impact with macroeconomic policy unless they are funded at the level of the Swedish active labor market program.

The thrust of the present book is not to favor consistently accommodative fiscal and monetary policies. The responsibility for the prolonged recession of the early 1990s is substantially due to excessive fiscal pump-priming by some national governments amidst the long-term economic expansion of the 1980s. In contrast, more responsible fiscal and monetary policies fostered by steps toward economic and monetary union have helped several European Community countries to set their financial houses in better order and to be in a better position to participate in a European resurgence.[98] Efforts at accomodation need be coordinated or harmonized at the global and regional levels in order to prevent the frustration of necessary national efforts.

Yet there is a glaring absence of concern for unemployment trends in many of the most important reports and statements from the IMF, the OECD, and their counterparts in major Western governments. Monetary policy is periodically allowed to tighten abruptly and severely—effectively planning and implementing higher levels of unemployment. Although accommodative monetary and fiscal policies cannot alone assure a strong climate for economic growth, profits, and employment, an overly restrictive approach to monetary and/or fiscal policies can certainly negate strategies that include commitments to rights and to active labor market policies.

Macroeconomic policies embodied in the financial stabilization and conditionality efforts of the IMF and other agencies and banks involved with the extension of credit to many Third World and other governments often have a severe negative impact on employment,

---

98. See *The Economist*, December 14, 1991, p. 52. Pressures for fiscal and monetary policy coordination and constraint delayed accommodative national policies in Western Europe in 1992 and 1993. "The Economics of European Disintegration," *The Economist*, May 22, 1993, p. 56.

especially in the short term. Further, the negative effect on employment of a global debt problem that peaked several years ago at approximately one trillion U.S. dollars has been and continues to be enormous. While some significant momentum for partial write-offs of debt has accelerated in the more realistic political and economic environment of recent years, Japan and other lending states continue to place limits on the amelioration of this central problem. Debt has helped throw much of East-Central Europe and Africa into depression, and it continues to threaten economic and political progress in Latin America. It also constrains export opportunities to each of those region, and thus limits economic growth in even the strongest export-oriented economies. Lending for financial stabilization as well as debt reduction strategies must be influenced much more than they presently are by considerations of employment stability and growth.

Industrial, Investment, and Trade Policy. Industrial, foreign investment, competition, and trade policies raise difficult problems from an employment perspective insofar as the maximization of advantage for national industries may well result in beggar-thy-neighbor results. Yet each of these policy areas needs to be pursued in the interest of growth and full employment at the national, regional, and global levels.

A full recognition of the realities of global interdependence requires a global approach to both industrial and trade policy that maximizes employment growth and stability. Appropriate industrial policies can steer countries and regions toward more competitive export postures and can help assure rising living standards for the average worker. Combined with progressive human resource development they can stimulate viable home-grown industries and attract the most appropriate direct multinational investment. The European Community offers a model of how substantial human resource and regional development funds can be channeled through international authorities. Bargaining by national governments at critical political junctures facilitated both substantial augmentation of such resources and increased hopes for future competitiveness in weaker member states and their most vulnerable or underdeveloped regions.

In the aftermath of the Cold War an effective global employment regime will have to incorporate similar ideas in order to prevent the renewed transformation of national economic conflicts into political and even military ones. The most positive scenarios for a more viable global economic community also depend on some constraints on the existing efforts of major exporting countries to compete to displace each other in particular national and regional markets. A closely related source of economic conflict is the increasingly costly competition to use public resources for export stimulation and to promote research and development breakthroughs by home-based firms. With the end of the overarching Cold War it is possible to anticipate a transition from such unrestrained economic competition to new political and military conflicts. At the root of such conflict may be a grave concern for employment security in the three existing centers of economic power as well as in other regions.

Employment and the Welfare State. William Beveridge and Richard Titmuss are among the most prominent of the writers who focused on the reciprocal impacts of social welfare and employment policies. Among the most penetrating recent analysis of this relationship is Gösta Esping-Andersen's *The Three Worlds of Welfare Capitalism*. In this and other works Esping-Andersen portrays three models through which "welfare regimes" have integrated or failed to integrate employment and welfare policies and goals. He distinguishes a cluster of welfare states as liberal, another as corporatist-statist, and a third as social democratic.[99] Virtually every advanced welfare state is viewed as sharing attributes of more than one approach but fitting primarily into one or the other. Esping-Andersen finds that "Of the many social institutions that are likely to be directly shaped and ordered by the welfare state, working life, employment, and the labor market are perhaps the most important."[100] The welfare state is traced as a major employer, as a facilitator of labor turnover and rationalization, and as a device for negotiating deferred compensation through the social wage. He concludes with the view that the contemporary welfare state is a powerful societal mechanism that decisively shapes the future in terms of the structure of employment as well as other critical aspects of societal change.

With this impressive book as context, it is possible to conceive of changes in welfare states that can maximize human resources and promote full employment. Especially given the recent difficulties even in Swedish welfare and labor market policies, no one country can serve as a clear model. The real need is to examine all aspects of the welfare state mix with minimal ideological blinders.

The utility of such programs often depends on fine tuning and planning. Early retirement measures that connect the labor market and pension systems may or may not prove productive to governments and firms, depending on such factors as whether resulting vacant positions are refilled. National health care delivery systems (or non-systems) may save jobs through controlled government and firm out-

99. Gösta Esping-Anderson, *The Three Worlds of Welfare Capitalism* (Princeton, NJ: Princeton University Press, 1990), p. 27.
100. Ibid., p. 141.

lays. Bad health insurance systems prevent desired mobility among workers whose insurance is tied to a particular employer. International interest in such issues has increased our knowledge of such larger and smaller consequences as well as the menu of social welfare and labor market measures that work in particular social, cultural, and political contexts.

Active Labor Market and Education Policies. Active labor market policies are among the most important measures developed directly in response to the fear or actuality of high unemployment. They are often discussed separately from education policies but should be understood as needing to be integrally linked to educational efforts from preschool to adult. No country that seeks to compete for multinational investment and shares of markets for sophisticated technology can afford not to effectively prepare its children for each level of education; maintain high expectations and standards at all levels and in all educational tracks; provide the large proportion of secondary school graduates who do not advance to higher education with communication skills and flexible knowledge of technology; ensure a smooth transition from school to employment; establish lifelong opportunities for necessary further education and retraining; assure the full commitments of various levels of government, as well as employers and labor unions; target those groups with the least relevant skills and the least opportunities in the present and future labor market; and provide innovative higher education that gives full due to science, technology, and the communication and human relations skills of the liberal arts.

Critical knowledge about education and active labor market policy must be learned from diverse societies and needs to be adapted to each particular country with concern for its cultural, social, economic, and political distinctiveness. The purpose of a given country's program may well be served by a very different structure in another society. As such, certain imperative goals need be accepted while methods are experimented with. The structure for effective training can be an American community college, a German apprenticeship program, or a training center of the Swedish Labor Market Board. Whether from public, trade union, or corporate contributions of funding and training, programs need be developed that enable the changing labor force to meet the challenges determined by international competition.

Appropriate models and ideas are not in short supply. The Kreisky Commission Report embodies but one excellent blueprint. While perhaps demonstrating overattachment to such labor-supported solutions as work hour reductions, it is anything but parochial in its endorsement of broad education together with lifelong retraining, its focus on the need to further stimulate investment and employment in such areas as environmental protection, infrastructure, and information technologies, and its call to target backward regions as well as such groups as the long-term unemployed, foreign workers, racial minorities, women, and the disabled. In this last theme it merges with the "Active Society" emphasis of the OECD. Clearly, countries with low birth rates and rapidly aging populations can hardly afford to concentrate on measures that reduce the size of their labor force. As the new U.S. Clinton administration reviews its options for labor market policy it will have as much international experience to review as exists in the health care field. It may also benefit from extensive national and IGO efforts to evaluate particular measures. This is a policy area that will profit from a highly pragmatic orientation, stressing proven experience with such measures as apprenticeships for youths, required corporate investments in training, and tax incentives for the employment and retention of targeted groups. Better labor market policy requires the careful study of past weaknesses and failures as successful national programs are selectively adapted to national and regional cultures and needs.[101]

Development Policy. There is a need to greatly augment the role that employment plays in national and intergovernmental development policies. The contributions of the ILO in technical assistance related to labor markets have always been marginal, and the major lending IGOs have not yet developed a sufficient emphasis on human resource development. There is no question that vast opportunities exist to remove impediments to economic growth through structural liberalization, including privatization and removal of barriers to direct investment and to importation of various goods. Yet the painful transitions that are being experienced are exacerbated by the lack of adequate social protection for the unemployed and for the poor, who lose direct or indirect subsidies for basic goods. More attention needs to be given, as has been explicit in the current East-Central European transitions, to developing critical national and regional systems and structures that can sustain trade, monetary stability, and labor markets.

The overall need is for regime and global policy development that incorporates and integrates each of these policy areas in order to overcome the fragmentation of IGO roles and ensure the necessary social learning, development of norms and rules, resource redistribution, and technical assistance. The result needs to be a social and human rights regime as well as one for economic policy. Global policy

101. For a rather hardheaded collection of papers written from a U.S. perspective see D. Lee Bawden and Felicity Skidmore, eds., *Rethinking Employment Policy* (Washington, DC: Urban Institute Press, 1989).

needs to reach well beyond the present politics of comparative disadvantage in order to maximize a far greater degree of social justice and to modify the inevitable pain that results from unrestrained and unequal economic power. This can be accomplished best with a largely new approach to intergovernmental activity affecting employment, one that looks at the global needs of the 1990s and beyond, much as Western Europe looked hard at its needs in the late 1980s and early 1990s.

Industrialization and affluence created the possibilities for realizing the long-advocated ideal of a guarantee of paid work as a human right. The impact and memory of the global depression of the 1930s, combined with World War II, made this goal popular and timely. Then the faltering of dreams of much greater affluence beginning in the 1970s weakened the power and feasibility of the idea. Declining labor movements, forced to shift from proactive to defensive and protective measures, weakened the base of support. Market-based ideologies were restored to prominence and power, and shifted the ground on which the struggle was fought. Association of full employment and the right to employment with the Soviet system in an era of intensified Cold War further eroded the base of support.

Yet the ideas of full employment and the right to paid work remain part of the political language of our times, partly because they have been endorsed in international declarations, conventions, and recommendations. They also gain from new experience with post-Communist mass unemployment, persistent high levels of unemployment in many OECD countries, and increasing awareness of unemployment as an aspect of Third World poverty. Fortunately, the knowledge needed to formulate measures that can help countries and regions to approach full employment continues to be discovered and disseminated, much of this through international processes. The national, regional, and global programs that have been designed to promote employment constitute a wealth of experience to be adapted and integrated with a wide array of other social and economic policy initiatives.

Appendix I. International Labor Organization

Convention No. 122
Convention Concerning Employment Policy[1]

The General Conference of the International Labour Organisation,

Having been convened at Geneva by the Governing Body of the International Labour Office, and having met in its Forty-eighth Session on 17 June 1964, and

Considering that the Declaration of Philadelphia recognises the solemn obligation of the International Labour Organisation to further among the nations of the world programmes which will achieve full employment and the raising of standards of living, and that the Preamble to the Constitution of the International Labour Organisation provides for the prevention of unemployment and the provision of an adequate living wage, and

Considering further that under the terms of the Declaration of Philadelphia it is the responsibility of the International Labour Organisation to examine and consider the bearing of economic and financial policies upon employment policy in the light of the fundamental objective that "all human beings, irrespective of race, creed or sex, have the right to pursue both their material well-being and their spiritual development in conditions of freedom and dignity, of economic security and equal opportunity", and

Considering that the Universal Declaration of Human Rights provides that "everyone has the right to work, to free choice of employment, to just and favourable conditions of work and to protection against unemployment", and

1. Adopted July 9, 1964, date of coming into force: July 15, 1966. Source: International Labour Organisation, *Conventions and Recommendations Adopted by the International Labour Conference, 1919–1966* (Geneva: International Labour Office, 1966), pp. 1097–1099.

Noting the terms of existing international labour Conventions and Recommendations of direct relevance to employment policy, and in particular of the Employment Service Convention and Recommendation, 1948, the Vocational Guidance Recommendation, 1949, the
Vocational Training Recommendation, 1962, and the Discrimination
(Employment and Occupation) Convention and Recommendation,
1958, and
Considering that these instruments should be placed in the wider framework of an international programme for economic expansion on the
basis of full, productive and freely chosen employment, and
Having decided upon the adoption of certain proposals with regard to
employment policy, which are included in the eighth item on the
agenda of the session, and
Having determined that these proposals shall take the form of an international Convention,
adopts this ninth day of July of the year one thousand nine hundred and sixty-
four the following Convention, which may be cited as the Employment Policy
Convention, 1964:

Article 1

1. With a view to stimulating economic growth and development, raising
levels of living, meeting manpower requirements and overcoming unemployment and underemployment, each Member shall declare and pursue, as a
major goal, an active policy designed to promote full, productive and freely
chosen employment.

2. The said policy shall aim at ensuring that—
(a) there is work for all who are available for and seeking work;
(b) such work is as productive as possible;
(c) there is freedom of choice of employment and the fullest possible opportunity for each worker to qualify for, and to use his skills and endowments
in, a job for which he is well suited, irrespective of race, colour, sex,
religion, political opinion, national extraction or social origin.

3. The said policy shall take due account of the stage and level of economic
development and the mutual relationships between employment objectives
and other economic and social objectives, and shall be pursued by methods that
are appropriate to national conditions and practices.

Article 2

Each Member shall, by such methods and to such extent as may be appropriate under national conditions—
(a) decide on and keep under review, within the framework of a co-ordinated
economic and social policy, the measures to be adopted for attaining the
objectives specified in Article 1;
(b) take such steps as may be needed, including when appropriate the establishment of programmes, for the application of these measures.

Article 3

In the application of this Convention, representatives of the persons
affected by the measures to be taken, and in particular representatives of
employers and workers, shall be consulted concerning employment policies,

with a view to taking fully into account their experience and views and securing their full co-operation in formulating and enlisting support for such policies.

Article 4

The formal ratifications of this Convention shall be communicated to the Director-General of the International Labour Office for registration.

Article 5

1. This Convention shall be binding only upon those Members of the International Labour Organisation whose ratifications have been registered with the Director-General.

2. It shall come into force twelve months after the date on which the ratifications of two Members have been registered with the Director-General.

3. Thereafter, this Convention shall come into force for any Member twelve months after the date on which its ratification has been registered.

Article 6

1. A Member which has ratified this Convention may denounce it after the expiration of ten years from the date on which the Convention first comes into force, by an act communicated to the Director-General of the International Labour Office for registration. Such denunciation shall not take effect until one year after the date on which it is registered.

2. Each Member which has ratified this Convention and which does not, within the year following the expiration of the period of ten years mentioned in the preceding paragraph, exercise the right of denunciation provided for in this Article, will be bound for another period of ten years and, thereafter, may denounce this Convention at the expiration of each period of ten years under the terms provided for in this Article.

Article 7

1. The Director-General of the International Labour Office shall notify all Members of the International Labour Organisation of the registration of all ratifications and denunciations communicated to him by the Members of the Organisation.

2. When notifying the Members of the Organisation of the registration of the second ratification communicated to him, the Director-General shall draw the attention of the Members of the Organisation to the date upon which the Convention will come into force.

Article 8

The Director-General of the International Labour Office shall communicate to the Secretary-General of the United Nations for registration in accordance with Article 102 of the Charter of the United Nations full particulars of all ratifications and acts of denunciation registered by him in accordance with the provisions of the preceding Articles.

Article 9

At such times as it may consider necessary the Governing Body of the International Labour Office shall present to the General Conference a report on the working of this Convention and shall examine the desirability of placing on the agenda of the Conference the question of its revision in whole or in part.

Article 10

1. Should the Conference adopt a new Convention revising this Convention in whole or in part, then, unless the new Convention otherwise provides,
(a) the ratification by a Member of the new revising Convention shall *ipso jure* involve the immediate denunciation of this Convention, notwithstanding the provisions of Article 6 above, if and when the new revising Convention shall have come into force;
(b) as from the date when the new revising Convention comes into force, this Convention shall cease to be open to ratification by the Members.
2. This Convention shall in any case remain in force in its actual form and content for those Members which have ratified it but have not ratified the revising Convention.

Article 11

The English and French versions of the text of this Convention are equally authoritative.

Recommendation No. 122
Recommendation concerning Employment Policy[1]

The General Conference of the International Labour Organisation,
Having been convened at Geneva by the Governing Body of the International Labour Office, and having met in its Forty-eighth Session on 17 June 1964, and
Considering that the Declaration of Philadelphia recognises the solemn obligation of the International Labour Organisation to further among the nations of the world programmes which will achieve full employment and the raising of standards of living, and that the Preamble to the Constitution of the International Labour Organisation provides for the prevention of unemployment and the provision of an adequate living wage, and
Considering further that under the terms of the Declaration of Philadelphia it is the responsibility of the International Labour Organisation to examine and consider the bearing of economic and financial policies upon employment policy in the light of the fundamental objective that "all human beings, irrespective of race, creed or sex, have the right to pursue both their material well-being and their spiritual development in conditions of freedom and dignity, of economic security and equal opportunity", and
Considering that the Universal Declaration of Human Rights provides that "everyone has the right to work, to free choice of employment, to just and favourable conditions of work and to protection against unemployment", and
Noting the terms of existing international labour Conventions and Recommendations of direct relevance to employment policy, and in par-

1. Adopted July 9, 1964. Source: International Labour Organisation, *Conventions and Recommendations Adopted by the International Labour Conference, 1919–1966* (Geneva: International Labour Office, 1966), pp. 1100–1111.

ticular of the Employment Service Convention and Recommendation, 1948, the Vocational Guidance Recommendation, 1949, the Vocational Training Recommendation, 1962, and the Discrimination (Employment and Occupation) Convention and Recommendation, 1958, and

Considering that these instruments should be placed in the wider framework of an international programme for economic expansion on the bais of full, productive and freely chosen employment, and

Having decided upon the adoption of certain proposals with regard to employment policy, which are included in the eighth item on the agenda of the session, and

Having determined that these proposals shall take the form of a Recommendation,

adopts this ninth day of July of the year one thousand nine hundred and sixty-four the following Recommendation, which may be cited as the Employment Policy Recommendation, 1964:

I. Objectives of Employment Policy

1.(1) With a view to stimulating economic growth and development, raising levels of living, meeting manpower requirements and overcoming unemployment and underemployment, each Member should declare and pursue, as a major goal, an active policy designed to promote full, productive and freely chosen employment.

(2) The said policy should aim at ensuring that—

(a) there is work for all who are available for and seeking work;
(b) such work is as productive as possible;
(c) there is freedom of choice of employment and the fullest possible opportunity for each worker to qualify for, and to use his skills and endowments in, a job for which he is well suited, irrespective of race, colour, sex, religion, political opinion, national extraction or social origin.

(3) The said policy should take due account of the stage and level of economic development and the mutual relationships between employment objectives and other economic and social objectives, and should be pursued by methods that are appropriate to national conditions and practice.

II. General Principles of Employment Policy

2. The aims of employment policy should be clearly and publicly defined, wherever possible in the form of quantitative targets for economic growth and employment.

3. Representatives of employers and workers and their organisations should be consulted in formulating policies for the development and use of human capacities, and their co-operation should be sought in the implementation of such policies, in the spirit of the Consultation (Industrial and National Levels) Recommendation, 1960.

4.(1) Employment policy should be based on analytical studies of the present and future size and distribution of the labour force, employment, unemployment and underemployment.

(2) Adequate resources should be devoted to the collection of statistical data, to the preparation of analytical studies and to the distribution of the results.

5.(1) Each Member should recognise the importance of building up the means of production and developing human capacities fully, for example through education, vocational guidance and training, health services and housing, and should seek and maintain an appropriate balance in expenditure for these different purposes.

(2) Each Member should take the necessary measures to assist workers, including young people and other new entrants to the labour force, in finding suitable and productive employment and in adapting themselves to the changing needs of the economy.

(3) In the application of this Paragraph particular account should be taken of the Vocational Guidance Recommendation, 1949, the Vocational Training Recommendation, 1962, and the Employment Service Convention and Recommendation, 1948.

6.(1) Employment policy should be co-ordinated with, and carried out within the framework of, over-all economic and social policy, including economic planning or programming in countries where these are used as instruments of policy.

(2) Each Member should, in consultation with and having regard to the autonomy and responsibility in certain of the areas concerned of employers and workers and their organisations, examine the relationship between measures of employment policy and other major decisions in the sphere of economic and social policy, with a view to making them mutually reinforcing.

7.(1) Where there are persons available for and seeking work for whom work is not expected to be available in a reasonably short time, the government should examine and explain in a public statement how their needs will be met.

(2) Each Member should, to the fullest extent permitted by its available resources and level of economic development, adopt measures taking account of international standards in the field of social security and of Paragraph 5 of this Recommendation to help unemployed and underemployed persons during all periods of unemployment to meet their basic needs and those of their dependants and to adapt themselves to opportunities for further useful employment.

III. General and Selective Measures of Employment Policy

General Considerations

8. Employment problems attributable to fluctuations in economic activity, to structural changes and especially to an inadequate level of activity should be dealt with by means of—
(a) general measures of economic policy; and
(b) selective measures directly connected with the employment of individual workers or categories of workers.

9. The choice of appropriate measures and their timing should be based on careful study of the causes of unemployment with a view to distinguishing the different types.

General Measures: Long Term

10. General economic measures should be designed to promote a continuously expanding economy possessing a reasonable degree of stability, which provides the best environment for the success of selective measures of employment policy.

General Measures: Short Term

11.(1) Measures of a short-term character should be planned and taken to prevent the emergence of general unemployment or underemployment associated with an inadequate level of economic activity, as well as to counterbalance inflationary pressure associated with a lack of balance in the employment market. At times when these conditions are present or threaten to appear, action should be taken to increase or, where appropriate, to reduce private consumption, private investment and/or government current or investment expenditure.

(2) In view of the importance of the timing of counter-measures, whether against recession, inflation or other imbalances, governments should, in accordance with national constitutional law, be vested with powers permitting such measures to be introduced or varied at short notice.

Selective Measures

12. Measures should be planned and taken to even out seasonal fluctuations in employment. In particular, appropriate action should be taken to spread the demand for the products and services of workers in seasonal occupations more evenly throughout the year or to create complementary jobs for such workers.

13.(1) Measures should be planned and taken to prevent the emergence and growth of unemployment or underemployment resulting from structural changes, and to promote and facilitate the adaptation of production and employment to such changes.

(2) For the purpose of this Recommendation the term "structural change" means long-term and substantial change taking the form of shifts in demand, of the emergence of new sources of supply, national or foreign (including supplies of goods from countries with lower costs of production) or of new techniques of production, or of changes in the size of the labour force.

(3) The dual objective of measures of adaptation to structural changes should be—

(a) to obtain the greatest benefit from economic and technical progress;
(b) to protect from financial or other hardship groups and individuals whose employment is affected by structural changes.

14.(1) To this end, and to avoid the loss of production entailed by delays in filling vacancies, Members should establish and adequately finance programmes to help workers to find and fit themselves for new jobs.

(2) Such programmes should include—

(a) the operation of an effective employment service, taking account of the provisions of the Employment Service Convention and Recommendation, 1948;
(b) the provision or encouragement of training and retraining facilities designed to enable workers to acquire the qualifications needed for lasting employment in expanding occupations, taking account of the provisions of the Vocational Training Recommendation, 1962;
(c) the co-ordination of housing policy with employment policy, by the provision of adequate housing and community facilities in places where there are job vacancies, and the provision of removal grants for workers and their dependants by the employer or out of public funds.

15. Special priority should be given to measures designed to remedy the serious, and in some countries growing, problem of unemployment among young people. In the arrangements for young persons envisaged in the Employment Service Convention and Recommendation, 1948, the Vocational Guidance Recommendation, 1949, and the Vocational Training Recommendation, 1962, full account should be taken of the trends of structural change, so as to ensure the development and the use of the capacities of young persons in relation to the changing needs of the economy.

16. Efforts should be made to meet the particular needs of categories of persons who encounter special difficulties as a result of structural change or for other reasons, such as older workers, disabled persons and other workers who may find it particularly difficult to change their places of residence or their occupations.

17. Special attention should be given to the employment and income needs of lagging regions and of areas where structural changes affect large numbers of workers, in order to bring about a better balance of economic activity throughout the country and thus to ensure a productive utilisation of all resources.

18.(1) When structural changes of exceptional magnitude occur, measures of the kinds provided for in Paragraphs 13 to 17 of this Recommendation may need to be accompanied by measures to avoid large-scale, sudden dislocation and to spread the impact of the change or changes over a reasonable period of time.

(2) In such cases governments, in consultation with all concerned, should give early consideration to the determination of the best means, of a temporary and exceptional nature, to facilitate the adaptation to the structural changes of the industries affected, and should take action accordingly.

19. Appropriate machinery to promote and facilitate the adaptation of production and employment to structural changes, with clearly defined responsibilities in regard to the matters dealt with in Paragraphs 13 to 18 of this Recommendation, should be established.

20.(1) Employment policy should take account of the common experience that, as a consequence of technological progress and improved productivity, possibilities arise for more leisure and intensified educational activities.

(2) Efforts should be made to take advantage of these possibilities by methods appropriate to national conditions and practice and to conditions in each industry; these methods may include—
(a)   reduction of hours of work without a decrease in wages, within the framework of the Reduction of Hours of Work Recommendation, 1962;
(b)   longer paid holidays;
(c)   later entry into the labour force, combined with more advanced education and training.

IV. Employment Problems Associated with Economic Underdevelopment

Investment and Income Policy

21. In developing countries employment policy should be an essential element of a policy for promoting growth and fair sharing of national incomes.

22. With a view to achieving a rapid expansion of production, investment and employment, Members should seek the views and active participation of

employers and workers, and their organisations, in the elaboration and application of national economic development policy, and of the various aspects of social policy, in accordance with the Consultation (Industrial and National Levels) Recommendation, 1960.

23.(1) In countries where a lack of employment opportunities is associated with a shortage of capital, all appropriate measures should be taken to expand domestic savings and to encourage the inflow of financial resources from other countries and from international agencies, with a view to increasing productive investment without prejudicing the national sovereignty or the economic independence of the recipient countries.

(2) In order to utilise the resources available to these countries rationally and to increase employment therein as far as possible, it would be desirable for them to co-ordinate their investments and other development efforts with those of other countries, especially in the same region.

Promotion of Industrial Employment

24.(1) Members should have regard to the paramount need for the establishment of industries, public or private, which are based on available raw materials and power, which correspond to the changing pattern of demand in domestic and foreign markets and which use modern techniques and appropriate research, in order to create additional employment opportunities on a long-term basis.

(2) Members should make every effort to reach a stage of industrial development which ensures, within the framework of a balanced economy, the maximum economic production of finished products, utilising local manpower.

(3) Particular attention should be given to measures promoting efficient and low-cost production, diversification of the economy and balanced regional economic development.

25. Besides promoting modern industrial development, Members should, subject to technical requirements, explore the possibility of expanding employment by—
(a) producing, or promoting the production of, more goods and services requiring much labour;
(b) promoting more labour-intensive techniques, in circumstances where these will make for more efficient utilisation of available resources.

26. Measures should be taken—
(a) to promote fuller utilisation of existing industrial capacity to the extent compatible with the requirements of domestic and export markets, for instance by more extensive introduction of multiple shifts, with due regard to the provision of amenities for workers on night shift and to the need for training a sufficient number of key personnel to permit efficient operation of multiple shifts;
(b) to create handicrafts and small-scale industries and to assist them to adapt themselves to technological advances and changes in market conditions so that they will be able to provide increasing employment without becoming dependent on such protective measures or special privileges as would impede economic growth; to this end the development of co-operatives should be encouraged and efforts should be made to establish a complementary relationship between small-scale and large-scale industry and to develop new outlets for the products of industry.

Promotion of Rural Employment

27.(1) Within the framework of an integrated national policy, countries in which there is much rural underemployment should place special emphasis on a broadly based programme to promote productive employment in the rural sector by a combination of measures, institutional and technical, relying as fully as possible on the efforts of the persons concerned. Such a programme should be founded on adequate study of the nature, prevalence and regional distribution of rural underemployment.

(2) Major objectives should be to create incentives and social conditions favourable to fuller utilisation of local manpower in rural development, and to improve productivity and quality of output. Means appropriate to local conditions should be determined, where possible, by adequate research and the instigation of multi-purpose pilot projects.

(3) Special attention should be devoted to the need for promoting opportunities for productive employment in agriculture and animal husbandry.

(4) Institutional measures for the promotion of productive employment in the rural section should include agrarian reforms, adapted to the needs of the country, including land reform and improvement of land tenure; reform in methods of land taxation; extension of credit facilities; development of improved marketing facilities; and promotion of co-operative organisation in production and marketing.

Population Growth

28. Countries in which the population is increasing rapidly, and especially those in which it already presses heavily on the economy, should study the economic, social and demographic factors affecting population growth with a view to adopting economic and social policies that make for a better balance between the growth of employment opportunities and the growth of the labour force.

V. ACTION BY EMPLOYERS AND WORKERS AND THEIR ORGANISATIONS

29.(1) Employers and workers in the public and private sectors, and their organisations, should take all practicable measures to promote the achievement and maintenance of full, productive and freely chosen employment.

(2) In particular, they should—

(a) consult one another, and as appropriate the competent public authorities, employment services or similar institutions, as far in advance as possible, with a view to working out mutually satisfactory adjustments to changes in the employment situation;

(b) study trends in the economic and employment situation, and in technical progress, and propose as appropriate, and in good time, such action by governments and by public and private undertakings as may safeguard within the framework of the general interest the employment security and opportunities of the workers;

(c) promote wider understanding of the economic background, of the reasons for changes in employment opportunities in specific occupations, industries or regions, and of the necessity of occupational and geographical mobility of manpower;

(d) strive to create a climate which, without prejudicing national sovereignty, economic independence or freedom of association, will encourage increased investment from both domestic and foreign sources, with positive effects on the economic growth of the country;

(e) provide or seek the provision of facilities such as training and retraining facilities, and related financial benefits;

(f) promote wage, benefit and price policies that are in harmony with the objectives of full employment, economic growth, improved standards of living and monetary stability, without endangering the legitimate objectives pursued by employers and workers and their organisations; and

(g) respect the principle of equality of opportunity and treatment in employment and occupation, taking account of the provisions of the Discrimination (Employment and Occupation) Convention and Recommendation, 1958.

(3) In consultation and co-operation as appropriate with workers' organisations and/or representatives of workers at the level of the undertaking, and having regard to national economic and social conditions, measures should be taken by undertakings to counteract unemployment, to help workers find new jobs, to increase the number of jobs available and to minimise the consequences of unemployment; such measures may include—

(a) retraining for other jobs within the undertaking;

(b) transfers within the undertaking;

(c) careful examination of, and action to overcome, obstacles to increasing shift work;

(d) the earliest possible notice to workers whose employment is to be terminated, appropriate notification to public authorities, and some form of income protection for workers whose employment has been terminated, taking account of the provisions of the Termination of Employment Recommendation, 1963.

VI. International Action to Promote Employment Objectives

30. Members, with the assistance as appropriate of intergovernmental and other international organisations, should co-operate in international action to promote employment objectives, and should, in their internal economic policy, seek to avoid measures which have a detrimental effect on the employment situation and the general economic stability in other countries, including the developing countries.

31. Members should contribute to all efforts to expand international trade as a means of promoting economic growth and expansion of employment opportunities. In particular, they should take all possible measures to diminish unfavourable repercussions on the level of employment of fluctuations in the international terms of trade and of balance-of-payment in other countries, in particular in

32.(1) Industrialised countries should, in their economic policies, including policies for economic co-operation and for expanding demand, take into account the need for increased employment in other countries, in particular in the developing countries.

(2) They should, as rapidly as their circumstances permit, take measures to accommodate increased imports of products, manufactured, processed and semi-processed as well as primary, that can be economically produced in developing countries, thus promoting mutual trade and increased employment in the production of exports.

33. International migration of workers for employment which is consistent with the economic needs of the countries of emigration and immigration, including migration from developing countries to industrialized countries, should be facilitated, taking account of the provisions of the Migration for Employment Convention and Recommendation (Revised), 1949, and the Equality of Treatment (Social Security) Convention, 1962.

34.(1) In international technical co-operation through multilateral and bilateral channels special attention should be paid to the need to develop active employment policies.

(2) To this end, such co-operation should include—

(a) advice in regard to employment policy and employment market organisation as essential elements in the field of general development planning and programming; and

(b) co-operation in the training of qualified local personnel, including technical personnel and management staff.

(3) Technical co-operation programmes relating to training should aim at providing the developing countries with suitable facilities for training within the country or region. They should also include adequate provision for the supply of equipment. As a complementary measure, facilities should also be provided for the training of nationals of developing countries in industrialised countries.

(4) Members should make all efforts to facilitate the release for suitable periods, both from governmental and non-governmental employment, of highly qualified experts in the various fields of employment policy for work in developing countries. Such efforts should include arrangements to make such release attractive to the experts concerned.

(5) In the preparation and implementation of technical co-operation programmes, the active participation of employers' and workers' organisations in the countries concerned should be sought.

35. Members should encourage the international exchange of technological processes with a view to increasing productivity and employment, by means such as licensing and other forms of industrial co-operation.

36. Foreign-owned undertakings should meet their staffing needs by employing and training local staff, including management and supervisory personnel.

37. Arrangements should be made, where appropriate on a regional basis, for periodical discussions and exchange of experience of employment policies, particularly employment policies in developing countries, with the assistance as appropriate of the International Labour Office.

VII. Suggestions Concerning Methods of Application

38. In applying the provisions of this Recommendation, each Member of the International Labour Organisation and the employers' and workers' organisations concerned should be guided, to the extent possible and desirable, by the suggestions concerning methods of application set forth in the Annex.

Annex
Suggestions Concerning Methods of Application

I. General and Selective Measures of Employment Policy

1.(1) Each Member should—

(a) make continuing studies of the size and distribution of the labour force and the nature and extent of unemployment and underemployment and trends therein, including, where possible, analyses of—

(i)   the distribution of the labour force by age, sex, occupational group, qualifications, regions and economic sectors; probable future trends in each of these; and the effects of demographic factors, particularly in developing countries with rapid population growth, and of technological change on such trends;

(ii) the volume of productive employment currently available and likely to be available at different dates in the future in different economic sectors, regions and occupational groups, account being taken of projected changes in demand and productivity;

(b)   make vigorous efforts, particularly through censuses and sample surveys, to improve the statistical data needed for such studies;

(c)   undertake and promote the collection and analysis of current indicators of economic activity, and the study of trends in the evolution of new techniques in the different sectors of industry both at home and abroad, particularly as regards automation, with a view, *inter alia,* to distinguishing short-term fluctuations from longer-term structural changes;

(d)   make short-term forecasts of employment, underemployment and unemployment sufficiently early and in sufficient detail to provide a basis for prompt action to prevent or remedy either unemployment or shortages of labour;

(e)   undertake and promote studies of the methods and results of employment policies in other countries.

(2) Members should make efforts to provide those responsible for collective bargaining with information on the results of studies of the employment situation undertaken in the International Labour Office and elsewhere, including studies of the impact of automation.

2. Attainment of the social objectives of employment policy requires co-ordination of employment policy with other measures of economic and social policy, in particular measures affecting—

(a)   investment, production and economic growth;

(b)   the growth and distribution of incomes;

(c)   social security;

(d)   fiscal and monetary policies, including anti-inflationary and foreign exchange policies; and

(e)   the promotion of freer movement of goods, capital and labour between countries.

3. With a view to promoting stability of production and employment, consideration should be given to the possibility of making more use of fiscal or quasi-fiscal measures designed to exert an automatic stabilising influence and to maintain a satisfactory level of consumer income and investment.

4. Measures designed to stabilise employment may further include—

(a)   fiscal measures in respect of tax rates and investment expenditure;

(b)   stimulation, or restraint, of economic activity by appropriate measures of monetary policy;

(c)   increased, or reduced, expenditure on public works or other public investment of a fundamental nature, for example roads, railways, harbours, schools, training centres and hospitals; Members should plan during periods of high employment to have a number of useful but postponable public works projects ready to be put into operation in times of recession;

(d)   measures of a more specific character, such as increased government orders to a particular branch of industry in which recession threatens to provoke a temporary decline in the level of activity.

5. Measures to even out seasonal fluctuations in employment may include—

(a) the application of new techniques to make it possible for work to be carried out under conditions in which it would have been impracticable without these techniques;

(b) the training of workers in seasonal occupations for complementary occupations;

(c) planning to counteract seasonal unemployment or underemployment; special attention should be given to the co-ordination of the activities of the different public authorities and private enterprises concerned with building and construction operations, so as to ensure continuity of activity to meet the employment needs of workers.

6.(1) The nature of the special difficulties which may be encountered as a result of structural changes by the categories of persons referred to in Paragraph 16 of the Recommendation should be ascertained by the competent authority and appropriate action recommended.

(2) Special measures should be taken to provide suitable work for these groups and to alleviate hardship.

(3) In cases where older or disabled workers face great difficulty in adjusting to structural changes, adequate benefits for such workers should be provided within the framework of the social security system, including, where appropriate, retirement benefits at an age below that normally prescribed.

7.(1) When structural changes affect large numbers of workers concentrated in a particular area and especially if the competitive strength of the area as a whole is impaired, Members should provide, and should, by the provision of effective incentives and consultation with the representatives of employers and workers, encourage individual enterprises to provide, additional employment in the area, based on comprehensive policies of regional development.

(2) Measures taken to this end may include—

(a) the diversification of existing undertakings or the promotion of new industries;

(b) public works or other public investment including the expansion or the setting up of public undertakings;

(c) information and advice to new industries as to conditions of establishment;

(d) measures to make the area more attractive to new industries, for example through the redevelopment or improvement of the infrastructure, or through the provision of special loan facilities, temporary subsidies or temporary tax concessions or of physical facilities such as industrial estates;

(e) preferential consideration in the allocation of government orders;

(f) appropriate efforts to discourage excessive industrial concentration.

(3) Such measures should have regard to the type of employment which different areas, by reason of their resources, access to markets and other economic factors, are best suited to provide.

(4) The boundaries of areas which are given special treatment should be defined after careful study of the probable repercussions on other, particularly neighbouring, areas.

II. Employment Problems Associated with Economic Underdevelopment

8. Measures to expand domestic saving and encourage the inflow of financial resources from other countries, with a view to increasing productive investment, may include—

(a) measures, consistent with the provisions of the Forced Labour Convention, 1930, and the Abolition of Forced Labour Convention, 1957, and taken within the framework of a system of adequate minimum labour standards and in consultation with employers and workers and their organisations, to use available labour, with a minimum complement of scarce resources, to increase the rate of capital formation;

(b) measures to guide savings and investment from unproductive uses to uses designed to promote economic development and employment;

(c) measures to expand savings—
   (i) through the curtailment of non-essential consumption, with due regard to the need for maintaining adequate incentives; and
   (ii) through savings schemes, including contributory social security schemes and small savings schemes;

(d) measures to develop local capital markets to facilitate the transformation of savings into productive investment;

(e) measures to encourage the reinvestment in the country of a reasonable part of the profits from foreign investments, as well as to recover and to prevent the outflow of national capital with a view to directing it to productive investment.

9.(1) Measures to expand employment by the encouragement of labour-intensive products and techniques may include—

(a) the promotion of labour-intensive methods of production by means of—
   (i) work study to increase the efficiency of modern labour-intensive operations;
   (ii) research and dissemination of information about labour-intensive techniques, particularly in public works and construction;

(b) tax concessions and preferential treatment in regard to import or other quotas to undertakings concerned;

(c) full exploration of the technical, economic and organisational possibilities of labour-intensive construction works, such as multi-purpose river valley development projects and the building of railways and highways.

(2) In determining whether a particular product or technique is labour-intensive, attention should be given to the proportions in which capital and labour are employed not merely in the final processes, but in all stages of production, including that of materials, power and other requirements; attention should be given also to the proportions in which increased availability of a product will generate increased demand for labour and capital respectively.

10. Institutional measures for the promotion of productive employment in the rural sector may, in addition to those provided for in Paragraph 27 of the Recommendation, include promotion of community development programmes, consistent with the provisions of the Forced Labour Convention, 1930, and the Abolition of Forced Labour Convention, 1957, to evoke the active participation of the persons concerned, and in particular of employers and workers and their organisations, in planning and carrying out local economic and social development projects, and to encourage the use in such

projects of local manpower, materials and financial resources that might otherwise remain idle or unproductively used.

11. Means appropriate to local conditions for the fuller utilisation of local manpower in rural development may include—
(a) local capital-construction projects, particularly projects conducive to a quick increase in agricultural production, such as small and medium irrigation and drainage works, the construction of storage facilities and feeder roads and the development of local transport;
(b) land development and settlement;
(c) more labour-intensive methods of cultivation, expansion of animal husbandry and the diversification of agricultural production;
(d) the development of other productive activities, such as forestry and fishing;
(e) the promotion of rural social services such as education, housing and health services;
(f) the development of viable small-scale industries and handicrafts in rural areas, such as local processing of agricultural products and manufacture of simple consumers' and producers' goods needed in the area.

12.(1) In pursuance of Paragraph 5 of the Recommendation, and taking account of the provisions of the Vocational Training Recommendation, 1962, developing countries should endeavour to eradicate illiteracy and promote vocational training for workers in all sectors, as well as appropriate professional training for scientific, technical and managerial personnel.

(2) The necessity of training instructors and workers in order to carry out the improvement and modernisation of agriculture should be taken into account.

Recommendation 169
Recommendation Concerning Employment Policy[1]

The General Conference of the International Labour Organisation,

Having been convened at Geneva by the Governing Body of the International Labour Office, and having met in its Seventieth Session on 6 June 1984, and

Noting the existing international standards contained in the Employment Policy Convention and Recommendation, 1964, as well as in other international labour instruments relating to certain categories of workers, in particular the Workers with Family Responsibilities Convention and Recommendation, 1981, the Older Workers Recommendation, 1980, the Migration for Employment Convention and Recommendation (Revised), 1949, the Migrant Workers (Supplementary Provisions) Convention, 1975, and the Migrant Workers Recommendation, 1975,

Recalling the responsibility of the International Labour Organisation, resulting from the Declaration of Philadelphia, to examine and consider the bearing of economic and financial policies upon employ-

1. Adopted June 26, 1984. Source: International Labour Conference, 70th Sess., *Record of the Proceedings* (Geneva: International Labour Office, 1984), pp. XVIII–XXXV.

ment policy in the light of the fundamental objective that "all human beings, irrespective of race, creed or sex, have the right to pursue both their material well-being and their spiritual development in conditions of freedom and dignity, of economic security and equal opportunity",

Recalling that the International Covenant on Economic, Social and Cultural Rights, adopted by the United Nations General Assembly in 1966, provides for the recognition of inter alia "the right to work, which includes the right of everyone to the opportunity to gain his living by work which he freely chooses or accepts", and for the taking of appropriate steps to achieve progressively the full realisation of, and to safeguard, this right,

Recalling also the provisions of the Convention on the Elimination of All Forms of Discrimination against Women, adopted by the United Nations General Assembly in 1979,

Recognising, in the light of increasing interdependence within the world economy and of low economic growth rates in recent years, the need to co-ordinate economic, monetary and social policies at the national and international levels, to strive for the reduction of disparities between developed and developing countries and for the establishment of the new international economic order, in order to make the fullest possible use of resources for development and for the creation of employment opportunities, and thus to combat unemployment and underemployment,

Noting the deterioration of employment opportunities in most industrialised and developing countries and expressing the conviction that poverty, unemployment and inequality of opportunity are unacceptable in terms of humanity and social justice, can provoke social tension and thus create conditions which can endanger peace and prejudice the exercise of the right to work, which includes free choice of employment, just and favourable conditions of work and protection against unemployment,

Considering that the Employment Policy Convention and Recommendation, 1964, should be placed in the wider framework of the Declaration of Principles and Programme of Action adopted in 1976 by the Tripartite World Conference on Employment, Income Distribution and Social Progress and the International Division of Labour, and of the resolution concerning follow-up to the World Employment Conference adopted by the International Labour Conference in 1979,

Having decided upon the adoption of certain proposals with regard to employment policy which is the fourth item on the agenda of the session, and Having determined that these proposals shall take the form of a Recommendation supplementing the Employment Policy Convention and Recommendation, 1964:

adopts this twenty-sixth day of June of the year one thousand nine hundred and eighty-four the following Recommendation, which may be cited as the Employment Policy (Supplementary Provisions) Recommendation, 1984.

I. General Principles of Employment Policy

1. The promotion of full, productive and freely chosen employment provided for in the Employment Policy Convention and Recommendation,

1964, should be regarded as the means of achieving in practice the realisation of the right to work.

2. Full recognition by Members of the right to work should be linked with the implementation of economic and social policies, the purpose of which is the promotion of full, productive and freely chosen employment.

3. The promotion of full, productive and freely chosen employment should be the priority in, and an integral part of, economic and social policies of Members and, where appropriate, their plans for the satisfaction of the basic needs of the population.

4. Members should give special attention to the most efficient means of increasing employment and production and draw up policies and, if appropriate, programmes designed to facilitate the increased production and fair distribution of essential goods and services and the fair distribution of income throughout the country, with a view to satisfying the basic needs of the population in accordance with the Declaration of Principles and Programme of Action of the World Employment Conference.

5. In accordance with national practice, the policies, plans and programmes referred to in Paragraphs 3 and 4 of this Recommendation should be drawn up and implemented in consultation and co-operation with the organisations of employers and workers and other organisations representative of the persons concerned, particularly those in the rural sector covered by the Rural Workers' Organisations Convention and Recommendation, 1975.

6. Economic and financial policies, at both the national and international levels, should reflect the priority to be attached to the goals referred to in Paragraphs 3 and 4 of this Recommendation.

7. The policies, plans and programmes referred to in Paragraphs 3 and 4 of this Recommendation should aim at eliminating any discrimination and ensuring for all workers equal opportunity and treatment in respect of access to employment, conditions of employment, wages and income, vocational guidance and training and career development.

8. Members should take measures to combat effectively illegal employment, that is employment which does not comply with the requirements of national laws, regulations and practice.

9. Members should take measures to enable the progressive transfer of workers from the informal sector, where it exists, to the formal sector to take place.

10. Members should adopt policies and take measures which, while taking account of national law and practice, should—

(a) facilitate adjustment to structural change at the global, sectoral and enterprise levels and the re-employment of workers who have lost their jobs as a result of structural and technological changes; and

(b) safeguard the employment or facilitate the re-employment of workers affected in the case of sale, transfer, closure or relocation of a company, establishment or equipment.

11. In accordance with national law and practice, the methods of giving effect to employment policies might include negotiating collective agreements on questions having a bearing on employment such as—

(a) the promotion and safeguarding of employment;

(b) the economic and social consequences of restructuring and rationalisation of branches of economic activity and undertakings;

(c) the reorganisation and reduction of working time;

(d) the protection of particular groups; and
(e) information on economic, financial and employment issues.

12. Members should, after consultation with the organisations of employers and workers, take effective measures to encourage multinational enterprises to undertake and promote in particular the employment policies set forth in the Tripartite Declaration of Principles concerning Multinational Enterprises and Social Policy, 1977, and to ensure that negative effects of the investments of multinational enterprises on employment are avoided and that positive effects are encouraged.

13. In view of increasing interdependence within the world economy, Members should, in addition to the measures taken at the national level, strengthen international co-operation in order to ensure the success of the fight against unemployment.

II. Population Policy

14.(1) While ensuring that sufficient employment opportunities exist, development and employment policies might, where appropriate and in accordance with national law and practice, include population policies and programmes designed to ensure promotion of family welfare and family planning through programmes of information and voluntary education on population issues.

(2) Members, particularly developing countries, in collaboration with both national and international non-governmental organisations might—
(a) pay particular attention in their population policies and programmes to educating actual and potential parents on the benefits of family planning;
(b) in rural areas, increase the number of health facilities and community centres offering family planning services and the number of trained personnel to provide these services; and
(c) in urban areas, pay particular attention to the urgent need to develop appropriate infrastructures and improve living conditions, especially in slum areas.

III. Employment of Youth and Disadvantaged Groups and Persons

15. In the context of an overall employment policy, Members should adopt measures to respond to the needs of all categories of persons frequently having difficulties in finding lasting employment, such as certain women, certain young workers, disabled persons, older workers, the long-term unemployed and migrant workers lawfully within their territory. These measures should be consistent with the provisions of international labour Conventions and Recommendations relating to the employment of these groups and with the conditions of employment established under national law and practice.

16. While taking account of national conditions and in accordance with national law and practice, the measures referred to in Paragraph 15 of this Recommendation might include, inter alia—
(a) general education accessible to all and vocational guidance and training programmes to assist these persons to find work and to improve their employment opportunities and their income;
(b) the creation of a training system linked with both the educational system and the world of work;
(c) counselling and employment services to assist individuals to enter the

labour market and to help them to find employment which corresponds to their skills and aptitudes;

(d) programmes which create gainful employment in specific regions, areas or sectors;
(e) programmes of adjustment to structural change;
(f) measures of continuing training and retraining;
(g) measures of vocational rehabilitation;
(h) assistance for voluntary mobility; and
(i) programmes for the promotion of self-employment and workers' co-operatives.

17.(1) Other special measures should be taken for young people. In particular—

(a) public and private institutions and undertakings should be encouraged to engage and to train young people by means appropriate to national conditions and practice;
(b) although priority should be given to integrating young persons into regular employment, special programmes might be set up with a view to employing young people on a voluntary basis for the execution of community projects, in particular local projects having a social character, bearing in mind the provisions of the Special Youth Schemes Recommendation, 1970;
(c) special programmes should be set up in which training and work alternate so as to assist young people in finding their first job;
(d) training opportunities should be adapted to technical and economic development and the quality of training should be improved;
(e) measures should be taken to ease the transition from school to work and to promote opportunities for employment on completion of training;
(f) research on employment prospects should be promoted as a basis for a rational vocational training policy; and
(g) the safety and health of young workers should be protected.

(2) The measures referred to in subparagraph (1) of this Paragraph should be carefully monitored to ensure that they result in beneficial effects on young people's employment.

(3) These measures should be consistent with the provisions of international labour Conventions and Recommendations relating to the employment of young persons and with the conditions of employment established under national law and practice.

18. Incentives appropriate to national conditions and practice might be provided in order to facilitate the implementation of the measures referred to in Paragraphs 15 to 17 of this Recommendation.

19. In accordance with national law and practice, full and timely consultations should be held on the formulation, application and monitoring of the measures and programmes referred to in Paragraphs 15 to 18 of this Recommendation between the competent authorities and the organisations of employers and workers and other organisations concerned.

IV. TECHNOLOGY POLICIES

20. One of the major elements of national development policy should be to facilitate the development of technology as a means of increasing productive potential and achieving the major development objectives of creation of em-

ployment opportunities and the satisfaction of basic needs. Technology policies should, taking into account the stage of economic development, contribute to the improvement of working conditions and reduction of working time, and include measures to prevent loss of jobs.

21. Members should—

(a) encourage research on the selection, adoption and development of new technologies and on their effects on the volume and structure of employment, conditions of employment, training, job content and skill requirements; and

(b) encourage research on the technologies most appropriate to the specific conditions of countries, by ensuring the involvement of independent research institutes.

22. Members should endeavour to ensure by appropriate measures—

(a) that the education and training systems, including schemes for retraining, offer workers sufficient opportunities for adjusting to altered employment requirements resulting from technological change;

(b) that particular attention is given to the best possible use of existing and future skills; and

(c) that negative effects of technological changes on employment, working and living conditions and on occupational safety and health are eliminated to the extent possible, in particular through the incorporation of ergonomic, safety and health considerations at the design stage of new technologies.

23. Members should, through all methods suited to national conditions and practice, promote the use of appropriate new technologies and assure or improve liaison and consultation between the different units and organisations concerned with these questions and the representative organisations of employers and workers.

24. The organisations of employers and workers concerned and undertakings should be encouraged to assist in the dissemination of general information on technological choices, in the promotion of technological linkages between large-scale and small-scale undertakings and in the setting up of relevant training programmes.

25. In accordance with national practice, Members should encourage employers' and workers' organisations to enter into collective agreements at national, sectoral or undertaking levels on the social consequences of the introduction of new technologies.

26. Members should, as far as possible and in accordance with national law and practice, encourage undertakings, when introducing into their operations technological changes which are liable to have major effects upon workers in the undertaking—

(a) to associate workers and/or their representatives in the planning, introduction and use of new technologies, that is to inform them of the opportunities offered by and the effects of such new technologies and to consult them in advance with a view to arriving at agreements;

(b) to promote a better organisation of working time and a better distribution of employment;

(c) to prevent and mitigate to the greatest extent practicable any adverse effects of the technological changes on workers; and

(d) to promote investments in technology that would encourage, directly or indirectly, the creation of employment and contribute to a progressive increase in production and the satisfaction of the basic needs of the population.

V. Informal Sector

27.(1) National employment policy should recognise the importance as a provider of jobs of the informal sector, that is economic activities which are carried on outside the institutionalised economic structures.

(2) Employment promotion programmes should be elaborated and implemented to encourage family work and independent work in individual workshops, both in urban and rural areas.

28. Members should take measures to promote complementary relationships between the formal and informal sectors and to provide greater access of undertakings in the informal sector to resources, product markets, credit, infrastructure, training facilities, technical expertise and improved technologies.

29.(1) While taking measures to increase employment opportunities and improve conditions of work in the informal sector, Members should seek to facilitate its progressive integration into the national economy.

(2) Members should take into account that integration of the informal sector into the formal sector may reduce its ability to absorb labour and generate income. Nevertheless, they should seek progressively to extend measures of regulation to the informal sector.

VI. Small Undertakings

30. National employment policy should take account of the importance of small undertakings as providers of jobs, and recognise the contribution of local employment creation initiatives to the fight against unemployment and to economic growth. These undertakings, which can take diverse forms, such as small traditional undertakings, co-operatives and associations, offer employment opportunities, especially for workers who have particular difficulties.

31. After consultation and in co-operation with employers' and workers' organisations, Members should take the necessary measures to promote complementary relationships between the undertakings referred to in Paragraph 30 of this Recommendation and other undertakings, to improve working conditions in these undertakings, and to improve their access to product markets, credit, technical expertise and advanced technology.

VII. Regional Development Policies

32. In accordance with national law and practice, Members should recognise the importance of balanced regional development as a means of mitigating the social and employment problems created by the unequal distribution of natural resources and the inadequate mobility of the means of production, and of correcting the uneven spread of growth and employment between regions and areas within a country.

33. Measures should be taken, after consultation and in co-operation with the representatives of the populations concerned and in particular with the organisations of employers and workers, with a view to promoting employment in underdeveloped or backward areas, declining industrial and agricultural areas, frontier zones and, in general, parts of the country which have not benefited satisfactorily from national development.

34. Taking account of national conditions and of each Member's plans and programmes, the measures referred to in Paragraph 33 of this Recommendation might include, inter alia—

(a) creating and developing growth poles and growth centres with good prospects for generating employment;

(b) developing and intensifying regional potential taking into account the human and natural resources of each region and the need for coherent and balanced regional development;

(c) expanding the number and size of medium-sized and small towns in order to counterbalance the growth of large cities;

(d) improving the availability and distribution of and access to essential services required for meeting basic needs;

(e) encouraging the voluntary mobility of workers within each region and between different regions of the country by appropriate social welfare measures, while making an effort to promote satisfactory living and working conditions in their areas of origin;

(f) investing in improvements to the regional infrastructures, services and administrative structures, including the allocation of the necessary staff and the provision of training and retraining opportunities; and

(g) promoting the participation of the community in the definition and implementation of regional development measures.

VIII. PUBLIC INVESTMENT AND SPECIAL PUBLIC WORKS PROGRAMMES

35. Members might implement economically and socially viable public investment and special public works programmes, particularly with a view to creating and maintaining employment and raising incomes, reducing poverty and better meeting basic needs in areas of widespread unemployment and underemployment. Such programmes should, where possible and appropriate—

(a) pay special attention to the creation of employment opportunities for disadvantaged groups;

(b) include rural and urban infrastructure projects as well as the construction of facilities for basic-needs satisfaction in rural, urban and suburban areas, and increased productive investments in sectors such as energy and telecommunications;

(c) contribute to raising the standard of social services in fields such as education and health;

(d) be designed and implemented within the framework of development plans where they exist and in consultation with the organisations of employers and workers concerned;

(e) identify the persons whom the programmes are to benefit, determine the available manpower and define the criteria for project selection;

(f) ensure that workers are recruited on a voluntary basis;

(g) ensure that manpower is not diverted from other productive activities;

(h) provide conditions of employment consistent with national law and practice, and in particular with legal provisions governing access to employment, hours of work, remuneration, holidays with pay, occupational safety and health and compensation for employment injuries; and

(i) facilitate the vocational training of workers engaged in such programmes as well as the retraining of those who, because of structural changes in production and employment, have to change their jobs.

IX. International Economic Co-Operation and Employment

36. Members should promote the expansion of international trade in order to help one another to attain employment growth. To this end, they should co-operate in international bodies which are engaged in facilitating sustainable and mutually beneficial increases in international trade, technical assistance and investment.

37. Bearing in mind their responsibilities in relation to other competent international bodies Members should, with a view to ensuring the effectiveness of employment policies, adopt the following objectives:

(a) to promote the growth of production and world trade in conditions of economic stability and growing employment, within the context of international co-operation for development and on the basis of equality of rights and mutual advantage;

(b) to recognise that the interdependence between States, resulting from the increasing integration of the world economy, should help to create a climate in which States can, wherever appropriate, define joint policies designed to promote a fair distribution of the social costs and benefits of structural adjustment as well as a fairer international distribution of income and wealth, in such a way as to enable developing countries to absorb the increase in their labour force, and the developed countries to raise their levels of employment and reduce the adjustment cost for the workers concerned;

(c) to co-ordinate national policies concerning trade and structural change and adjustment so as to make possible a greater participation of developing countries in world industrial production within an open and fair world trading system, to stabilise commodity prices at remunerative levels which are acceptable to both producers and consumers, and to encourage investment in the production and processing of commodities in developing countries;

(d) to encourage the peaceful resolution of disputes among nations and negotiated arms reduction agreements which will achieve security for all nations, as well as the progressive transfer of expenditure on armaments and the reconversion of the armaments industry to the production of essential goods and services, especially those which satisfy the basic needs of the population and the needs of developing countries;

(e) to seek agreement on concerted action at the international level with a view to improving the international economic system, especially in the financial sphere, so as to promote employment in developed as well as developing countries;

(f) to increase mutual economic and technical co-operation, especially between countries at different levels of economic development and with different social and economic systems, through exchange of experience and the development of complementary capacities, particularly in the fields of employment and human resources and the choice, development and transfer of technology in accordance with mutually accepted law and practice concerning private property rights;

(g) to create conditions for sustained, non-inflationary growth of the world economy, and for the establishment of an improved international monetary system which would lead to the establishment of the new international economic order; and

(h) to ensure greater stability in exchange rates, a reduction of the debt burden of developing countries, the provision of long-term, low-cost financial assistance to developing countries and the adoption of adjustment policies which promote employment and the satisfaction of basic needs.

38. Members should—

(a) promote the transfer of technologies with a view to enabling developing countries to adopt, on fair and reasonable commercial terms, those which are most appropriate for the promotion of employment and the satisfaction of basic needs; and

(b) take appropriate measures for the creation and maintenance of employment and for the provision of training and retraining opportunities. Such measures might include the establishment of national, regional or international readjustment funds for the purpose of assisting in the positive adjustment of industries and workers affected by changes in the world economy.

X. INTERNATIONAL MIGRATION AND EMPLOYMENT

39. Members, taking account of international labour Conventions and Recommendations on migrant workers, should, where international migration takes place, adopt policies designed—

(a) to create more employment opportunities and better conditions of work in countries of emigration so as to reduce the need to migrate to find employment; and

(b) to ensure that international migration takes place under conditions designed to promote full, productive and freely chosen employment.

40. Members which habitually or repeatedly admit significant numbers of foreign workers with a view to employment should, when such workers come from developing countries, endeavour to co-operate more fully in the development of such countries, by appropriate intensified capital movements, the expansion of trade, the transfer of technical knowledge and assistance in the vocational training of local workers, in order to establish an effective alternative to migration for employment and to assist the countries in question in improving their economic and employment situation.

41. Members which habitually or repeatedly experience significant outflows of their nationals for the purpose of employment abroad should, provided that such measures are not inconsistent with the right of everyone to leave any country including his own, take measures by means of legislation, agreements with employers' and workers' organisations, or in any other manner consistent with national conditions and practice, to prevent malpractices at the stage of recruitment or departure liable to result in illegal entry to, or stay or employment in, another country.

42. Developing emigration countries, in order to facilitate the voluntary return of their nationals who possess scarce skills, should—

(a) provide the necessary incentives; and

(b) enlist the co-operation of the countries employing their nationals as well as of the International Labour Office and other international or regional bodies concerned with the matter.

43. Members, both countries of employment and countries of origin, should take appropriate measures to—

(a) prevent abuse in the recruitment of labour for work abroad;

(b) prevent the exploitation of migrant workers; and

(c) ensure the full exercise of the rights to freedom of association and to organise and bargain collectively.

44. Members, both countries of employment and countries of origin, should, when it is necessary, taking fully into account existing international labour Conventions and Recommendations on migrant workers, conclude bilateral and multilateral agreements covering issues such as right of entry and stay, the protection of rights resulting from employment, the promotion of education and training opportunities for migrant workers, social security, and assistance to workers and members of their families wishing to return to their country of origin.

Appendix II. Organization for Economic Cooperation and Development

Resolution of the Council
on Manpower Policy as a Means for the Promotion of Economic Growth[1]

THE COUNCIL

Having regard to Articles 1, 2 and 5(b) of the Convention on the Organisation for Economic Co-operation and Development of 14th December 1960;

Having regard to the attached Report[2] of the Manpower and Social Affairs Committee of 19th March 1964 on Manpower Policy as a Means for the Promotion of Economic Growth (hereinafter called the « Report »);

On the proposal of the Manpower and Social Affairs Committee;

I. APPROVES the Report.

II. RECOMMENDS that Member countries proceed—in the near future and as part of their development activities and their efforts to attain the growth target of the Organisation—to a re-examination of their manpower policies in the light of the Report with a view to increasing their ability to solve employment problems created by technical and economic change.

III. RECOMMENDS that Member countries in carrying out this re-examination should undertake any appropriate consultations, particularly with management and labour organisations.

IV. REQUESTS Member countries to report to the Organisation on action taken by them to implement this Recommendation, not later than by 30th June 1965.

---

1. May 21, 1964 (cf. C/M(64)10 (Final), Item 84—Doc. No. C(64) 48 (Final)). Source: Organisation for Economic Co-operation and Development, *Acts of the Organisation* 4 (Paris: OECD, 1964), pp. 185–195.

2. Not included in the present volume.

MANPOWER POLICY AS A MEANS FOR THE PROMOTION OF ECONOMIC GROWTH

1. Manpower policy should be given an important role in the pursuance of economic growth by contributing both to the increase of the productive capacity of the economy and to its utilisation. Along with the basic programme for education and training of youth there is need for training programmes for persons of all working ages to help meet demands for new skills and adaptation to changes in the industrial structure. Along with scientific and technical progress there is need for measures to promote acceptance of new techniques by all concerned. Along with fiscal and monetary policies designed to maintain high levels of employment and business activity in general terms, there is need for more specialised and selective measures, creating jobs in labour surplus areas and encouraging the flow of manpower from such areas to expanding and productive industries.

2. By promoting the mutual adjustment of manpower needs and resources, an active manpower policy has the special advantage of being expansionist with regard to employment and production but anti-inflationary with regard to costs and prices.

3. The diversification of production, the increasing volume of technical research and innovations, the efforts to liberalise and expand international trade, and the appearance of a number of new countries as producers in the world market for industrial products tend to increase the multiplicity of economic changes, perhaps also their severity. If the necessary adjustments do not take place rapidly there is a risk that they will give rise to economic contractions and unemployment. If the adjustments are not carried out in forms acceptable to those who are most immediately affected, protective and restrictive reactions can be expected. Since the benefits of such change accrue to the community as a whole, the community should bear a significant part of the costs of adjustment to economic and technical change and should also act to reduce the burden of such adjustment.

4. Countries sometimes accept the burden of large direct or indirect subsidies of measures of protection to maintain employment in declining and less productive sectors. Public money could often be better used to facilitate and stimulate workers' moving and retraining for better jobs or the establishment of industries with positive prospects in areas facing employment difficulties. Expenditure of the types envisaged here for the improvement of human resources and their readjustment should not be regarded as a cost to society, but rather as a sound « investment in adaptation ». At the same time they promote important social values by increasing the individual's freedom in the choice of an occupation or workplace and his security against loss of income.

5. In view of the interdependence of national economies it is advantageous for an individual country if in all other countries high employment prevails, economic progress continues, and negative repercussions and restrictive reactions to technical and economic change are avoided. Consequently the O.E.C.D. countries have a joint interest in exploring solutions to employment problems.

6. The Manpower and Social Affairs Committee therefore consider that Member countries should undertake a specific re-examination of their manpower policies in the near future. Some specific measures and programmes which should normally be part of an active manpower policy are indicated in the following paragraphs. It is understood that in devising such a manpower

policy due regard must be given to the level of economic development and the institutional background, which may vary from country to country, and to the consequent differences in degrees of priority which have to be given to various elements. It is nevertheless desirable that all Member countries undertake parallel efforts to make progress in this field. Manpower policy should be made one of the main elements of economic policy in the pursuit of the O.E.C.D. growth target; at the same time the social aspects of such a policy should always be borne in mind.

7. *Policy-making and Administration.* A central policy body, or adequate co-ordination between different existing agencies is essential to formulate overall policy, to determine general directives, to identify strategic activities in the light of changing needs, and to initiate and develop new programmes and services. The Manpower authorities should strive to ensure that the objectives of the national manpower programmes are fully recognised by all relevant sectors of government and that the employment objectives everywhere are given the high priority they deserve from the point of view of economic, political and human interests.

8. *Participation of Employers' and Workers' Organisations.* Employers and workers, through the development of manpower programmes on a plant, establishment, or industry basis, can make an important contribution to the promotion of economic growth. Such programmes, which will vary widely in both form and nature among industries and countries, can frequently be stimulated through appropriate labour-management-government consultation and co-operation. To be effective, such consultation must spring from an appreciation of the role employers and workers and their organisations can play in promoting economic growth and improvement in standards of all people.

9. *Co-ordination of Manpower and Other Economic Policies.* Different types of measures should be predominant depending on whether the period is one of inflationary pressures or one when a business recession or restrictive policies for maintaining the balance of payments and price stability tend to reduce employment and hamper growth. The manpower authorities should constantly be prepared for rapid and timely action according to circumstances. This presupposes a high degree of information about economic trends in various parts of the economy, including contacts with employers to get advance notice about changes in the employment outlook. During slack periods, if timing and other factors support their effectiveness, public works and the provision of socially-needed public services should be used, possibly as part of a policy to increase the general level of demand. Such works, as well as local or general arrangements to influence employment in private enterprise must be prepared in advance, so that they can be utilised at the right moment. Seasonal employment variations might also be counteracted by administrative influence upon the starting of building and construction projects or financial incentives to stimulate employment during the slack season.

10. *The Employment Service.* This should be an institution promoting the effective functioning of the labour market as a whole in respect of all categories of workers. It must be given sufficient resources, including qualified personnel and attractive premises so as to gain the confidence of all sectors and classes of employees and employers. It should be capable of providing adequate description of jobs and of qualifications of applicants, vocational guidance and occupational counselling services, and inter-regional clearing of vacancies. It

should also be able to administer special programmes designed to encourage geographical and occupational mobility and social adjustment. These programmes should apply to all categories of workers, whether employed, underemployed, or unemployed, so as to promote optimum utilisation of manpower.

11. *Human Resource Development, Including Vocational Training and Retraining.* One important element of an active manpower policy is to see to it that human resources are developed to such an extent that the achievement of desired rates of technological change will not be impeded through lack of workers with suitable skills. To a great extent, training opportunities are provided by employers, but public authorities must see to it that total training capacity is adequate for the economy as a whole. Probably an increasing part of the population will be required to change occupation during their life, as technology progresses. Adult training and retraining facilities should be provided on an increasing scale, both within private industries and in educational institutions, in order to promote the necessary shifts and adjustments. Everybody needing and wishing to acquire new skills should be given the opportunity to qualify for the new and better jobs. It should be realised that the best preparation for later occupational shifts is a good basic education and technical training for the young, which takes account of the needs of modern technology.

12. *Geographical Mobility.* Geographical mobility would be promoted by better information to workers about job openings outside the home area, but in many cases economic and other hindrances to desirable mobility are considerable. The employment services should be authorised to provide travel and resettlement allowances to offset these hindrances. Co-operation with housing authorities and special efforts for solving housing problems in expansive areas will often be appropriate to create better conditions for a rational reallocation of the labour force. Measures should be taken to facilitate the social adjustment and integration of people settling in a new area, in particular those coming from very different environments, such as international migrants and rural workers going to urban industries.

13. *Regional Development.* A well-rounded manpower programme requires adequate measures to bring jobs to workers. Programmes for encouraging employment in depressed and underdeveloped areas should be established, with due regard to sound principles of economic development. Such programmes may include fiscal advantages, loans for new investment, and other incentives to private enterprise, as well as public undertakings. The administrative agencies should be equipped to aid local community organisations in their economic development programmes and to co-ordinate such programmes with national economic aims.

14. *Employment of Marginal Groups.* Many groups now intermittently or permanently outside the labour force can be helped to participate in useful employment through such aids as rehabilitation, retraining, special job arrangements and efforts to reduce prejudice against their employment. Such measures can be particularly efficient when shortages of labour exist or are impending.

15. *Financial Provisions for Readjustments.* Adequate unemployment benefits and compensation in case of redundancy as well as the special allowances for persons undertaking resettlement, retraining, rehabilitation, and other readjustments, are recommended as facilitating economic change with favourable results for the economic position, physical well-being, or the morale of

workers. They would promote rational placement in new jobs and positive attitudes to progressive changes and should therefore be regarded as valuable not only for the individual but for the economy as a whole.

16. *Special Problems of Developing Countries.* It is understood that a solution of the employment problems of Member countries in process of development, which generally have to cope with extensive underemployment in rural areas, must depend to a great extent upon the possibilities of achieving the accumulation of capital necessary for the creation of new industries and adequate public investments. Any development plan, however, must contain an appreciation, based upon an analysis of demographic and other internal conditions and on the experiences of the already more industrialised countries, of the various manpower requirements which such a plan involves and the ways and means through which the population of underdeveloped regions can be adapted to modern life. Co-operation between manpower and education authorities— always necessary—is of particular importance in these cases.

17. *Summary.* The pursuance of a programme on these lines would mean action in the following directions:

(a) A more comprehensive employment service, which can be utilised by employees and employers of all categories.

(b) An increased degree of preparedness for preventive or remedial action against employment disturbances.

(c) Substantial enlargement of adult training facilities and reforms in the general education and training system to meet the rapidly changing needs of modern technology.

(d) Forecasting of future occupational requirements, to act as a guide for developing education and training programmes.

(e) The introduction or reinforcement of specific means for encouraging desirable geographical mobility.

(f) More systematic support of industrial expansion in backward or depressed areas with development possibilities.

(g) The intensification of measures to make it easier for marginal groups to take up and keep gainful occupation.

(h) The development of income security programmes, such as unemployment and redundancy compensation and special adjustment allowances.

Recommendation of the Council on a General Employment and Manpower Policy[1]

The COUNCIL,

Having regard to Articles 1, 2, 5(b) of the Convention on the Organisation for Economic Co-operation and Development of 14th December 1960;

Having regard to the Recommendation of the Council of 21st May 1964 on Manpower Policy as a Means for the Promotion of Economic Growth [Doc. No. C(64)48(Final)];

1. Adopted March 5, 1976 (c.f. C/M/(76)4(Final), Item 46(a), (b) and (c)—Doc. No. C(76)37). Source: Organisation for Economic Co-operation and Development, *Acts of the Organisation* 16 (Paris: OECD, 1976), pp. 31–35. Notes marked * are from the original document; numbered notes are from the present volume.

Having regard to the Report of 11th June 1975 of the Manpower and Social Affairs Committee on Future Orientation of OECD Activity in the Field of International Migration and, in particular, the Annex thereto [Doc. No. C(75)104];

Having regard to the Report of the Manpower and Social Affairs Committee on a General Employment and Manpower Policy of 3rd March 1976 (hereinafter called the "Report of the Manpower and Social Affairs Committee") [Doc. No. MAS/MIN(76)6 Annex and Corrigendum];

On the proposal of the Manpower and Social Affairs Committee at Ministerial Level of 4th and 5th March 1976;

I. ENDORSES the views expressed in the Report of the Manpower and Social Affairs Committee:

II. RECOMMENDS that Member countries periodically examine, in the light of the report of the Manpower and Social Affairs Committee, their general employment and manpower policy so as to attain the objective of full employment, in particular by:

(a) continuing implementation of the principles of an active manpower policy contained in the Recommendation of the Council of 21st May 1964, referred to above, reinforced by a general and positive strategy for creating and maintaining employment and improved conditions of working life for all those who are able and want to work, with the support of relevant economic, employment, manpower and social policies;

(b) the close linking of employment and manpower policy and general economic policy, with the aim of achieving full employment objectives and improved quality of working life in the context of social and economic progress;

(c) systematic use and evaluation as appropriate of selective employment and manpower measures, with the objective of achieving and maintaining high levels of employment and balance between the supply and demand of labour in ways which contribute as much as possible to the struggle against inflation;

(d) special assistance to disadvantaged groups to enter, remain in or return to employment, thereby promoting more equity in the distribution of employment opportunities and income;

(e) balanced development of income maintenance, and of positive manpower utilisation measures which ensure the earliest possible return to employment, on the basis that it is preferable to spend money on activities which contribute to the expansion of employment;

(f) international co-operation in order that national employment and manpower policies and free international trade and investment are mutually consistent, so as to minimise the social costs of adjusting workers to structural changes which result from changing patterns of international trade;

(g) implementation between the OECD countries concerned of the guiding principles* for facilitating the orientation of migration policies and their concertation at international level;

* As formulated in the Report of the Manpower and Social Affairs Committee on the Future Orientation of the Activity of the Organisation in the Field of International Migration referred to above, the OECD countries concerned being defined as those which have adhered to the Council's Decision governing the employment of nationals of Member countries (Doc. Nos. C(56)258, OECD/C(61)5).

(h) organisational arrangements within national administrations for the co-ordination of all elements of policy affecting employment and manpower, in particular so that manpower authorities may help to ensure that the various elements of an employment strategy are taken into account in all fields of social and economic life;

(i) continuing co-operation and involvement of workers, employers and their representatives as an important aspect of total manpower and employment policy.

III. INVITES Member countries to report to the Organisation on steps taken by them to implement this Recommendation, not later than the 31st March 1977 and subsequently at intervals to be determined by the Manpower and Social Affairs Committee.

In adopting this Recommendation, the Council:

1. AGREED to its derestriction;

2. NOTED the statement by the Secretary-General on the conclusions resulting from the meeting of the Manpower and Social Affairs Committee at Ministerial level;

3. NOTED the statements by the Delegates for Switzerland and Portugal.

Appendix III. Council of Europe

European Social Charter[1]

The Governments signatory hereto, being Members of the Council of Europe,

Considering that the aim of the Council of Europe is the achievement of greater unity between its Members for the purpose of safeguarding and realising the ideals and principles which are their common heritage and of facilitating their economic and social progress, in particular by the maintenance and further realisation of human rights and fundamental freedoms;

Considering that in the European Convention for the Protection of Human Rights and Fundamental Freedoms signed at Rome on 4th November 1950, and the Protocol thereto signed at Paris on 20th March 1952, the member States of the Council of Europe agreed to secure to their populations the civil and political rights and freedoms therein specified;

Considering that the enjoyment of social rights should be secured without discrimination on grounds of race, colour, sex, religion, political opinion, national extraction or social origin;

Being resolved to make every effort in common to improve the standard of living and to promote the social well-being of both their urban and rural populations by means of appropriate institutions and actions,

Have agreed as follows:

PART I

The Contracting Parties accept as the aim of their policy, to be pursued by all appropriate means, both national and international in character, the attainment of conditions in which the following rights and principles may be effectively realised:

1. Everyone shall have the opportunity to earn his living in an occupation freely entered upon.

1. Signed October 18, 1961, entered into force February 26, 1965, E.T.S. No. 35 (1961); 529 U.N.T.S. 89, No. 7659 (1965). Source: Directorate of Information, Council of Europe, *European Social Charter* (Strasbourg: Council of Europe, 1967), pp. 3–20 (reprinted, with appendix, in Council of Europe, *European Conventions and Agreements* [Strasbourg: Council of Europe, 1971], 1: 339–359).

2. All workers have the right to just conditions of work.

3. All workers have the right to safe and healthy working conditions.

4. All workers have the right to a fair remuneration sufficient for a decent standard of living for themselves and their families.

5. All workers and employers have the right to freedom of association in national or international organisations for the protection of their economic and social interests.

6. All workers and employers have the right to bargain collectively.

7. Children and young persons have the right to a special protection against the physical and moral hazards to which they are exposed.

8. Employed women, in case of maternity, and other employed women as appropriate, have the right to a special protection in their work.

9. Everyone has the right to appropriate facilities for vocational guidance with a view to helping him choose an occupation suited to his personal aptitude and interests.

10. Everyone has the right to appropriate facilities for vocational training.

11. Everyone has the right to benefit from any measures enabling him to enjoy the highest possible standard of health attainable.

12. All workers and their dependents have the right to social security.

13. Anyone without adequate resources has the right to social and medical assistance.

14. Everyone has the right to benefit from social welfare services.

15. Disabled persons have the right to vocational training, rehabilitation and resettlement, whatever the origin and nature of their disability.

16. The family as a fundamental unit of society has the right to appropriate social, legal and economic protection to ensure its full development.

17. Mothers and children, irrespective of marital status and family relations, have the right to appropriate social and economic protection.

18. The nationals of any one of the Contracting Parties have the right to engage in any gainful occupation in the territory of any one of the others on a footing of equality with the nationals of the latter, subject to restrictions based on cogent economic or social reasons.

19. Migrant workers who are nationals of a Contracting Party and their families have the right to protection and assistance in the territory of any other Contracting Party.

Part II

The Contracting Parties undertake, as provided for in Part III, to consider themselves bound by the obligations laid down in the following Articles and paragraphs.

Article 1
The right to work

With a view to ensuring the effective exercise of the right to work, the Contracting Parties undertake:

1. to accept as one of their primary aims and responsibilities the achievement and maintenance of as high and stable a level of employment as possible, with a view to the attainment of full employment;

2. to protect effectively the right of the worker to earn his living in an occupation freely entered upon;

3. to establish or maintain free employment services for all workers;

4. to provide or promote appropriate vocational guidance, training and rehabilitation.

Article 2
The right to just conditions of work

With a view to ensuring the effective exercise of the right to just conditions of work, the Contracting Parties undertake:

1. to provide for reasonable daily and weekly working hours, the working week to be progressively reduced to the extent that the increase of productivity and other relevant factors permit;

2. to provide for public holidays with pay;

3. to provide for a minimum of two weeks' annual holiday with pay;

4. to provide for additional paid holidays or reduced working hours for workers engaged in dangerous or unhealthy occupations as prescribed;

5. to ensure a weekly rest period which shall, as far as possible, coincide with the day recognised by tradition or custom in the country or region concerned as a day of rest.

Article 3
The right to safe and healthy working conditions

With a view to ensuring the effective exercise of the right to safe and healthy working conditions, the Contracting Parties undertake:

1. to issue safety and health regulations;

2. to provide for the enforcement of such regulations by measures of supervision;

3. to consult, as appropriate, employers' and workers' organisations on measures intended to improve industrial safety and health.

Article 4
The right to a fair remuneration

With a view to ensuring the effective exercise of the right to a fair remuneration, the Contracting Parties undertake:

1. to recognise the right of workers to a remuneration such as will give them and their families a decent standard of living;

2. to recognise the right of workers to an increased rate of remuneration for overtime work, subject to exceptions in particular cases;

3. to recognise the right of men and women workers to equal pay for work of equal value;

4. to recognise the right of all workers to a reasonable period of notice for termination of employment;

5. to permit deductions from wages only under conditions and to the extent prescribed by national laws or regulations or fixed by collective agreements or arbitration awards.

The exercise of these rights shall be achieved by freely concluded collective agreements, by statutory wage-fixing machinery, or by other means appropriate to national conditions.

Article 5
The right to organise

With a view to ensuring or promoting the freedom of workers and employers to form local, national or international organisations for the protection of their economic and social interests and to join those organisations, the Contracting Parties undertake that national law shall not be such as to impair, nor shall it be so applied as to impair, this freedom. The extent to which the guarantees provided for in this Article shall apply to the police shall be determined by national laws or regulations. The principle governing the application to the members of the armed forces of these guarantees and the extent to which they shall apply to persons in this category shall equally be determined by national laws or regulations.

Article 6
The right to bargain collectively

With a view to ensuring the effective exercise of the right to bargain collectively, the Contracting Parties undertake:

1. to promote joint consultation between workers and employers;

2. to promote, where necessary and appropriate, machinery for voluntary negotiations between employers or employers' organisations and workers' organisations, with a view to the regulation of terms and conditions of employment by means of collective agreements;

3. to promote the establishment and use of appropriate machinery for conciliation and voluntary arbitration for the settlement of labour disputes; and recognise:

4. the right of workers and employers to collective action in cases of conflicts of interest, including the right to strike, subject to obligations that might arise out of collective agreements previously entered into.

Article 7
The right of children and young persons to protection

With a view to ensuring the effective exercise of the right of children and young persons to protection, the Contracting Parties undertake:

1. to provide that the minimum age of admission to employment shall be 15 years, subject to exceptions for children employed in prescribed light work without harm to their health, morals or education;

2. to provide that a higher minimum age of admission to employment shall be fixed with respect to prescribed occupations regarded as dangerous or unhealthy;

3. to provide that persons who are still subject to compulsory education shall not be employed in such work as would deprive them of the full benefit of their education;

4. to provide that the working hours of persons under 16 years of age shall be limited in accordance with the needs of their development, and particularly with their need for vocational training;

5. to recognise the right of young workers and apprentices to a fair wage or other appropriate allowances;

6. to provide that the time spent by young persons in vocational training during the normal working hours with the consent of the employer shall be treated as forming part of the working day;

7. to provide that employed persons of under 18 years of age shall be entitled to not less than three weeks' annual holiday with pay;

8. to provide that persons under 18 years of age shall not be employed in night work with the exception of certain occupations provided for by national laws or regulations;

9. to provide that persons under 18 years of age employed in occupations prescribed by national laws or regulations shall be subject to regular medical control;

10. to ensure special protection against physical and moral dangers to which children and young persons are exposed, and particularly against those resulting directly or indirectly from their work.

Article 8
The right of employed women to protection

With a view to ensuring the effective exercise of the right of employed women to protection, the Contracting Parties undertake:

1. to provide either by paid leave, by adequate social security benefits or by benefits from public funds for women to take leave before and after childbirth up to a total of at least 12 weeks;

2. to consider it as unlawful for an employer to give a woman notice of dismissal during her absence on maternity leave or to give her notice of dismissal at such a time that the notice would expire during such absence;

3. to provide that mothers who are nursing their infants shall be entitled to sufficient time off for this purpose;

4.(a) to regulate the employment of women workers on night work in industrial employment;

(b) to prohibit the employment of women workers in underground mining, and, as appropriate, on all other work which is unsuitable for them by reason of its dangerous, unhealthy, or arduous nature.

Article 9
The right to vocational guidance

With a view to ensuring the effective exercise of the right to vocational guidance, the Contracting Parties undertake to provide or promote, as necessary, a service which will assist all persons, including the handicapped, to solve problems related to occupational choice and progress, with due regard to the individual's characteristics and their relation to occupational opportunity: this assistance should be available free of charge, both to young persons, including school children, and to adults.

Article 10
The right to vocational training

With a view to ensuring the effective exercise of the right to vocational training, the Contracting Parties undertake:

1. to provide or promote, as necessary, the technical and vocational training of all persons, including the handicapped, in consultation with employers' and workers' organisations, and to grant facilities for access to higher technical and university education, based solely on individual aptitude;

2. to provide or promote a system of apprenticeship and other systematic arrangements for training young boys and girls in their various employments;

3. to provide or promote, as necessary:

(a) adequate and readily available training facilities for adult workers;

(b) special facilities for the re-training of adult workers needed as a result of technological development or new trends in employment;

4. to encourage the full utilisation of the facilities provided by appropriate measures such as:

(a) reducing or abolishing any fees or charges;

(b) granting financial assistance in appropriate cases;

(c) including in the normal working hours time spent on supplementary training taken by the worker, at the request of his employer, during employment;

(d) ensuring, through adequate supervision, in consultation with the employers' and workers' organisations, the efficiency of apprenticeship and other training arrangements for young workers, and the adequate protection of young workers generally.

Article 11
The right to protection of health

With a view to ensuring the effective exercise of the right to protection of health, the Contracting Parties undertake, either directly or in co-operation with public or private organisations, to take appropriate measures designed *inter alia:*

1. to remove as far possible the causes of ill-health;

2. to provide advisory and educational facilities for the promotion of health and the encouragement of individual responsibility in matters of health;

3. to prevent as far as possible epidemic, endemic and other diseases.

Article 12
The right to social security

With a view to ensuring the effective exercise of the right to social security, the Contracting Parties undertake:

1. to establish or maintain a system of social security;

2. to maintain the social security system at a satisfactory level at least equal to that required for ratification of International Labour Convention (No. 102) Concerning Minimum Standards of Social Security;

3. to endeavour to raise progressively the system of social security to a higher level;

4. to take steps, by the conclusion of appropriate bilateral and multilateral agreements, or by other means, and subject to the conditions laid down in such agreements, in order to ensure:

(a) equal treatment with their own nationals of the nationals of other Contracting Parties in respect of social security rights, including the retention of benefits arising out of social security legislation, whatever movements the persons protected may undertake between the territories of the Contracting Parties;

(b) the granting, maintenance and resumption of social security rights by such means as the accumulation of insurance or employment periods completed under the legislation of each of the Contracting Parties.

Article 13
The right to social and medical assistance

With a view to ensuring the effective exercise of the right to social and medical assistance, the Contracting Parties undertake:

1. to ensure that any person who is without adequate resources and who is unable to secure such resources either by his own efforts or from other sources, in particular by benefits under a social security scheme, be granted adequate assistance, and, in case of sickness, the care necessitated by this condition;

2. to ensure that persons receiving such assistance shall not, for that reason, suffer from a diminution of their political or social rights;

3. to provide that everyone may receive by appropriate public or private services such advice and personal help as may be required to prevent, to remove, or to alleviate personal or family want;

4. to apply the provisions referred to in paragraphs 1, 2 and 3 of this Article on an equal footing with their nationals to nationals of other Contracting Parties lawfully within their territories, in accordance with their obligations under the European Convention on Social and Medical Assistance, signed at Paris on 11th December 1953.

Article 14
The right to benefit from social welfare services

With a view to ensuring the effective exercise of the right to benefit from social welfare services, the Contracting Parties undertake:

1. to promote or provide services which, by using methods of social work, would contribute to the welfare and development of both individuals and groups in the community, and to their adjustment to the social environment;

2. to encourage the participation of individuals and voluntary or other organisations in the establishment and maintenance of such services.

Article 15
The right of physically or mentally disabled persons to vocational training, rehabilitation and social resettlement

With a view to ensuring the effective exercise of the right of the physically or mentally disabled to vocational training, rehabilitation and resettlement, the Contracting Parties undertake:

1. to take adequate measures for the provision of training facilities, including, where necessary, specialised institutions, public or private;

2. to take adequate measures for the placing of disabled persons in employment, such as specialised placing services, facilities for sheltered employment and measures to encourage employers to admit disabled persons to employment.

Article 16
The right of the family to social, legal and economic protection

With a view to ensuring the necessary conditions for the full development of the family, which is a fundamental unit of society, the Contracting Parties undertake to promote the economic, legal and social protection of family life by such means as social and family benefits, fiscal arrangements, provision of family housing, benefits for the newly married, and other appropriate means.

Article 17
The right of mothers and children to social and economic protection

With a view to ensuring the effective exercise of the right of mothers and children to social and economic protection, the Contracting Parties will take all appropriate and necessary measures to that end, including the establishment or maintenance of appropriate institutions or services.

Article 18
The right to engage in a gainful occupation in the territory of other Contracting Parties

With a view to ensuring the effective exercise of the right to engage in a gainful occupation in the territory of any other Contracting Party, the Contracting Parties undertake:

1. to apply existing regulations in a spirit of liberality;
2. to simplify existing formalities and to reduce or abolish chancery dues and other charges payable by foreign workers or their employers;
3. to liberalise, individually or collectively, regulations governing the employment of foreign workers;

and recognise:

4. the right of their nationals to leave the country to engage in a gainful occupation in the territories of the other Contracting Parties.

Article 19
The right of migrant workers and their families to protection and assistance

With a view to ensuring the effective exercise of the right of migrant workers and their families to protection and assistance in the territory of any other Contracting Party, the Contracting Parties undertake:

1. to maintain or to satisfy themselves that there are maintained adequate and free services to assist such workers, particularly in obtaining accurate information, and to take all appropriate steps, so far as national laws and regulations permit, against misleading propaganda relating to emigration and immigration;
2. to adopt appropriate measures within their own jurisdiction to facilitate the departure, journey and reception of such workers and their families, and to provide, within their own jurisdiction, appropriate services for health, medical attention and good hygienic conditions during the journey;
3. to promote co-operation, as appropriate, between social services, public and private, in emigration and immigration countries;
4. to secure for such workers lawfully within their territories, insofar as such matters are regulated by law or regulations or are subject to the control of administrative authorities, treatment not less favourable than that of their own nationals in respect of the following matters:
   (a) remuneration and other employment and working conditions;
   (b) membership of trade unions and enjoyment of the benefits of collective bargaining;
   (c) accommodation;
5. to secure for such workers lawfully within their territories treatment not less favourable than that of their own nationals with regard to employment taxes, dues or contributions payable in respect of employed persons;
6. to facilitate as far as possible the reunion of the family of a foreign worker permitted to establish himself in the territory;
7. to secure for such workers lawfully within their territories treatment not less favourable than that of their own nationals in respect of legal proceedings relating to matters referred to in this Article;
8. to secure that such workers lawfully residing within their territories are not expelled unless they endanger national security or offend against public interest or morality;

9. to permit, within legal limits, the transfer of such parts of the earnings and savings of such workers as they may desire;

10. to extend the protection and assistance provided for in this Article to self-employed migrants insofar as such measures apply.

PART III

Article 20
Undertakings

1. Each of the Contracting Parties undertakes:

(a) to consider Part I of this Charter as a declaration of the aims which it will pursue by all appropriate means, as stated in the introductory paragraph of that Part;

(b) to consider itself bound by at least five of the following Articles of Part II of this Charter: Articles 1, 5, 6, 12, 13, 16 and 19;

(c) in addition to the Articles selected by it in accordance with the preceding sub-paragraph, to consider itself bound by such a number of Articles or numbered paragraphs of Part II of the Charter as it may select, provided that the total number of Articles or numbered paragraphs by which it is bound is not less than 10 Articles or 45 numbered paragraphs.

2. The Articles or paragraphs selected in accordance with sub-paragraphs (b) and (c) of paragraph 1 of this Article shall be notifed to the Secretary-General of the Council of Europe at the time when the instrument of ratification or approval of the Contracting Party concerned is deposited.

3. Any Contracting Party may, at a later date, declare by notification to the Secretary-General that it considers itself bound by any Articles or any numbered paragraphs of Part II of the Charter which it has not already accepted under the terms of paragraph 1 of this Article. Such undertakings subsequently given shall be deemed to be an integral part of the ratification or approval, and shall have the same effect as from the thirtieth day after the date of the notification.

4. The Secretary-General shall communicate to all the signatory Governments and to the Director-General of the International Labour Office any notification which he shall have received pursuant to this Part of the Charter.

5. Each Contracting Party shall maintain a system of labour inspection appropriate to national conditions.

PART IV

Article 21
Reports concerning accepted provisions

The Contracting Parties shall send to the Secretary-General of the Council of Europe a report at two-yearly intervals, in a form to be determined by the Committee of Ministers, concerning the application of such provisions of Part II of the Charter as they have accepted.

Article 22
Reports concerning provisions which are not accepted

The Contracting Parties shall send to the Secretary-General, at appropriate intervals as requested by the Committee of Ministers, reports relating to the provisions of Part II of the Charter which they did not accept at the time of their ratification or approval or in a subsequent notification. The Committee of Ministers shall determine from time to time in respect of which provisions such reports shall be requested and the form of the reports to be provided.

Article 23
Communication of copies

1. Each Contracting Party shall communicate copies of its reports referred to in Articles 21 and 22 to such of its national organisations as are members of the international organisations of employers and trade unions to be invited under Article 27, paragraph 2, to be represented at meetings of the Sub-committee of the Governmental Social Committee.

2. The Contracting Parties shall forward to the Secretary-General any comments on the said reports received from these national organisations, if so requested by them.

Article 24
Examination of the reports

The reports sent to the Secretary-General in accordance with Articles 21 and 22 shall be examined by a Committee of Experts, who shall have also before them any comments forwarded to the Secretary-General in accordance with paragraph 2 of Article 23.

Article 25
Committee of Experts

1. The Committee of Experts shall consist of not more than seven members appointed by the Committee of Ministers from a list of independent experts of the highest integrity and of recognised competence in international social questions, nominated by the Contracting Parties.

2. The members of the Committee shall be appointed for a period of six years. They may be reappointed. However, of the members first appointed, the terms of office of two members shall expire at the end of four years.

3. The members whose terms of office are to expire at the end of the initial period of four years shall be chosen by lot by the Committee of Ministers immediately after the first appointment has been made.

4. A member of the Committee of Experts appointed to replace a member whose term of office has not expired shall hold office for the remainder of his predecessor's term.

Article 26
Participation of the International Labour Organisation

The International Labour Organisation shall be invited to nominate a representative to participate in a consultative capacity in the deliberations of the Committee of Experts.

Article 27
Sub-committee of the Governmental Social Committee

1. The reports of the Contracting Parties and the conclusions of the Committee of Experts shall be submitted for examination to a Sub-committee of the Governmental Social Committee of the Council of Europe.

2. The Sub-committee shall be composed of one representative of each of the Contracting Parties. It shall invite no more than two international organisa-

tions of employers and no more than two international trade union organisations as it may designate to be represented as observers in a consultative capacity at its meetings. Moreover, it may consult no more than two representatives of international non-governmental organisations having consultative status with the Council of Europe, in respect of questions with which the organisations are particularly qualified to deal, such as social welfare, and the economic and social protection of the family.

3. The Sub-committee shall present to the Committee of Ministers a report containing its conclusions and append the report of the Committee of Experts.

Article 28
Consultative Assembly

The Secretary-General of the Council of Europe shall transmit to the Consultative Assembly the conclusions of the Committee of Experts. The Consultative Assembly shall communicate its views on these Conclusions to the Committee of Ministers.

Article 29
Committee of Ministers

By a majority of two-thirds of the members entitled to sit on the Committee, the Committee of Ministers may, on the basis of the report of the Sub-committee, and after consultation with the Consultative Assembly, make to each Contracting Party any necessary recommendations.

PART V

Article 30
Derogations in time of war or public emergency

1. In time of war or other public emergency threatening the life of the nation any Contracting Party may take measures derogating from its obligations under this Charter to the extent strictly required by the exigencies of the situation, provided that such measures are not inconsistent with its other obligations under international law.

2. Any Contracting Party which has availed itself of this right of derogation shall, within a reasonable lapse of time, keep the Secretary-General of the Council of Europe fully informed of the measures taken and of the reasons therefor. It shall likewise inform the Secretary-General when such measures have ceased to operate and the provisions of the Charter which it has accepted are again being fully executed.

3. The Secretary-General shall in turn inform the other Contracting Parties and the Director-General of the International Labour Office of all communications received in accordance with paragraph 2 of this Article.

Article 31
Restrictions

1. The rights and principles set forth in Part I when effectively realised, and their effective exercise as provided for in Part II, shall not be subject to any restrictions or limitations not specified in those Parts, except such as are prescribed by law and are necessary in a democratic society for the protection

of the rights and freedoms of others or for the protection of public interest, national security, public health, or morals.

2. The restrictions permitted under this Charter to the rights and obligations set forth herein shall not be applied for any purpose other than that for which they have been prescribed.

Article 32
Relations between the Charter and domestic law or international agreements

The provisions of this Charter shall not prejudice the provisions of domestic law or of any bilateral or multilateral treaties, conventions or agreements which are already in force, or may come into force, under which more favourable treatment would be accorded to the persons protected.

Article 33
Implementation by collective agreements

1. In member States where the provisions of paragraphs 1, 2, 3, 4 and 5 of Article 2, paragraphs 4, 6 and 7 of Article 7 and paragraphs 1, 2, 3 and 4 of Article 10 of Part II of this Charter are matters normally left to agreements between employers or employers' organisations and workers' organisations, or are normally carried out otherwise than by law, the undertakings of those paragraphs may be given and compliance with them shall be treated as effective if their provisions are applied through such agreements or other means to the great majority of the workers concerned.

2. In member States where these provisions are normally the subject of legislation, the undertakings concerned may likewise be given, and compliance with them shall be regarded as effective if the provisions are applied by law to the great majority of the workers concerned.

Article 34
Territorial application

1. This Charter shall apply to the metropolitan territory of each Contracting Party. Each signatory Government may, at the time of signature or of the deposit of its instrument of ratification or approval, specify, by declaration addressed to the Secretary-General of the Council of Europe, the territory which shall be considered to be its metropolitan territory for this purpose.

2. Any Contracting Party may, at the time of ratification or approval of this Charter or at any time thereafter, declare by notification addressed to the Secretary-General of the Council of Europe, that the Charter shall extend in whole or in part to a non-metropolitan territory or territories specified in the said declaration for whose international relations it is responsible or for which it assumes international responsibility. It shall specify in the declaration the Articles or paragraphs of Part II of the Charter which it accepts as binding in respect of the territories named in the declaration.

3. The Charter shall extend to the territory or territories named in the aforesaid declarations as from the thirtieth day after the date on which the Secretary-General shall have received notification of such declaration.

4. Any Contracting Party may declare at a later date by notification addressed to the Secretary-General of the Council of Europe, that, in respect of one or more of the territories to which the Charter has been extended in accordance with paragraph 2 of this Article, it accepts as binding any Articles

or any numbered paragraphs which it has not already accepted in respect of that territory or territories. Such undertakings subsequently given shall be deemed to be an integral part of the original declaration in respect of the territory concerned, and shall have the same effect as from the thirtieth day after the date of the notification.

5. The Secretary-General shall communicate to the other signatory Governments and to the Director-General of the International Labour Office any notification transmitted to him in accordance with this Article.

Article 35
Signature, ratification and entry into force

1. This Charter shall be open for signature by the Members of the Council of Europe. It shall be ratified or approved. Instruments of ratification or approval shall be deposited with the Secretary-General of the Council of Europe.

2. This Charter shall come into force as from the thirtieth day after the date of deposit of the fifth instrument of ratification or approval.

3. In respect of any signatory Government ratifying subsequently, the Charter shall come into force as from the thirtieth day after the date of deposit of its instrument of ratification or approval.

4. The Secretary-General shall notify all the Members of the Council of Europe and the Director-General of the International Labour Office, of the entry into force of the Charter, the names of the Contracting Parties which have ratified or approved it and the subsequent deposit of any instruments of ratification or approval.

Article 36
Amendments

Any Member of the Council of Europe may propose amendments to this Charter in a communication addressed to the Secretary-General of the Council of Europe. The Secretary-General shall transmit to the other Members of the Council of Europe any amendments so proposed, which shall then be considered by the Committee of Ministers and submitted to the Consultative Assembly for opinion. Any amendments approved by the Committee of Ministers shall enter into force as from the thirtieth day after all the Contracting Parties have informed the Secretary-General of their acceptance. The Secretary-General shall notify all the Members of the Council of Europe and the Director-General of the International Labour Office of the entry into force of such amendments.

Article 37
Denunciation

1. Any Contracting Party may denounce this Charter only at the end of a period of five years from the date on which the Charter entered into force for it, or at the end of any successive period of two years, and, in each case, after giving six months notice to the Secretary-General of the Council of Europe, who shall inform the other Parties and the Director-General of the International Labour Office accordingly. Such denunciation shall not affect the validity of the Charter in respect of the other Contracting Parties provided that at all times there are not less than five such Contracting Parties.

2. Any Contracting Party may, in accordance with the provisions set out in

the preceding paragraph, denounce any Article or paragraph of Part II of the Charter accepted by it provided that the number of Articles or paragraphs by which this Contracting Party is bound shall never be less than 10 in the former case and 45 in the latter and that this number of Articles or paragraphs shall continue to include the Articles selected by the Contracting Party among those to which special reference is made in Article 20, paragraph 1, sub-paragraph (b).

3. Any Contracting Party may denounce the present Charter or any of the Articles or paragraphs of Part II of the Charter, under the conditions specified in paragraph I of this Article in respect of any territory to which the said Charter is applicable by virtue of a declaration made in accordance with paragraph 2 of Article 34.

Article 38
Appendix

The Appendix to this Charter shall form an integral part of it.

In witness whereof, the undersigned, being duly authorised thereto, have signed this Charter.

Done at Turin, this 18th day of October 1961, in English and French, both texts being equally authoritative, in a single copy which shall be deposited within the archives of the Council of Europe. The Secretary-General shall transmit certified copies to each of the Signatories.

APPENDIX TO THE SOCIAL CHARTER

Scope of the Social Charter in terms of persons protected:

1. Without prejudice to Article 12, paragraph 4 and Article 13, paragraph 4, the persons covered by Articles 1 to 17 include foreigners only insofar as they are nationals of other Contracting Parties lawfully resident or working regularly within the territory of the Contracting Party concerned, subject to the understanding that these Articles are to be interpreted in the light of the provisions of Articles 18 and 19.

This interpretation would not prejudice the extension of similar facilities to other persons by any of the Contracting Parties.

2. Each Contracting Party will grant to refugees as defined in the Convention relating to the Status of Refugees, signed at Geneva on 28th July 1951, and lawfully staying in its territory, treatment as favourable as possible, and in any case not less favourable than under the obligations accepted by the Contracting Party under the said Convention and under any other existing international instruments applicable to those refugees.

Part I, Paragraph 18 and Part II, Article 18, paragraph 1

It is understood that these provisions are not concerned with the question of entry into the territories of the Contracting Parties and do not prejudice the provisions of the European Convention on Establishment, signed at Paris on 13th December 1955.

Part II, Article 1, paragraph 2

This provision shall not be interpreted as prohibiting or authorising any union security clause or practice.

Article 4, paragraph 4

This provision shall be so understood as not to prohibit immediate dismissal for any serious offence.

Article 4, paragraph 5

It is understood that a Contracting Party may give the undertaking required in this paragraph if the great majority of workers are not permitted to suffer deductions from wages either by law or through collective agreements or arbitration awards, the exceptions being those persons not so covered.

Article 6, paragraph 4

It is understood that each Contracting Party may, insofar as it is concerned, regulate the exercise of the right to strike by law, provided that any further restriction that this might place on the right can be justified under the terms of Article 31.

Article 7, paragraph 8

It is understood that a Contracting Party may give the undertaking required in this paragraph if it fulfils the spirit of the undertaking by providing by law that the great majority of persons under 18 years of age shall not be employed in night work.

Article 12, paragraph 4

The words "and subject to the conditions laid down in such agreements" in the introduction to this paragraph are taken to imply *inter alia* that with regard to benefits which are available independently of any insurance contribution a Contracting Party may require the completion of a prescribed period of residence before granting such benefits to nationals of other Contracting Parties.

Article 13, paragraph 4

Governments not Parties to the European Convention on Social and Medical Assistance may ratify the Social Charter in respect of this paragraph provided that they grant to nationals of other Contracting Parties a treatment which is in conformity with the provisions of the said Convention.

Article 19, paragraph 6

For the purpose of this provision, the term "family of a foreign worker" is understood to mean at least his wife and dependent children under the age of 21 years.

Part III

It is understood that the Charter contains legal obligations of an international character, the application of which is submitted solely to the supervision provided for in Part IV thereof.

Article 20, paragraph 1

It is understood that the "numbered paragraphs" may include Articles consisting of only one paragraph.

Part V, Article 30

The term "in time of war or other public emergency" shall be so understood as to cover also the *threat* of war.

Appendix IV. United Nations

International Covenant on Economic, Social and Cultural Rights[1]

PREAMBLE

The States Parties to the present Covenant,

Considering that, in accordance with the principles proclaimed in the Charter of the United Nations, recognition of the inherent dignity and of the equal and inalienable rights of all members of the human family is the foundation of freedom, justice and peace in the world,

Recognizing that these rights derive from the inherent dignity of the human person,

Recognizing that, in accordance with the Universal Declaration of Human Rights, the ideal of free human beings enjoying freedom from fear and want can only be achieved if conditions are created whereby everyone may enjoy his economic, social and cultural rights, as well as his civil and political rights,

Considering the obligation of States under the Charter of the United Nations to promote universal respect for, and observance of, human rights and freedoms,

Realizing that the individual, having duties to other individuals and to the community to which he belongs, is under a responsibility to strive for the promotion and observance of the rights recognized in the present Covenant,

Agree upon the following articles:

PART I

Article 1

1. All peoples have the right of self-determination. By virtue of that right they freely determine their political status and freely pursue their economic, social and cultural development.

2. All peoples may, for their own ends, freely dispose of their natural wealth and resources without prejudice to any obligations arising out of international economic co-operation, based upon the principle of mutual benefit, and international law. In no case may a people be deprived of its own means of subsistence.

---

1. Adopted and opened for signature December 16, 1966, entered into force January 3, 1976. U.N.G.A. Res. 2200A (XXI), 21 U.N. GAOR, Supp. No. 16, at 49, U.N. Doc. A/6316 (1967), 993 U.N.T.S. 3.

3. The States Parties to the present Covenant, including those having responsibility for the administration of Non-Self-Governing and Trust Territories, shall promote the realization of the right of self-determination, and shall respect that right, in conformity with the provisions of the Charter of the United Nations.

PART II

Article 2

1. Each State Party to the present Covenant undertakes to take steps, individually and through international assistance and co-operation, especially economic and technical, to the maximum of its available resources, with a view to achieving progressively the full realization of the rights recognized in the present Covenant by all appropriate means, including particularly the adoption of legislative measures.

2. The States Parties to the present Covenant undertake to guarantee that the rights enunciated in the present Covenant will be exercised without discrimination of any kind as to race, colour, sex, language, religion, political or other opinion, national or social origin, property, birth or other status.

3. Developing countries, with due regard to human rights and their national economy, may determine to what extent they would guarantee the economic rights recognized in the present Covenant to non-nationals.

Article 3

The States Parties to the present Covenant undertake to ensure the equal right of men and women to the enjoyment of all economic, social and cultural rights set forth in the present Covenant.

Article 4

The State Parties to the present Covenant recognize that, in the enjoyment of those rights provided by the State in conformity with the present Covenant, the State may subject such rights only to such limitations as are determined by law only in so far as this may be compatible with the nature of these rights and solely for the purpose of promoting the general welfare in a democratic society.

Article 5

1. Nothing in the present Covenant may be interpreted as implying for any State, group or person any right to engage in any activity or to perform any act aimed at the destruction of any of the rights or freedoms recognized herein, or at their limitation to a greater extent than is provided for in the present Covenant.

2. No restriction upon or derogation from any of the fundamental human rights recognized or existing in any country in virtue of law, conventions, regulations or custom shall be admitted on the pretext that the present Covenant does not recognize such rights or that it recognizes them to a lesser extent.

PART III

Article 6

1. The States Parties to the present Covenant recognize the right to work, which includes the right of everyone to the opportunity to gain his living by

work which he freely chooses or accepts, and will take appropriate steps to safeguard this right.

2. The steps to be taken by a State Party to the present Covenant to achieve the full realization of this right shall include technical and vocational guidance and training programmes, policies and techniques to achieve steady economic, social and cultural development and full and productive employment under conditions safeguarding fundamental political and economic freedoms to the individual.

Article 7

The States Parties to the present Covenant recognize the right of everyone to the enjoyment of just and favourable conditions of work which ensure, in particular:

(a) Remuneration which provides all workers, as a minimum, with:
   (i) Fair wages and equal renumeration for work of equal value without distinction of any kind, in particular women being guaranteed conditions of work not inferior to those enjoyed by men, with equal pay for equal work;
   (ii) A decent living for themselves and their families in accordance with the provisions of the present Covenant;
(b) Safe and healthy working conditions;
(c) Equal opportunity for everyone to be promoted in his employment to an appropriate higher level, subject to no considerations other than those of seniority and competence;
(d) Rest, leisure and reasonable limitation of working hours and periodic holidays with pay, as well as remuneration for public holidays.

Article 8

1. The States Parties to the present Covenant undertake to ensure:

(a) The right of everyone to form trade unions and join the trade union of his choice, subject only to the rules of the organization concerned, for the promotion and protection of his economic and social interests. No restrictions may be placed on the exercise of this right other than those prescribed by law and which are necessary in a democratic society in the interests of national security or public order or for the protection of the rights and freedoms of others;
(b) The right of trade unions to establish national federations or confederations and the right of the latter to form or join international trade-union organizations;
(c) The right of trade unions to function freely subject to no limitations other than those prescribed by law and which are necessary in a democratic society in the interests of national security or public order or for the protection of the rights and freedoms of others;
(d) The right to strike, provided that it is exercised in conformity with the laws of the particular country.

2. This article shall not prevent the imposition of lawful restrictions on the exercise of these rights by members of the armed forces or of the police or of the administration of the State.

3. Nothing in this article shall authorize States Parties to the International Labour Organisation Convention of 1948 concerning Freedom of Association and Protection of the Right to Organize to take legislative measures which

would prejudice, or apply the law in such a manner as would prejudice, the guarantees provided for in that Convention.

Article 9

The States Parties to the present Covenant recognize the right of everyone to social security, including social insurance.

Article 10

The States Parties to the present Covenant recognize that:

1. The widest possible protection and assistance should be accorded to the family, which is the natural and fundamental group unit of society, particularly for its establishment and while it is responsible for the care and education of dependent children. Marriage must be entered into with the free consent of the intending spouses.

2. Special protection should be accorded to mothers during a reasonable period before and after childbirth. During such period working mothers should be accorded paid leave or leave with adequate social security benefits.

3. Special measures of protection and assistance should be taken on behalf of all children and young persons without any discrimination for reasons of parentage or other conditions. Children and young persons should be protected from economic and social exploitation. Their employment in work harmful to their morals or health or dangerous to life or likely to hamper their normal development should be punishable by law. States should also set age limits below which the paid employment of child labour should be prohibited and punishable by law.

Article 11

1. The States Parties to the present Covenant recognize the right of everyone to an adequate standard of living for himself and his family, including adequate food, clothing and housing, and to the continuous improvement of living conditions. The States Parties will take appropriate steps to ensure the realization of this right, recognizing to this effect the essential importance of international co-operation based on free consent.

2. The States Parties to the present Covenant, recognizing the fundamental right of everyone to be free from hunger, shall take, individually and through international co-operation, the measures, including specific programmes, which are needed:

(a) To improve methods of production, conservation and distribution of food by making full use of technical and scientific knowledge, by disseminating knowledge of the principles of nutrition and by developing or reforming agrarian systems in such a way as to achieve the most efficient development and utilization of natural resources;

(b) Taking into account the problems of both food-importing and food-exporting countries, to ensure an equitable distribution of world food supplies in relation to need.

Article 12

The States Parties to the present Covenant recognize the right of everyone to the enjoyment of the highest attainable standard of physical and mental health.

2. The steps to be taken by the States Parties to the present Covenant to achieve the full realization of this right shall include those necessary for:
(a) The provision for the reduction of the stillbirth-rate and of infant mortality and for the healthy development of the child;
(b) The improvement of all aspects of environmental and industrial hygiene;
(c) The prevention, treatment and control of epidemic, endemic, occupational and other diseases;
(d) The creation of conditions which would assure to all medical service and medical attention in the event of sickness.

Article 13

1. The States Parties to the present Covenant recognize the right of everyone to education. They agree that education shall be directed to the full development of the human personality and the sense of its dignity, and shall strengthen the respect for human rights and fundamental freedoms. They further agree that education shall enable all persons to participate effectively in a free society, promote understanding, tolerance and friendship among all nations and all racial, ethnic or religious groups, and further the activities of the United Nations for the maintenance of peace.

2. The States Parties to the present Covenant recognize that, with a view to achieving the full realization of this right:
(a) Primary education shall be compulsory and available free to all;
(b) Secondary education in its different forms, including technical and vocational secondary education, shall be made generally available and accessible to all by every appropriate means, and in particular by the progressive introduction of free education;
(c) Higher education shall be made equally accessible to all, on the basis of capacity, by every appropriate means, and in particular by the progressive introduction of free education;
(d) Fundamental education shall be encouraged or intensified as far as possible for those persons who have not received or completed the whole period of their primary education;
(e) The development of a system of schools at all levels shall be actively pursued, an adequate fellowship system shall be established, and the material conditions of teaching staff shall be continuously improved.

3. The States Parties to the present Covenant undertake to have respect for the liberty of parents and, when applicable, legal guardians to choose for their children schools, other than those established by the public authorities, which conform to such minimum educational standards as may be laid down or approved by the State and to ensure the religious and moral education of their children in conformity with their own convictions.

4. No part of this article shall be construed so as to interfere with the liberty of individuals and bodies to establish and direct educational institutions, subject always to the observance of the principles set forth in paragraph 1 of this article and to the requirement that the education given in such institutions shall conform to such minimum standards as may be laid down by the State.

Article 14

Each State Party to the present Covenant which, at the time of becoming a Party, has not been able to secure in its metropolitan territory or other territories under its jurisdiction compulsory primary education, free of charge, undertakes, within two years, to work out and adopt a detailed plan of action for the progressive implementation, within a reasonable number of years, to be fixed in the plan, of the principle of compulsory education free of charge for all.

Article 15

1. The States Parties to the present Covenant recognize the right of everyone:
(a) To take part in cultural life;
(b) To enjoy the benefits of scientific progress and its applications;
(c) To benefit from the protection of the moral and material interests resulting from any scientific, literary or artistic production of which he is the author.

2. The steps to be taken by the States Parties to the present Covenant to achieve the full realization of this right shall include those necessary for the conservation, the development and the diffusion of science and culture.

3. The States Parties to the present Covenant undertake to respect the freedom indispensable for scientific research and creative activity.

4. The States Parties to the present Covenant recognize the benefits to be derived from the encouragement and development of international contacts and co-operation in the scientific and cultural fields.

PART IV

Article 16

1. The States Parties to the present Covenant undertake to submit in conformity with this part of the Covenant reports on the measures which they have adopted and the progress made in achieving the observance of the rights recognized herein.

2. (a) All reports shall be submitted to the Secretary-General of the United Nations, who shall transmit copies to the Economic and Social Council for consideration in accordance with the provisions of the present Covenant;
(b) The Secretary-General of the United Nations shall also transmit to the specialized agencies copies of the reports, or any relevant parts therefrom, from States Parties to the present Covenant which are also members of these specialized agencies in so far as these reports, or parts therefrom, relate to any matters which fall within the responsibilities of the said agencies in accordance with their constitutional instruments.

Article 17

1. The States Parties to the present Covenant shall furnish their reports in stages, in accordance with a programme to be established by the Economic and Social Council within one year of the entry into force of the present Covenant after consultation with the States Parties and the specialized agencies concerned.

2. Reports may indicate factors and difficulties affecting the degree of fulfilment of obligations under the present Covenant.

3. Where relevant information has previously been furnished to the

United Nations or to any specialized agency by any State Party to the present Covenant, it will not be necessary to reproduce that information, but a precise reference to the information so furnished will suffice.

Article 18
Pursuant to its responsibilities under the Charter of the United Nations in the field of human rights and fundamental freedoms, the Economic and Social Council may make arrangements with the specialized agencies in respect of their reporting to it on the progress made in achieving the observance of the provisions of the present Covenant falling within the scope of their activities. These reports may include particulars of decisions and recommendations on such implementation adopted by their competent organs.

Article 19
The Economic and Social Council may transmit to the Commission on Human Rights for study and general recommendation or, as appropriate, for information the reports concerning human rights submitted by States in accordance with articles 16 and 17, and those concerning human rights submitted by the specialized agencies in accordance with article 18.

Article 20
The States Parties to the present Covenant and the specialized agencies concerned may submit comments to the Economic and Social Council on any general recommendation under article 19 or reference to such general recommendation in any report of the Commission on Human Rights or any documentation referred to therein.

Article 21
The Economic and Social Council may submit from time to time to the General Assembly reports with recommendations of a general nature and a summary of the information received from the States Parties to the present Covenant and the specialized agencies on the measures taken and the progress made in achieving general observance of the rights recognized in the present Covenant.

Article 22
The Economic and Social Council may bring to the attention of other organs of the United Nations, their subsidiary organs and specialized agencies concerned with furnishing technical assistance any matters arising out of the reports referrred to in this part of the present Covenant which may assist such bodies in deciding, each within its field of competence, on the advisability of international measures likely to contribute to the effective progressive implementation of the present Covenant.

Article 23
The States Parties to the present Covenant agree that international action for the achievement of the rights recognized in the present Covenant includes such methods as the conclusion of conventions, the adoption of recommendations, the furnishing of technical assistance and the holding of regional meetings and technical meetings for the purpose of consultation and study organized in conjunction with the Governments concerned.

Article 24

Nothing in the present Covenant shall be interpreted as impairing the provisions of the Charter of the United Nations and of the constitutions of the specialized agencies which define the respective responsibilities of the various organs of the United Nations and of the specialized agencies in regard to the matters dealt with in the present Covenant.

Article 25

Nothing in the present Covenant shall be interpreted as impairing the inherent right of all peoples to enjoy and utilize fully and freely their natural wealth and resources.

PART V

Article 26

1. The present Covenant is open for signature by any State Member of the United Nations or member of any of its specialized agencies, by any State Party to the Statute of the International Court of Justice, and by any other State which has been invited by the General Assembly of the United Nations to become a party to the present Covenant.

2. The present Covenant is subject to ratification. Instruments of ratification shall be deposited with the Secretary-General of the United Nations.

3. The present Covenant shall be open to accession by any State referred to in paragraph 1 of this article.

4. Accession shall be effected by the deposit of an instrument of accession with the Secretary-General of the United Nations.

5. The Secretary-General of the United Nations shall inform all States which have signed the present Covenant or acceded to it of the deposit of each instrument of ratification or accession.

Article 27

1. The present Covenant shall enter into force three months after the date of the deposit with the Secretary-General of the United Nations of the thirty-fifth instrument of ratification or instrument of accession.

2. For each State ratifying the present Covenant or acceding to it after the deposit of the thirty-fifth instrument of ratification or instrument of accession, the present Covenant shall enter into force three months after the date of the deposit of its own instrument of ratification or instrument of accession.

Article 28

The provisions of the present Covenant shall extend to all parts of federal States without any limitations or exceptions.

Article 29

1. Any State Party to the present Covenant may propose an amendment and file it with the Secretary-General of the United Nations. The Secretary-General shall thereupon communicate any proposed amendments to the States Parties to the present Covenant with a request that they notify him whether they favour a conference of States Parties for the purpose of considering and voting upon the proposals. In the event that at least one third of the States Parties favours such a conference, the Secretary-General shall convene

the conference under the auspices of the United Nations. Any amendment adopted by a majority of the States Parties present and voting at the conference shall be submitted to the General Assembly of the United Nations for approval.

2. Amendments shall come into force when they have been approved by the General Assembly of the United Nations and accepted by a two-thirds majority of the States Parties to the present Covenant in accordance with their respective constitutional processes.

3. When amendments come into force they shall be binding on those States Parties which have accepted them, other States Parties still being bound by the provisions of the present Covenant and any earlier amendment which they have accepted.

Article 30

Irrespective of the notifications made under article 26, paragraph 5, the Secretary-General of the United Nations shall inform all States referred to in paragraph 1 of the same article of the following particulars:

(a) Signatures, ratifications and accessions under article 26;
(b) The date of the entry into force of the present Covenant under article 27 and the date of the entry into force of any amendments under article 29.

Article 31

1. The present Covenant, of which the Chinese, English, French, Russian and Spanish texts are equally authentic, shall be deposited in the archives of the United Nations.

2. The Secretary-General of the United Nations shall transmit certified copies of the present Covenant to all States referred to in article 26.

Appendix V. European Community

Protocol on Social Policy[1]

THE HIGH CONTRACTING PARTIES,

NOTING that 11 Member States, that is to say the Kingdom of Belgium, the Kingdom of Denmark, the Federal Republic of Germany, the Hellenic Republic, the Kingdom of Spain, the French Republic, Ireland, the Italian Republic, the Grand Duchy of Luxembourg, the Kingdom of the Netherlands and the Portuguese Republic, wish to continue along the path laid down in the 1989 Social Charter; that they have adopted among themselves an Agreement to this end; that this Agreement is annexed to this Protocol; that this Protocol and the said Agreement are without prejudice to the provisions of this Treaty, particularly those relating to social policy which constitute an integral part of the *acquis communautaire:*

1. Agree to authorize those 11 Member States to have recourse to the institutions, procedures and mechanisms of the Treaty for the purposes of taking among themselves and applying as far as they are concerned the acts and decisions required for giving effect to the abovementioned Agreement.

2. The United Kingdom of Great Britain and Northern Ireland shall not take part in the deliberations and the adoption by the Council of Commission proposals made on the basis of this Protocol and the abovementioned Agreement.

By way of derogation from Article 148(2) of the Treaty, acts of the Council which are made pursuant to this Protocol and which must be adopted by a qualified majority shall be deemed to be so adopted if they have received at least 44 votes in favour. The unanimity of the members of the Council, with the exception of the United Kingdom of Great Britain and Northern Ireland, shall be necessary for acts of the Council which must be adopted unanimously and for those amending the Commission proposal.

Acts adopted by the Council and any financial consequences other than administrative costs entailed for the institutions shall not be applicable to the United Kingdom of Great Britain and Northern Ireland.

1. Protocol signed February 7, 1992. Council and Commission of the European Communities, *Treaty on Economic Union* (Luxembourg: European Communities, 1992), p. 196.

3. This Protocol shall be annexed to the Treaty establishing the European Community.

Agreement on Social Policy Concluded Between the Member States of the European Community with the Exception of the United Kingdom of Great Britain and Northern Ireland.[1]

The undersigned 11 HIGH CONTRACTING PARTIES, that is to say the Kingdom of Belgium, the Kingdom of Denmark, the Federal Republic of Germany, the Hellenic Republic, the Kingdom of Spain, the French Republic, Ireland, the Italian Republic, the Grand Duchy of Luxembourg, the Kingdom of the Netherlands and the Portuguese Republic (hereinafter referred to as 'the Member States'),

WISHING to implement the 1989 Social Charter on the basis of the *acquis communautaire,*

CONSIDERING the Protocol on social policy,

HAVE AGREED as follows:

Article 1

The Community and the Member States shall have as their objectives the promotion of employment, improved living and working conditions, proper social protection, dialogue between management and labour, the development of human resources with a view to lasting high employment and the combating of exclusion. To this end the Community and the Member States shall implement measures which take account of the diverse forms of national practices, in particular in the field of contractual relations, and the need to maintain the competitiveness of the Community economy.

Article 2

1. With a view to achieving the objectives of Article 1, the Community shall support and complement the activities of the Member States in the following fields:

- improvement in particular of the working environment to protect workers' health and safety;
- working conditions;
- the information and consultation of workers;
- equality between men and women with regard to labour market opportunities and treatment at work;
- the integration of persons excluded from the labour market, without prejudice to Article 127 of the Treaty establishing the European Community (hereinafter referred to as 'the Treaty').

2. To this end, the Council may adopt, by means of directives, minimum requirements for gradual implementation, having regard to the conditions and technical rules obtaining in each of the Member States. Such directives shall avoid imposing administrative, financial and legal constraints in a way

1. Protocol and Agreement signed February 7, 1992. Council and Commission of the European Communities, *Treaty on European Union* (Luxembourg: European Communities, 1992), pp. 197–201.

which would hold back the creation and development of small and medium-sized undertakings.

The Council shall act in accordance with the procedure referred to in Article 189c of the Treaty after consulting the Economic and Social Committee.

3. However, the Council shall act unanimously on a proposal from the Commission, after consulting the European Parliament and the Economic and Social Committee, in the following areas:
- social security and social protection of workers;
- protection of workers where their employment contract is terminated;
- representation and collective defence of the interests of workers and employers, including co-determination, subject to paragraph 6;
- conditions of employment for third-country nationals legally residing in Community territory;
- financial contributions for promotion of employment and job-creation, without prejudice to the provisions relation to the Social Fund.

4. A Member State may entrust management and labour, at their joint request, with the implementation of directives adopted pursuant to paragraphs 2 and 3.

In this case, it shall ensure that, no later than the date on which a directive must be transposed in accordance with Article 189, management and labour have introduced the necessary measures by agreement, the Member State concerned being required to take any necessary measure enabling it at any time to be in a position to guarantee the results imposed by that directive.

5. The provisions adopted pursuant to this Article shall not prevent any Member State from maintaining or introducing more stringent protective measures compatible with the Treaty.

6. The provisions of this Article shall not apply to pay, the right of association, the right to strike or the right to impose lock-outs.

Article 3

1. The Commission shall have the task of promoting the consultation of management and labour at Community level and shall take any relevant measure to facilitate their dialogue by ensuring balanced support for the parties.

2. To this end, before submitting proposals in the social policy field, the Commission shall consult management and labour on the possible direction of Community action.

3. If, after such consultation, the Commission considers Community action advisable, it shall consult management and labour on the content of the envisaged proposal. Management and labour shall forward to the Commission an opinion or, where appropriate, a recommendation.

4. On the occasion of such consultation, management and labour may inform the Commission of their wish to initiate the process provided for in Article 4. The duration of the procedure shall not exceed nine months, unless the management and labour concerned and the Commission decide jointly to extend it.

Article 4

1. Should management and labour so desire, the dialogue between them at Community level may lead to contractual relations, including agreements.

2. Agreements concluded at Community level shall be implemented either in accordance with the procedures and practices specific to management and labour and the Member States or, in matters covered by Article 2, at the joint request of the signatory parties, by a Council decision on a proposal from the Commission.

The Council shall act by qualified majority, except where the agreement in question contains one or more provisions relating to one of the areas referred to in Article 2(3), in which case it shall act unanimously.

Article 5

With a view to achieving the objectives of Article 1 and without prejudice to the other provisions of the Treaty, the Commission shall encourage cooperation between the Member States and facilitate the coordination of their action in all social policy fields under this Agreement.

Article 6

1. Each Member State shall ensure that the principle of equal pay for male and female workers for equal work is applied.

2. For the purpose of this Article, 'pay' means the ordinary basic or minimum wage or salary and any other consideration, whether in cash or in kind, which the worker receives directly or indirectly, in respect of his employment, from his employer.

Equal pay without discrimination based on sex means:
(a) that pay for the same work at piece rates shall be calculated on the basis of the same unit of measurement;
(b) that pay for work at time rates shall be the same for the same job.

3. This Article shall not prevent any Member State from maintaining or adopting measures providing for specific advantages in order to make it easier for women to pursue a vocational activity or to prevent or compensate for disadvantages in their professional careers.

Article 7

The Commission shall draw up a report each year on progress in achieving the objectives of Article 1, including the demographic situation in the Community. It shall forward the report to the European Parliament, the Council and the Economic and Social Committee.

The European Parliament may invite the Commission to draw up reports on particular problems concerning the social situation.

DECLARATIONS

1. Declaration on Article 2(2)

The 11 High Contracting Parties note that in the discussion on Article 2(2) of the Agreement it was agreed that the Community does not intend, in laying down minimum requirements for the protection of the safety and health of employees, to discriminate in a manner unjustified by the circumstances against employees in small and medium-sized undertakings.

2. Declaration on Article 4(2)

The 11 High Contracting Parties declare that the first of the arrangements for application of the agreements between management and labour at Community level—referred to in Article 4(2)—will consist in developing, by collective bargaining according to the rules of each Member State, the content of the agreements, and that consequently this arrangement implies no obligation on the Member States to apply the agreements directly or to work out rules for their transposition, nor any obligation to amend national legislation in force to facilitate their implementation.

Bibliography

Adam, Jan, ed. *Employment Policies in the Soviet Union and Eastern Europe*. New York: St. Martin's Press, 1982.

Alston, Philip, and Katarina Tomaševski, eds. *The Right to Food*. Boston: M. Nijhoff, 1984.

Arendt, Hannah. *The Human Condition*. Chicago: University of Chicago Press, 1958.

Arneson, Richard J. "Is Work Special? Justice and the Distribution of Employment." *American Political Science Review* 84, 4 (December 1990).

Ascher, William. "New Development Approaches and the Adaptability of International Agencies: The Case of the World Bank." *International Organization* 37 (Summer 1983).

Ashford, Douglas E., ed. *History and Context in Comparative Public Policy*. Pittsburgh: University of Pittsburgh Press, 1992.

Ayres, Robert L. *Banking on the Poor: The World Bank and World Poverty*. Cambridge, MA: MIT Press, 1983.

Bailey, Stephen K. *Congress Makes a Law: The Story Behind the Employment Act of 1946*. New York: Columbia University Press, 1950.

Bakke, E. Wight. *The Unemployed Man: A Social Study*. New York: E. P. Dutton, 1934.

Baumer, Donald C. and Carl E. Van Horn. *The Politics of Unemployment*. Washington, DC: CQ, 1985.

Bawden, D. Lee and Felicity Skidmore, eds. *Rethinking Employment Policy*. Washington, DC: Urban Institute, 1989.

Beveridge, William H. *Full Employment in a Free Society*. New York: W. W. Norton, 1945.

Biersteker, Thomas J. "Reducing the Role of the State in the Economy: A Conceptual Exploration of IMF and World Bank Prescriptions." *International Studies Quarterly* 34, 4 (December 1990).

Blanc, Louis. *Organization of Work*. University of Cincinnati Studies, Series II, trans. by Marie Paula Dickore. Cincinnati, OH: University of Cincinnati, 1911.

Blanplain, Roger. *The OECD Guidelines for Multinational Enterprises and Labour Relations, 1982–84: Experience and Review*. Deventer: Kluwer, 1985.

Brandt Commission on International Development Issues. *Common Crisis North-South: Cooperation for World Recovery*. Cambridge, MA: MIT Press, 1983.

Brown, Peter G. and Douglas MacLean. *Human Rights and U.S. Foreign Policy: Principles and Applications.* Lexington, MA: Lexington Books, 1979.

Camps, Miriam. *Collective Management: The Reform of Global Economic Organizations.* New York: McGraw-Hill, 1981.

Camps, Miriam. *"First World" Relationships: The Role of the OECD* Paris: Atlantic Institute for International Affairs, 1975.

Caparoso, James A., ed. *A Changing International Division of Labor.* Boulder, CO: Lynne Reinner, 1987.

Cecchini, Paolo, with Michel Catinat and Alexis Jaequemin. *TheEuropean Challenge: 1992—The Benefits of a Single Market.* Aldershot, Eng.: Gower, 1988.

Claude, Richard Pierre and Burns H. Weston, eds. *Human Rights in the World Community: Issues and Action.* 2nd ed. Philadelphia: University of Pennsylvania Press, 1992.

Commission on Employment Problems in Europe. *A Programme for Full Employment in the 1990s.* New York: Pergamon Press, 1989.

Conference on Social Policies in the 1980s. *The Welfare State in Crisis.* Paris: OECD, 1981.

Cox, Robert W. *Production, Power and World Order: Social Forces in the Making of History.* New York: Columbia University Press, 1987.

Cox, Robert W. et al. *The Anatomy of Influence: Decision Making in International Organization.* New Haven, CT: Yale University Press, 1973.

Cranston, Maurice W. *What Are Human Rights?* London: Bodley Head, 1973.

Dahrendorf, Ralf. *The Modern Social Conflict: An Essay on the Politics of Liberty.* New York: Weidenfeld and Nicolson, 1988.

Dahrendorf, Ralf, ed. *Europe's Economy in Crisis.* New York: Holmes and Meier, 1982.

Deacon, Bob et al., *The New Eastern Europe: Social Policy Past, Present and Future.* London: Sage Publications, 1992.

Dierkes, Meinolf, Hans N. Weiler, and Ariane Berthoin Antal. *Comparative Policy Research: Learning from Experience.* New York: St. Martin's Press, 1987.

Donnelly, Jack. *Universal Human Rights in Theory and Practice.* Ithaca, NY: Cornell University Press, 1989.

———. "Human Rights and Human Dignity: An Analytic Critique of Non-Western Conceptions of Human Rights." *American Political Science Review* 76, 2 (June 1982).

———. "Human Rights as Natural Rights." *Human Rights Quarterly* 4, 3 (Summer 1982).

Dworkin, Ronald M. *Taking Rights Seriously.* Cambridge, MA: Harvard University Press, 1977.

Elster, Jon. "Is There (or Should There Be) a Right to Work?" In Amy Guttman, ed., *Democracy and the Welfare State.* Princeton, NJ: Princeton University Press, 1988.

Esping-Andersen, Gösta. *The Three Worlds of Welfare Capitalism.* Princeton, NJ: Princeton University Press, 1990.

Feinberg, Joel. *Rights, Justice, and the Bounds of Liberty: Essays in Social Policy.* Princeton, NJ: Princeton University Press, 1980.

Feinberg, Richard E., ed. *Between Two Worlds: The World Bank's Next Decade.* New Brunswick, NJ: Transaction Press, 1986.

Flora, Peter and Arnold J. Heidenheimer, eds. *The Development of Welfare States in Europe and America.* New Brunswick, NJ: Transaction, 1981.

Forrest, Alan. *The French Revolution and the Poor*. New York: St. Martin's Press, 1981.

Forsythe, David. *The Internationalization of Human Rights*. Lexington, MA: Lexington, 1991.

Frankel, Charles. *Human Rights and Foreign Policy*. New York: Foreign Policy Association, 1978. Headline Series No. 241 .

Friedrich, Carl J. "Rights, Liberties, Freedoms: A Reappraisal." *American Political Science Review* 57, 4 (December 1963).

Galenson, Walter. *The International Labor Organization: An American View*. Madison: University of Wisconsin Press, 1981.

Garraty, John A. *Unemployment in History: Economic Thought and Public Policy*. New York: Harper and Row, 1978.

Ghai, Dharam P., ed. *The IMF and the South: The Social Impact of Crisis and Adaptation*. Atlantic Highlands, NJ: Zed/ Humanities, 1992.

Gibbons, William J. and Gerald C. Treacy, eds. *Seven Great Encyclicals*. Glen Rock, NJ: Paulist Press, 1963.

Gilder, George. *Wealth and Poverty*. New York: Basic Books, 1981.

Ginsburg, Helen. *Full Employment and Public Policy: The United States and Sweden*. Lexington, MA: Lexington Books, 1983.

Ginzberg, Eli. *Good Jobs, Bad Jobs, No Jobs*. Cambridge, MA: Harvard University Press, 1979.

Gourevitch, Peter A. *Politics in Hard Times*. Ithaca, NY: Cornell University Press, 1986.

Grieves, Forest, ed. *Transnationalism in World Politics and Business*. New York: Pergamon, 1979.

Gross, Bertram and Alfred Pfaller, eds. *Unemployment: A Global Challenge*. Vol. 492 of The Annals of the American Academy of Political and Social Science. Newbury Park, CA: Sage Publications, 1987.

Gunderson, Morley, Noah M. Meltz, and Sylvia Ostry, eds. *Unemployment: International Perspectives*. Toronto: University of Toronto Press, 1987.

Gwin, Catherine C., Richard E. Feinberg, and contributors. *Pulling Together: The International Monetary Fund in a Multipolar World*. New Brunswick, NJ: Transaction Books, 1989.

Haas, Ernst B. *Beyond the Nation-State: Functionalism and International Organization*. Stanford, CA: Stanford University Press, 1964.

———. *When Knowledge is Power*. Berkeley: University of California Press, 1990.

———. *Global Evangelism Rides Again: How to Protect Human Rights Without Really Trying*. Berkeley, CA: Institute of International Studies, 1978.

Haas, Peter M., ed. *Knowledge, Power, and International Policy Coordination*. Special issue of *International Organization* 46 (Winter 1992).

Harris, David. *The European Social Charter*. Charlottesville: University of Virginia Press, 1984.

Harvey, Philip. *Securing the Right to Employment: Social Welfare and the Unemployed in the United States*. Princeton, NJ: Princeton University Press, 1989.

Hayek, Friedrich A. *The Constitution of Liberty*. Chicago: University of Chicago Press, 1960.

———. *The Road to Serfdom*. Chicago: University of Chicago Press, 1944.

Heclo, Hugh. *Modern Social Politics in Britain and Sweden: From Relief to Income Maintenance*. New Haven, CT: Yale University Press, 1974.

Heidenheimer, Arnold J., Hugh Heclo, and Carolyn Teich Adams. *Comparative Public Policy: The Politics of Social Choice in Europe and America*. 2nd ed. New York: St. Martin's Press, 1983.

Henkin, Louis. *The Rights of Man Today*. Boulder, CO: Westview Press, 1978.

Hill, Christopher. *The World Turned Upside Down: Radical Ideas During the English Revolution*. New York: Viking, 1972.

Himmelfarb, Gertrude. *The Idea of Poverty: England in the Early Industrial Age*. New York: Alfred Knopf, 1984.

Humphrey, John P. *Human Rights and the United Nations: A Great Adventure*. Dobbs Ferry, NY: Transnational Books, 1984.

Imber, Mark F. *The USA, ILO, UNESCO and IAEA: Politicization and Withdrawal in the Specialized Agencies*. New York: St. Martin's Press, 1989.

Independent Commission of the South on Development Issues. *The Challenge to the South: A Report of the South Commission*. New York: Oxford University Press, 1990.

Independent Commission on International Development Issues. *North-South, a Programme for Survival: Report of the Independent Commission on International Development Issues*. Cambridge, MA: MIT Press, 1980.

International Labour Organisation. *Employment and Poverty in a Troubled World: Report of a Meeting of High-Level Experts on Employment*. Geneva: International Labour Office, 1985.

———. *World Recession and Global Interdependence: Effects on Employment, Poverty and Policy Formation in Developing Countries*. Geneva: International Labour Office, 1987.

International Monetary Fund et al. *A Study of the Soviet Economy*, Vol. 2. Paris: International Monetary Fund, World Bank, OECD, and European Bank for Reconstruction and Development, 1991.

Jacobson, Harold K. *Networks of Interdependence: International Organizations and the Global Political System*. New York: Alfred Knopf, 1979.

Jahoda, Marie, Paul Lazarsfeld, and Hans Zeisel. *Marienthal: The Sociography of an Unemployed Community*. Chicago: Aldine Atherton, 1971.

Jenks, C. Wilfred. *Social Justice in the Law of Nations: The ILO Impact After Fifty Years*. London: Oxford University Press, 1970.

Joyce, James Avery. *World Labour Rights and Their Protection*. New York: St. Martin's Press, 1980.

Kaus, Mickey. *The End of Equality*. New York: Basic Books, 1992.

Kelvin, Peter and Joanna Jarrett. *Unemployment, Its Social Psychological Effects: A Commentary on the Literature*. Cambridge: Cambridge University Press, 1985.

Kennedy, Paul. *Preparing for the Twenty-First Century*. New York: Random House, 1993.

Krasner, Stephen D., ed. *International Regimes*. Ithaca, NY: Cornell University Press, 1983.

Landy, E. A. *The Effectiveness of International Supervision: Thirty Years of I.L.O. Experience*. Dobbs Ferry, NY: Oceana, 1966.

Layton-Henry, Zig, ed. *The Political Rights of Migrant Workers in Western Europe*. Newbury Park, CA: Sage Publications, 1990.

Lekachman, Robert. *The Age of Keynes*. New York: Random House, 1966.

Lindbeck, Assar. *Swedish Economic Policy*. Berkeley: University of California Press, 1974.

Lubin, Carol and Anne Winslow. *Social Justice for Women: The International Labor Organization and Women*. Durham, NC: Duke University Press, 1990.

Macdonald, Ronald St. John, Douglas M. Johnston, and Gerald L. Morris, eds. *The International Law and Policy of Human Welfare*. Alphen aan den Rijn, Netherlands: Sijthoff & Noordhoff, 1978.

Marshall, T. H. *Class, Citizenship, and Social Development*. Garden City, NY: Doubleday, 1964.

Mayer, Jean. "The Concept of the Right to Work in International Standards and the Legislation of ILO Member States." *International Labour Review* 124 (1985).

McCracken, Paul W. *Towards Full Employment and Price Stability: Summary of a Report*. Paris: OECD, 1977.

McDougal, Myres S., Harold D. Lasswell, and Lung-chu Chen. *Human Rights and World Public Order*. New Haven, CT: Yale University Press, 1980.

Meehan, Elizabeth. "Sex Equality Policies in the European Community." *Journal of European Integration* 13, 2–3 (Winter–Spring 1990).

Meron, Theodor, ed. *Human Rights in International Law: Legal and Policy Issues*. Oxford: Clarendon Press, 1984.

Morse, David A. *The Origin and Evolution of the I.L.O. and Its Role in the World Community*. Ithaca, NY: Cornell University, New York State School of Industrial and Labor Relations, 1969.

Mosley, Paul, Jane Harrigan, and John Toye. *Aid and Power: The World Bank and Policy-Based Lending*. London: Routledge, 1991.

Mower, A. Glen, Jr. *International Cooperation for Social Justice: Global and Regional Protection of Economic and Social Rights*. Westport, CT: Greenwood Press, 1985.

———. *Regional Human Rights: A Comparative Study of West European and Inter-American Systems*. New York: Greenwood Press, 1991.

Nagel, Stuart, ed. *Symposium on Global Policy Studies*, special issue of *International Political Science Review* 11, 3 (July 1990).

Nickel, James W. "Is There a Human Right to Employment?" *Philosophical Forum* 10 (1978–79).

———. *Making Sense of Human Rights: Philosophical Reflections on the Universal Declaration of Human Rights*. Berkeley: University of California Press, 1987.

Nisbet, Robert. *History of the Idea of Progress*. New York: Basic Books, 1980.

Nozick, Robert. *Anarchy, State, and Utopia*. New York: Basic Books, 1974.

Onuf, Nicholas G. and V. Spike Peterson. "Human Rights from an International Regimes Perspective." *Journal of International Affairs* 38 (Winter 1984).

Organisation for Economic Cooperation and Development. *The Challenge of Unemployment: A Report to Labour Ministers*. Paris: OECD, 1982.

———. *The Changing Course of International Migration*. Paris: OECD, 1993.

———. *Interdependence and Cooperation in Tomorrow's World*. Paris: OECD, 1987.

———. *Labour Market Flexibility: Report by a High-Level Group of Experts to the Secretary-General*. Paris: OECD, 1986.

———. *Labour Market Policies for the 1990s*. Paris: OECD, 1990.

———. *A Medium Term Strategy for Employment and Manpower Policies*. Paris: OECD, 1978.

———. *Positive Adjustment Policies: Managing Structural Change*. Paris: OECD, 1983.

Osakwe, Christopher. *The Participation of the Soviet Union in Universal International Organizations*. Leiden: Sijthoff, 1972.

Pence, Gregory E. "Toward a Theory of Work." *Philosophical Forum* 10 (1978–79).

Pierre, Andrew J., ed. *Unemployment and Growth in the Western Economies*. New York: Council on Foreign Relations, 1984.

Plant, Raymond. "Welfare and the Value of Liberty." *Government and Opposition* 20, 1 (1985).

Plant, Raymond with Harry Lesser and Peter Taylor-Gooby. *Political Philosophy and Social Welfare: Essays on the Normative Basis of Welfare Provision*. London: Routledge and Kegan Paul, 1980.

Polanyi, Karl. *The Great Transformation*. Boston: Beacon Press, 1957.

Prechal, Sacha and Noreen Burrows. *Gender Discrimination Law of the European Community*. Aldershot, Eng.: Dartmouth, 1990.

Putnam, Robert D. and Nicholas Bayne. *Hanging Together: Cooperation and Conflict in the Seven-Power Summits*. Rev. ed. Cambridge, MA: Harvard University Press, 1987.

Ratner, Ronnie Steinberg. *Equal Employment Policy for Women*. Philadelphia: Temple University Press, 1980.

Reich, Robert. *The Work of Nations: Preparing Ourselves for 21st Century Capitalism*. New York: Knopf, 1991.

Richardson, Jeremy and Roger Henning, eds. *Unemployment: Policy Responses of Western Democracies*. Beverly Hills, CA: Sage Publications, 1984.

Rimlinger, Gaston V. *Welfare Policy and Industrialization in Europe, America and Russia*. New York: John Wiley, 1971.

Rist, Ray C. *Finding Work: Cross National Perspectives on Employment and Training*. Philadelphia: Falmer, 1986.

Rosen, Sumner M. "Protecting Labor Rights in Market Economies," *Human Rights Quarterly* 14, 3 (August 1992): 371–382.

Salomé, Bernard, ed. *Fighting Urban Unemployment in Developing Countries*. Paris: OECD, 1989.

Schmidt, Manfred G. "The Politics of Unemployment: Rates of Unemployment and Labor Market Policy." *West European Politics* 7 (July 1984).

Sewell, John W. and Stuart K. Tucker, eds. *Growth, Exports and Jobs in a Changing World*. New Brunswick, NJ: Transaction Books, 1988.

Shklar, Judith N. *American Citizenship: The Quest for Inclusion*. Cambridge, MA: Harvard University Press, 1991.

Shue, Henry. *Basic Rights: Subsistence, Affluence, and U.S. Foreign Policy*. Princeton, NJ: Princeton University Press, 1980.

Sidell, Scott. *The IMF and Third-World Political Instability: Is There a Connection?* New York: St. Martin's Press, 1988.

Siegel, Richard L. and Leonard B. Weinberg, *Comparing Public Policies: United States, Soviet Union and Europe*. Homewood, IL: Dorsey, 1977.

Soroos, Marvin S. *Beyond Sovereignty: The Challenge of Global Policy*. Columbia: University of South Carolina Press, 1986.

Squire, Lyn. *Employment Policy in Developing Countries: A Survey of Issues and Evidence*. New York: Oxford University Press, 1981.

Standing, Guy. *Unemployment and Labour Market Flexibility: The United Kingdom*. Geneva: International Labour Office, 1986.

Standing, Guy and Gyorgy Sziracki. "Introduction: Labour Market Issues in Eastern Europe's Transition." *International Labour Review* 130, 2 (1991).

Symposium: The Implementation of the International Covenant on Economic, Social and Cultural Rights. *Human Rights Quarterly* 9, 2 (May 1987).

Taylor, Paul G. *The Limits of European Integration*. New York: Columbia University Press, 1983.

Taylor, Paul G. and A. J. R. Groom, eds. *International Institutions at Work*. New York: St. Martin's Press, 1986.

Teague, Paul and John Grahl. "European Community Labour Market Policy: Present Scope and Future Direction." *Journal of European Integration* 13, 1 (Winter 1989).

Thomas, Vinod et al. *Restructuring Economies in Distress: Policy Reform and the World Bank*. New York: Oxford University Press, 1991.

Tipton, John Bruce. *Participation of the United States in the International Labor Organization*. Champaign, IL: University of Illinois, Institute of Labor and Industrial Relations, 1959.

Tolley, Howard, Jr. *The U.N. Commission on Human Rights*. Boulder, CO: Westview Press, 1987.

Tsoukalis, Loukas. *The New European Community: The Politics and Economics of Integration* New York: Oxford University Press, 1992.

Valticos, Nicolas X. *International Labour Law*. Deventer, Netherlands: Kluwer, 1979.

Vasak, Karel and Philip Alston, eds. *The International Dimensions of Human Rights*. 2 vols. Westport, CT: Greenwood Press, 1982.

Venturini, Patrick. *1992: The European Social Dimension*. Luxembourg: European Communities, 1989.

Wilensky, Harold L. *The Welfare State and Equality: Structural and Ideological Roots of Public Expenditures*. Berkeley: University of California Press, 1975.

Williams, Shirley. *A Job to Live: The Impact of Tomorrow's Technology on Work and Society*. New York: Viking Penguin, 1985.

Winch, Donald. *Economics and Policy: A Historical Study*. London: Hodder and Stoughton, 1969; New York: Walker, 1970.

Ziskind, David. "Forced Labor in the Law of Nations." *Comparative Labor Law* 3 (1980).

Index

United Nations (*cont.*)
 Cultural Organization, 93; General Assembly, 90, 168; International Covenant on Economic, Social, and Cultural Rights,14, 25, 25n, 26, 55, 65, 68n, 69, 75, 90, 95, 96, 133, 170; Secretariat, 68, Third Committee (Social, Humanitarian and Cultural) of the General Assembly, 14, 66, 68, 70, 70n, 75; Universal Declaration of Human Rights, 14, 55, 65, 72, 79, 141
United States, 7, 51, 57n, 58, 60, 66, 67, 146, 182; 1946 Employment Act, 59, 59n, 84; Comprehensive Employment and Training Act, 74n, 84; Democratic Party, 164; Department of Commerce, 95; Department of Labor, 95n; employment policies, 74n, 121, 163; foreign policy, 87n; Humphrey-Hawkins Full Employment Act, 84; Knights of Labor, 46n; public policy, 49n, 106; State of the Union Address (1945), 59
utopian: approaches, 31; concepts, 40, 73n; musings, 29; proposals, 164

Valticos, Nicolas X., 79n
van der Ven, J. J. M., 74, 74n
Vasak, Karel, 24n
Venezuelan Constitution, 61
vocational training programs, 15, 70, 126, 130
Vogel, Heinrich, 83n, 111n
Vranken, Martin, 83

wage slavery, 39
Walker, Samuel, 3n
Wallace, Helen, 176n
Walterskirchen, Ewald, 159n
war, 49, 54, 55, 188; influence of on social and economic policy, 25, 59
Webb, Beatrice and Sidney, 57, 57n
Weiler, Hans N., 49n

Weimar Germany, 57
Weinberg, Leonard B., 49n
Weinraub, Bernard, 150n
Weissbrodt, David, 168n, 170n
Welch, Claude E., Jr., 87n
welfare: benefits, 10; policy, 24n, 25; rights, 49; welfare state, 8, 19, 23, 27n, 29n, 40, 41, 48n, 49n, 74n, 75, 161, 166, 188
Wellman, Carl, 26
Wells, H. G. 63, 63n
West Germany. *See* German Federal Republic
Western Europe, 5, 13, 57, 58, 59, 64, 67, 74, 83, 183, 191
Weston, Burns, 24n
White Paper on Employment Policy, 59
Whiteside, Noel, 8, 8n
Wiarda, Howard J., 60n
Wigforss, Ernst, 64
Wilensky, Harold L., 49n
Williams, Shirley, 8
Wilson, Jeanne L., 150n
Winch, Donald, 57, 57n
Winstanley, Gerard, 30
Wiseberg, Laurie, 81n
worktime reduction, 125
World Bank, 6n, 12, 108, 127–28, 141–42, 157, 167
World War I, 113
World War II, 58, 72, 74, 98, 113, 191

Yeltsin, Boris, 156
Yemin, Edward, 82n
Young, Oran R., 104
Yugoslavia, 150

Zeisel, Hans, 8, 8n
Ziskind, David, 132n
Zivs, Samuel, 38n
Zysman, John, 174n

University of Pennsylvania Press
Pennsylvania Studies in Human Rights
Bert B. Lockwood, Jr., Series Editor
Professor and Director, Urban Morgan Institute for Human Rights,
University of Cincinnati College of Law

Advisory Board

Marjorie Agosin
Philip Alston
Kevin Boyle
Richard P. Claude
David Weissbrodt

George J. Andreopoulos, editor. *Genocide: Conceptual and Historical Dimensions.*
  1994
Abdullahi Ahmed An-Na'im, editor. *Human Rights in Cross-Cultural Perspectives:*
  A Quest for Consensus. 1991
Iain Guest. *Behind the Disappearances: Argentina's Dirty War Against Human Rights*
  and the United Nations. 1990
Thomas B. Jabine and Richard P. Claude, editors. *Human Rights and Statistics:*
  Getting the Record Straight. 1991
Menno T. Kamminga. *Inter-State Accountability for Violations of Human Rights.*
  1992
Richard Lewis Siegel. *Employment and Human Rights: The International Dimen-*
  sion. 1994
Tolley, Howard B. *The International Commission of Jurists: Global Advocates for*
  Human Rights. 1994

This book was set in Baskerville and Eras typefaces. Baskerville was designed by John Baskerville at his private press in Birmingham, England, in the eighteenth century. The first typeface to depart from oldstyle typeface design, Baskerville has more variation between thick and thin strokes. In an effort to insure that the thick and thin strokes of his typeface reproduced well on paper, John Baskerville developed the first wove paper, the surface of which was much smoother than the laid paper of the time. The development of wove paper was partly responsible for the introduction of typefaces classified as modern, which have even more contrast between thick and thin strokes.

Eras was designed in 1969 by Studio Hollenstein in Paris for the Wagner Typefoundry. A contemporary script-like version of a sans-serif typeface, the letters of Eras have a monotone stroke and are slightly inclined.

Printed on acid-free paper.